Assessment Essentials

Catherine A. Palomba
Trudy W. Banta

Assessment
Essentials

Planning, Implementing, and Improving Assessment in Higher Education

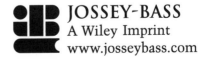

JOSSEY-BASS
A Wiley Imprint
www.josseybass.com

Published by Jossey-Bass
A Wiley Imprint
989 Market Street, San Francisco, CA 94103-1741   www.josseybass.com

Jossey-Bass books and products are available through most bookstores. To contact Jossey-Bass directly call our Customer Care Department within the U.S. at 800-956-7739, outside the U.S. at 317-572-3986 or fax 317-572-4002.

Jossey-Bass also publishes its books in a variety of electronic formats. Some content that appears in print may not be available in electronic books.

Library of Congress Cataloging-in-Publication Data

Palomba, Catherine A., date.
    Assessment essentials : planning, implementing, and improving assessment in higher education / Catherine A. Palomba, Trudy W. Banta.—1st ed.
    Includes bibliographical references and index.
    ISBN 0-7879-4180-8
    1. Universities and colleges—United States—Examinations.   I. Banta, Trudy W.   II. Title.   III. Series.
    LB2366.2.P35   1999
    378.1'664—dc21

                                                                    98-58122

FIRST EDITION
HB Printing   10 9 8 7 6

The Jossey-Bass
Higher and Adult Education Series

Contents

To our essentials:
Neil, Mary Frances, and Nick;
Holly and Logan

Preface

As Ernest L. Boyer has noted, higher education is "one of the greatest hopes for intellectual and civic progress in this country" yet it is seen by many as "part of the problem rather than the solution" (1997, pp. 81, 85). Pressure has come from several directions for campuses to look carefully at student learning, articulate learning objectives, set high standards for accomplishment, and assess whether students have met these standards (Wingspread Group on Higher Education, 1993). Most campuses, including public and private institutions, community colleges, comprehensive campuses, and research universities, have responded to this pressure.

Although only a small number of campuses were engaged in assessment of educational programs fifteen years ago, now nearly every campus carries out assessment-related projects (El-Khawas, 1995). Reflecting the predominantly local nature of assessment, a great number of faculty and staff have been called upon to design and carry out assessment activities and have become in the process strong advocates for assessment.

Many current practitioners learned about assessment along the way by attending conferences and workshops, exchanging ideas, and taking advantage of available resources. These individuals have developed and implemented creative approaches to assessment. As a result of their great willingness to communicate with one another about what does and does not work, assessment today is not the same as it was fifteen years ago. Some of what was once conventional wisdom is not anymore. Rather than relying heavily on large-scale assessment projects that often seemed unrelated to regular instructional activities, faculty, staff, and students have developed a variety of assessment approaches that closely reflect everyday campus activities.

We, the authors, have been fortunate to be part of this growth and change. For several years, both of us have worked with faculty and staff engaged in assessment projects and learned a great deal from them. This book grew out of our desire to share some of what we have learned and to create a vehicle for faculty and staff to exchange information and ideas with each other. The book's twelve chapters present a look at assessment as it is currently practiced and offer some guidance about how to plan an assessment program, how to carry it out, and how to use its results to improve academic and cocurricular programs.

Because we believe strongly that faculty and staff can learn from each other regardless of their disciplines, we began our book-writing efforts by inviting practitioners from various fields of study to send us examples of their assessment work. Thanks to their generous responses, we have gathered examples from more than seventy campuses. We have also selected examples from articles that have appeared in published sources, including *Assessment Update*, the bimonthly newsletter edited by Trudy Banta, and *Assessment in Practice*, authored by Banta, Jon Lund, Karen Black, and Frances Oblander. These examples have been woven into the chapters to illustrate the variety of assessment approaches under way on college and university campuses. Our examples come from all kinds of institutions: community colleges, liberal arts colleges, and comprehensive, doctoral, and research universities. The common thread is that the institution is engaged in assessment activities. As our examples show, the conversations and thoughtfulness that mark assessment on college and university campuses reflect great concern for the educational process and speak well for the future of assessment.

Audiences

As we wrote the book we tried to keep in mind faculty and staff members who are new to assessment and have been asked to assume responsibility for assessment activities. Perhaps they have been asked to serve on an assessment committee, to write plans for assessing a course they are teaching, or to help other faculty and staff become involved in assessment. This book should help newcomers become acquainted with the way assessment is practiced on campuses today. Faculty and staff who are more experienced with assessment will also, we hope, find some value in the perspective we offer. We may discuss some methodological details that are new to these individuals. Because their understanding of assessment is critical to its success, we hope that administrators too can benefit from our description of assessment.

Review of the Contents

Chapter One presents six *assessment essentials*. These strategies include developing learning goals and objectives; planning for assessment; involving faculty, staff, and students in assessment; selecting and designing methods; reporting and using results; and assessing the assessment program. These six essentials, common to successful assessment programs, provide the foundation for the chapters that follow. Chapter Two includes both a discussion about developing goals and objectives for learning and a description of assessment planning. Chapter Three presents ideas about encouraging involvement in assessment. Although the focus is on faculty and students, the ideas about involving faculty apply to professional staff as well.

Chapter Four contains background information about selecting and designing instruments. We stress the idea of carefully articulating selection criteria before methods and techniques are chosen. We also offer some approaches for developing local methods. Chapters Five through Seven contain additional information about various assessment techniques. Each of these chapters contains suggestions for implementing particular methods, as well as examples of their use on university and college campuses. Chapter Five describes performance assessment, including portfolios. Chapter Six presents information about the use of objective tests, classroom assignments, and classroom assessment for collecting assessment information. Chapter Seven describes the use of surveys, focus groups, and other qualitative methods. Although several of our chapters are concerned with assessment methods, we believe that methods and measurement should not drive assessment. What is most important is the collaboration and discussion that surround the assessment process.

Chapters Eight through Ten apply the information presented about processes and approaches to particular circumstances. Chapter Eight concentrates on the various ways assessment techniques can be used to determine if students are ready for the workplace or for further education. Chapter Nine contains a discussion of the assessment process as it applies to general education. One chapter is not enough to cover all of the many approaches used to assess general education on campuses today. Thus we simply tried to present a glimpse of various campus practices. Because faculty in many disciplines find themselves wrestling with how to define and assess critical thinking, we do offer an in-depth discussion of assessment as it applies to this important area of learning. Chapter Ten describes approaches to assessing various aspects of campus experiences and environment, such as curriculum design and out-of-class learning. Chapter Eleven addresses ways to report and use assessment information. In Chapter Twelve we return to some of the ideas presented earlier; the purpose of the chapter is to remind readers of the many choices they must make as they carry out assessment programs. As faculty, staff, and students consider these choices, their assessment programs take shape.

We do not advocate any one approach or technique to answer the assessment questions raised throughout the book; we have tried to lay out several possibilities for discussion purposes. In order for each chapter to stand alone, there is some repetition among the chapters. For example, the chapter on general education returns to some of the planning issues raised in Chapter Two. We have tried to keep this to a minimum. We hope there is something in each chapter that will enrich each reader's understanding of assessment.

Acknowledgments

This book reflects the work of the many, many individuals who are practicing assessment on college campuses, both those who sent us contributions and those who have described their work elsewhere at conferences and in publications. It also reflects the thinking of assessment practitioners who have helped form assessment at universities and colleges. For example, we found ourselves referring frequently to the work of Peter Ewell; others are cited throughout the pages as well. We acknowledge their leadership.

In addition, we thank the faculty and staff on our own campuses who have worked so hard on assessment and been generous in sharing their ideas and concerns. We have drawn liberally from the work they have done to illustrate points we make in the text. For instance, several examples come from Ball State University's College of Business, which has been an assessment leader in its own discipline.

We also want to thank several individuals who have been extremely helpful in shaping and preparing the manuscript, including Brian Pickerill and Becky Black at Ball State University and Karen Black, Jane Lambert, Emily Ward, Cheyenne Walker, and Victoria McBee at Indiana University–Purdue University Indianapolis. Their help has been invaluable in countless ways.

April 1999   Catherine A. Palomba
                                                    Muncie, Indiana

                                                    Trudy W. Banta
                                                    Indianapolis, Indiana

The Authors

Catherine A. Palomba is director of the Offices of Academic Assessment and Institutional Research at Ball State University. Catherine joined the administrative staff of Ball State in 1985 and became a director in 1991. Between 1980 and 1985, she was a research analyst at the Center for Naval Analyses in Alexandria, Virginia, where she did manpower research for the Marine Corps. In the 1970s, Catherine was an associate professor of economics at West Virginia University, where she received two awards as a West Virginia University Outstanding Teacher. She has published refereed articles in several journals, including *The Journal of Law and Economics* and *The Southern Economic Journal*. Palomba earned her master's degree (1966) in economics from the University of Minnesota and her Ph.D. (1969) from Iowa State University. She has given presentations about assessment at several college campuses and assessment conferences. Ball State University's assessment program has been featured in a recent monograph about campus practices and has been recognized by the American Productivity and Quality Center as a "best practice" institution for assessing learning outcomes.

Trudy W. Banta is vice chancellor for planning and institutional improvement and professor of higher education at Indiana University–Purdue University Indianapolis. Prior to assuming her current position in 1992, Banta was director of the Center for Assessment

Research and Development and professor of education at the University of Tennessee, Knoxville. She has developed and coordinated thirteen national conferences and ten international conferences on the topic of assessing quality in higher education. She has consulted with faculty and administrators in thirty-six states and Puerto Rico and has given invited addresses on outcomes assessment at national conferences in China, France, Germany, Canada, and Spain. Since 1983, Banta has edited six published volumes on assessment, contributed nineteen chapters to published works, and written more than eighty articles and reports. She is the founding editor of *Assessment Update*, a bimonthly periodical published by Jossey-Bass since 1989. Banta holds an Ed.D. in educational psychology from the University of Tennessee, Knoxville. Among her honors are an award from the National Council on Measurement in Education in 1984 for outstanding use of measurement technology, recognition in 1988 for contributions to the field of assessment by the American Association for Higher Education, and recognition in 1997 by the American Productivity and Quality Center for leadership of one of six programs exemplifying best practice in using management information in decision making.

Assessment Essentials

1

The Essentials of
Successful Assessment

ASSESS *(v.)*: to examine carefully

Assessment is a process that focuses on student learning, a process that involves reviewing and reflecting on practice as academics have always done, but in a more planned and careful way. In the mid-1980s educators as well as the public began to recognize the need for assessment in higher education. Reports such as the National Institute of Education's *Involvement in Learning* (1984), the Association of American Colleges' *Integrity in the College Curriculum* (1985), and the National Governors Association's *Time for Results* (1986) focused keen attention on the preparation of college graduates. Were they learning what they should be learning? Were they able to apply specialized knowledge and skills in the workplace, or as they sought further education? Were they able to communicate well and solve problems?

Only a handful of institutions, including Alverno College, Truman State University (then Northeast Missouri State University), and the University of Tennessee, Knoxville, were in a position to respond quickly to these questions. In 1973, Alverno's faculty and administrators reshaped their curriculum around eight crosscutting abilities including communication, analysis, and social interaction. Their focus then, as now, was on individual student learning as demonstrated by performance on faculty-designed instruments. The administration at Truman State University was an early advocate of value-added assessment, using standardized tests to compare growth in student knowledge between the freshman and sophomore years. Soon Truman State faculty also began to use writing evaluations and examinations in the major to assess their students and programs. Assessment at the University of Tennessee, Knoxville included department-level activities, standardized testing, and opinion surveys that had been initiated in response to state-level performance funding (Mentkowski, 1988; Mentkowski and Doherty, 1984; Banta, 1985; Hutchings and Marchese, 1990; McClain and Krueger, 1985).

Other early assessment practitioners included faculty at Miami-Dade Community College in Florida, Kean College in New Jersey, King's College in Pennsylvania, and James Madison University in Virginia. King's College focused on the individual student learner and on course-embedded assessment—assessment located within courses. James Madison emphasized cross-campus collaboration involving faculty and student-affairs professionals particularly in efforts to examine the effects of out-of-class activities on learning and development (Erwin, 1991; Hutchings and Marchese, 1990; Ewell, 1991). Thus, early efforts involved a diverse mix of campuses and approaches.

In fall 1988, Secretary of Education William Bennett issued an executive order requiring all federally approved accreditation organizations to include in their criteria for accreditation evidence of institutional outcomes (U.S. Department of Education, 1988). During the next several years, regional associations issued specific directives for institutional accreditation, and discipline-specific bodies created guidelines for program accreditation. State governments also became involved, with two-thirds now "in the assessment business" (Ewell, 1998).

By 1989, nearly 70 percent of campuses had assessment activities under way, according to *Campus Trends* data from the American Council on Education (El-Khawas, 1989). Administrators at many campuses turned first to commercially available standardized tests, although faculty-designed alternatives such as portfolios and capstone course projects quickly appeared. By 1990, a strong interest in "closer to the classroom" methods was already in evidence (Hutchings and Marchese, 1990, p. 23). The number of universities and colleges engaged in assessment has increased substantially in the past decade. In 1995, according to *Campus Trends* data, 94 percent of institutions had assessment activities under way and 90 percent had increased their activities as compared to five years earlier. Rather than relying on nationally available instruments, most institutions (86 percent) reported using local measures and nearly 70 percent were developing portfolios (El-Khawas, 1995).

As a result of these trends, increasing numbers of faculty have been called upon to participate in assessment. Some assume leadership roles, serving on campuswide committees charged with planning the institution's overall approach to assessment or designing a program to assess general education. A greater number are involved at the department level helping to design and carry out assessment of programs or courses for majors. Attendance at national, regional, and discipline-specific assessment conferences attests to continued interest in sharing assessment information. In fact, for more than a decade, the number of participants at the American Association for Higher Education's annual assessment conference has topped one thousand. This book is designed to fill some of the continuing need for information about assessment.

A Definition of Assessment

Assessment is intimately linked to an institution's mission and learning goals. Thus, the definition of assessment used on any particular campus may not work well on other campuses. In order to gain the most benefit from assessment, faculty and administrators at each institution must develop their own understanding of assessment.

With this caution in mind, the authors offer the following definition of assessment, adapted from one provided by Marchese in 1987.

> Assessment is the systematic collection, review, and use of information about educational programs undertaken for the purpose of improving student learning and development.

Assessment is more than the collection of data. To make assessment work, educators must be purposeful about the information they collect. As a basis for data gathering, they must clarify their goals and objectives for learning and be aware of where these goals and objectives are addressed in the curriculum. After data are gathered, educators must examine and use assessment results to improve educational programs (Marchese, 1987, 1997a; Hutchings, Marchese, and Wright, 1991).

Hutchings and Marchese (1990) suggest that the meaning of assessment is captured best by its key questions. What should college graduates know, be able to do, and value? Have the graduates of our institutions acquired this learning? What, in fact, are the contributions of the institution and its programs to student growth? How can student learning be improved? When individuals involved in assessment become confused about its purposes, it helps to return to these key questions.

Assessment as addressed in this book is often referred to as "student outcomes" assessment. This expression places emphasis on student learning and development as opposed to faculty evaluation or comprehensive program review, but it can be misleading. Remembering the difference between *intended* outcomes, as described in statements of expectations for students, and *actual* outcomes, as reflected in the results of assessment activities, is helpful. In order to place emphasis on the notion of improvement, Patrick Terenzini (1989) suggests focusing on assessing progress rather than outcomes.

Assessing outcomes implies a finality; assessing progress suggests there is time and opportunity to improve. The strong early focus of assessment programs on measuring outcomes was quickly deemphasized. Although Alexander Astin (1985, 1991) helped refocus thinking about higher education away from resources such as library holdings and student SAT scores toward educational outputs such as knowledge, skills, and values, he also argued that the results of education must be understood in relationship to both inputs and environment. It became clear that knowing where students wind up is only part of the story; information about where they start and what they encounter along the way is also necessary. Without this context it is difficult to use outcome results for improvement (Hutchings and Marchese, 1990). Questions about student experiences need to be considered in planning assessment programs. What kinds of courses do students take? What opportunities are available for out-of-class learning and development?

Programmatic Assessment

The overriding purpose of assessment is to understand how educational programs are working and to determine whether they are contributing to student growth and development. Hence, the ultimate emphasis of assessment is on programs rather than on individual students. At its most useful, assessment provides information about students as a group—information that can be aggregated across sections of a single course and is meaningful across courses. Assessment indicates what the experiences of students add up to, and what these experiences, in turn, imply about educational programs. Assessment enables educators to examine whether the curriculum makes sense in its entirety and whether students, as a result of all their experiences, have the knowledge, skills, and values that graduates should possess. Programmatic assessment helps determine whether students can integrate learning from individual courses into a coherent whole. It is interested in the cumulative effects of the educational process. Rather than just documenting the achievement of individual students, programmatic assessment tells about the overall learning, growth, and development of groups of students as a result of all of their educational experiences. It looks at programs in a holistic way (Hutchings and Marchese, 1990; Ratcliff, 1994).

Assessment Essentials

In order for an assessment program to be successful, several strategies must be practiced. In fact, the six strategies presented here are so pervasive to the ongoing effectiveness of assessment that they can be described as *assessment essentials*.

Agree on Goals and Objectives for Learning

Reaching agreement about goals and objectives for learning and having an understanding of where and how they are addressed in the curriculum is essential to successful assessment. This foundation guides the selection of assessment instruments and facilitates the use of assessment results. It also provides explicit information to students and the public about the aims of higher education.

As a starting point for assessment, faculty must consider the institution's values, goals, and vision (Banta, Lund, Black, and Oblander, 1996). Some campuses are especially committed to experiential education, some value knowledge and understanding of computers, others value service learning. Bloomfield College focuses on preparing students to assume leadership roles in a multicultural society. Carnegie Mellon University identifies information science as a core competence around which social science and science fields are developed (Dill, 1997; Leslie and Fretwell, 1996). Regional accreditors have required their members to make their educational goals clear, public, and appropriate to higher education. Thus, mission statements may capture the special qualities that graduates are expected to possess. Although campus studies indicate that the content of mission statements is often vague and empty, competitive pressures may force institutions to become more focused and specific in their mission statements and in the ways they convey them to the public (Dill, 1997). Assessment itself is a strong factor in pushing institutions toward clarity of purpose (Nichols, 1995b; Banta, Lund, Black, and Oblander, 1996).

Developing learning goals and objectives for general education necessarily involves a group of campus representatives who describe the knowledge, skills, and values graduates should possess regardless of their discipline. Agreement about the role of general education on campus will guide this discussion. Faculty who are developing goals and objectives for the major will be most concerned with the standards of the field but will likely consider learning objectives traditionally associated with general education programs such as valuing lifelong learning or working cooperatively. Reaching agreement about educational aims may take considerable time. Although many faculty develop statements about what they want students to learn in specific courses, current statements about what students should know after they have completed the courses in a program may not exist.

Design and Implement a Thoughtful
Approach to Assessment Planning

At either the institutional or department level, members of the committee or task force charged with developing an approach to assessment need to begin with a discussion about its purposes. Several authors distinguish between activities aimed at improvement and those aimed at demonstration of accountability (Erwin, 1991; Ewell, 1991; Terenzini, 1989). These categories are often referred to as *formative* and *summative* evaluations. The first is meant to "form" the program or performance, the second to make judgments about it. Formative assessment is conducted during the life of a program (or performance) with the purpose of providing feedback that can be used to modify, shape, and improve the program (or performance.) Summative assessment is conducted after a program has been in operation for awhile, or at its conclusion, to make judgments about its quality or worth compared to previously defined standards for performance. If activities are to continue or be repeated, the results of summative assessment can be used to help form the program (or performance) for the future (Gardiner, 1989; Ewell, 1991; Farmer and Napieralski, 1997).

Although the overall focus of the assessment movement has centered on improvement of educational programs, elements of summative assessment are in practice on college campuses, not only in responding to external accreditors and state governments, but also in internal structures. For example, general education assessment programs that are course-based may include an evaluation of whether courses should remain in the program. These reviews should contain strong elements of formative as well as summative assessment. As Marcia Mentkowski (1998) points out, assessment is a "set of processes designed to improve, demonstrate, and inquire about student learning outcomes" (p. 1). Assessment clearly has multiple purposes.

The terms formative and summative assessment are applied to activities focused on individual students as well as those focused on overall programs. Summative assessment activities aimed at students include such things as junior-level writing competence exams and comprehensive exams in the major that must be passed for advancement or certification. Formative assessment measures include performance reviews accompanied by feedback, perhaps provided by a panel of experts (who may also certify the work). The strongly held current view that students should learn from assessment has increased the use of formative assessment approaches focused on individual students.

One of the major tasks faced by assessment planners is the development of a planning document. An assessment plan captures agreement about what matters, gives direction for actions, and provides a means to determine if progress is being made. Creating a plan helps the institution or program see the big picture of assessment, including its who, what, when, and why. The plan need not be elaborate. It may be a simple time line or a matrix of activities, but there needs to be agreement at the institution and within departments about the overall objectives of an assessment program and how it will be carried out.

Although regional accrediting bodies now ask their members to have written assessment plans at the institutional level, emphasis should be on the process and discussion that produces and carries out the plan rather than on the document itself. Many institutional planners have learned the value of strategic process-oriented planning and the flexibility it brings to dealing with organizational change (Chaffee and Jacobson, 1997; Rowley, Lujan, and Dolence, 1997). Individuals involved in assessment planning can adopt strategic planning methods such as brainstorming, seeking input, and revising.

Institutions may have assessment plans or designs at several levels, including campus, program, course, and classroom. Assessment at each level can provide information for the others and may reflect a variety of purposes. For example, a department assessment plan aimed at improvement may reflect institutional reporting requirements and those of one or more disciplinary accrediting bodies.

An important consideration when planning an assessment program is to link the results of assessment to other educational processes such as curriculum review and planning and budgeting. Some academic programs require that proposals for curriculum change be accompanied by relevant assessment information. Insisting that assessment information be provided in support of budgeting requests is another approach for linking assessment to decision making.

Involve Individuals from On and Off Campus

Students and faculty, as well as administrators and professional staff, need to be represented in planning and carrying out assessment. Alumni, employers, and community members also can make valuable contributions. Widespread engagement helps guarantee that assessment will focus on the most important learning issues and maximizes the likelihood that assessment information will be used. Although degrees of involvement will vary among individuals, extensive awareness about what assessment is and what it is trying to accomplish must exist.

A key to assessment success is involving faculty in the process. Given their responsibility for designing and delivering the curriculum, faculty members' voices are absolutely essential in framing the questions and areas of inquiry that are the heart of assessment. Faculty development efforts are necessary in helping individuals understand the purposes and methods of assessment. Attendance at conferences and on-campus seminars, brown-bag lunches, and faculty workshops are only a few of the many approaches that can be used for this purpose. But beyond awareness, faculty must assume responsibility for designing, implementing, and carrying out the assessment program. Whether by serving on committees or task forces, or by simply engaging in assessment work by themselves or with others, faculty must be involved. An assessment program driven by administrators or professional staff without a strong role for faculty has little chance of success.

Because information collected from students provides much of the raw material for assessment, it is easy to see students as passive participants in the process and to take their role for granted. But students, too, need to understand the purposes of assessment and to be involved in making choices about how the program is designed and implemented. By serving on committees, critiquing projects, and facilitating data collection, students can become partners in assessment. Likewise, external groups such as graduates, employers, and community members have much to offer. For example, they can help articulate learning goals and objectives, participate in data-gathering activities, and critique assessment results.

The way an institution is organized to carry out assessment is an important factor in assessment's acceptance on campus. All successful programs have leadership from key individuals. Some create a central assessment office. Elsewhere, responsibilities for assessment are added to existing responsibilities of faculty or administrators. In addition, most institutions create a campuswide assessment committee with responsibilities for planning and facilitating the program. Assessment coordinators or committees may be appointed in individual departments. Regardless of the exact model, a representative mix of individuals needs to be involved.

Inviting individuals to serve on campuswide committees is only one of many possibilities for engaging members of the campus community. Any opportunities for exchanging ideas and concerns about assessment can be helpful. For example, at Austin Peay State University the associate vice president for planning and institutional effectiveness participates in an annual meeting with each department to discuss assessment information with faculty (Rudolph, 1996).

Select or Design and Implement
Data Collection Approaches

To select among assessment instruments, faculty must discuss and establish their selection criteria and become familiar with various assessment methods. The most important selection criterion is whether the method will provide useful information—information that indicates whether students are learning and developing in ways faculty have agreed are important. Assessment methods must be linked to goals and objectives for learning and to the instructional activities that support these goals. For example, future teachers should be observed interacting with students, not simply examined with a multiple-choice test.

Assessment methods (also called techniques or instruments) include both *direct* and *indirect* approaches. Direct measures of learning require students to display their knowledge and skills as they respond to the instrument itself. Objective tests, essays, presentations, and classroom assignments all meet this criterion. Indirect methods such as surveys and interviews ask students to reflect on their learning rather than to demonstrate it. Many assessment programs include exit surveys or interviews of graduating seniors, alumni surveys of recent or long-term graduates, or both. These allow faculty to hear from their students about how their programs are working or what could be improved. They also yield details about instructional or curricular strengths that direct measures alone cannot provide. Nevertheless, when selecting specific assessment techniques, activities that directly assess learning must be included if the assessment program is to have credibility.

Direct assessment techniques include both *objective tests* where students select a response from among those provided and *performance measures* where students generate their own responses. Performance measures range from essay questions included on multiple-choice exams to comprehensive portfolios containing material accumulated over time. These measures allow students to demonstrate skills as well as knowledge.

A further distinction that may be made is between *quantitative* methods that rely on numerical scores or ratings and *qualitative* methods that rely on descriptions rather than numbers. The latter include ethnographic field studies, logs, journals, participant observations, and open-ended questions on interviews and surveys. The goal of qualitative methods is to provide a narration or description about what is occurring with emphasis on illuminating the meaning of behavior (Kinnick and Walleri, 1995). Faculty who ask seniors to write about important learning experiences and then prepare an overall summary of prevalent themes are using a qualitative approach.

Because of the rich information they provide, current trends in assessment include increased use of performance measures and qualitative approaches. Educators increasingly believe that assessment itself should contribute to learning (Wright, 1997; Kinnick and Walleri, 1995; Marchese, 1998). Over time, educational research has identified conditions that are beneficial to student learning. The premise of assessment is that all educators, not just educational researchers, care about whether their students learn. Based on that premise, faculty and staff who select and design assessment strategies need to consider what is known about learning. Because learning is enhanced by doing, it makes sense to design assessment strategies that actively engage students. Such methods should also allow students the chance to receive feedback and respond to it. All assessment practitioners need not be educational researchers, but they should ask focused questions about each assessment strategy. Will it, by itself, enhance student learning? Will it provide students with opportunities for self-evaluation?

In addition to the methods chosen, faculty must decide when information will be collected. From students at entry, midpoint, or exit? From alumni one, two, or five years after graduation? If students are the source, faculty must decide how the information will affect student progress. Will it be required or graded? The site of data collection must also be determined. One possibility is to create (or take advantage of) data-collection opportunities outside the classroom. For example, all students can be required to attend a special session to complete a writing competence exam. Taking advantage of orientation to administer an entry-level test is another example. Within majors, students can be required to participate in specially designed performances or to attend sessions to complete national tests of competence in their field. The current trend is to collect assessment information within the classroom, not simply for convenience but because of the opportunity this provides to use already in-place assignments and coursework for assessment purposes. The latter approach, called "course-embedded" assessment (Ewell, 1991; Wright, 1997), involves taking a second look at materials generated in the classroom so that, in addition to providing a basis for grading students, these materials allow faculty to evaluate their approaches to instruction and course design. In addition to being cost-efficient, course-embedded assessment is least likely to suffer from problems related to student motivation. A variant involves designing exam questions, case study exercises, or other assignments that are inserted into classroom work for the explicit purpose of providing group-level information. The specific approach that is used needs to reflect the overall purposes of the assessment program.

Examine, Share, and Act on Assessment Findings

Assessment should foster conditions in which meaningful questions are raised and addressed and in which assessment evidence is valued and used. Well-chosen assessment methods will produce information that can lead to improvement. However, the information must be analyzed and shared before it can provide a basis for action. Various assessment audiences and their needs must be considered. Often, separate reports are required to serve distinct audiences.

Regional accrediting associations, accrediting bodies in the disciplines, and state governments all have distinct reporting needs that frequently affect the content and timing of assessment programs. Accrediting bodies generally provide outlines that must be followed when submitting reports, and at least twenty state governments require information in the form of performance indicators (Ewell, 1998).

Current and future students, as well as their parents, are often interested in the performance of academic institutions. Potential students may request job placement figures as they select their campus or major. Employers, community leaders, and donors may value assessment information as well. Detailed project reports probably will not suit the needs of these audiences, but highlights of assessment findings may be well received.

Internal audiences, including committees and task forces, may have specific requests. At some institutions, the faculty senate requires all seniors to engage in performance assessment within their majors and asks faculty in the programs to report on the results. At other campuses, faculty have designed general education assessment programs that contain specific reporting requirements for instructors who are teaching courses in the program (Pitts, Lowe, Ranieri, and Palomba, 1997).

Where possible, assessment programs should produce information that can be shared with several audiences for a variety of purposes. For example, results from a writing competence exam can provide information to students about their progress, help assess the overall effectiveness of the general education program, and provide disaggregated data to individual academic programs about the progress of their majors. The best assessment programs share timely information in varied ways, including project reports, theme reports, and feedback to students.

Regularly Reexamine the Assessment Process

Assessment is about learning. Much of what is learned is about the assessment process itself. Attention to the way assessment is carried out invariably points to opportunities for improvement. Although a regular meeting each year should be reserved for discussion about the way the program is functioning, introspection about assessment should occur throughout the process, not just intermittently.

The strategies highlighted in this chapter provide direction for assessing assessment. For example, faculty can examine the program to see if important constituencies are involved, if clear statements of learning objectives are available, if methods are meaningfully aligned with goals, and if results are being integrated into curriculum and budget decisions. Exhibit 1.1 includes these important characteristics and can be used to monitor an assessment program.

The Joint Committee on Standards for Educational Evaluation (1994) has established several standards for program evaluation that can be applied or adapted by a committee charged with evaluating an assessment program. These standards are organized around the following four attributes:

1. *Utility,* including identification of stakeholders, credibility of evaluators, pertinence of information, and clarity and timeliness of reporting

2. *Feasibility,* including practicality of procedures, political viability, and cost effectiveness

Exhibit 1.1. Characteristics of a Good Assessment Program

A good assessment program does the following:

❑ Asks important questions
❑ Reflects institutional mission
❑ Reflects programmatic goals and objectives for learning
❑ Contains a thoughtful approach to assessment planning
❑ Is linked to decision making about the curriculum
❑ Is linked to processes such as planning and budgeting
❑ Encourages involvement of individuals from on and off campus
❑ Contains relevant assessment techniques
❑ Includes direct evidence of learning
❑ Reflects what is known about how students learn
❑ Shares information with multiple audiences
❑ Leads to reflection and action by faculty, staff, and students
❑ Allows for continuity, flexibility, and improvement in assessment

3. *Propriety,* including service to participants, community, and society, respect for the rights of those involved, and provisions for complete and fair assessment

4. *Accuracy,* including program documentation, use of valid and reliable procedures, appropriate analysis, impartial reporting, and justified conclusions

An important consideration in evaluating an assessment program is whether it provides for both continuity and flexibility. Assessment information is most helpful to the decision-making process if it is provided in a consistent format over a period of time. If the same test or survey is administered across a series of semesters, educators can see trends in the results and can more confidently identify issues or make necessary changes. Collecting the same information before and after an academic program has been modified allows decision makers to judge more readily if the modification had an impact.

Although continuity is important in an assessment program, so too is flexibility. Viewing the assessment process itself as dynamic rather than fixed encourages experimentation and helps overcome the fear that a measure will become a permanent fixture regardless of its value (Ratcliff, 1994). This is one reason why multiple measures are recommended. With multiple measures, a nonproductive method can be dropped without having to start data collection from scratch. In addition, finding similar results with more than one assessment measure increases confidence in changing academic programs. For example, faculty may be more willing to require additional library work if both senior surveys and research papers demonstrate a need.

The Interrelated Nature of the Strategies

The six strategies just described are *essential* in order to capture the benefits of assessment. Although they are presented as steps, the strategies are not necessarily sequential. In many cases they will occur simultaneously as a set of interrelated actions. For example, it takes widespread involvement to create and carry out a meaningful assessment planning process. Likewise, faculty may begin to rethink their curriculum goals as they select and implement assessment techniques. As with other systems at work, when practicing assessment it pays to remember that often, "Reality is made up of circles" rather than straight lines (Senge, 1990, p. 73).

A Continuing Case for Assessment

Despite the assessment activities that are occurring on college and university campuses, questioning of higher education continues. Issues such as expanded government regulation, intensified competition, new modes of delivery, greater diversity in clientele, and growing concerns for learners and learning needs constitute an increasingly complex context for higher education (Peterson, Dill, and Mets, 1997). Demands for efficiency compete with those for effectiveness. Issues of access compete with those of cost. Peter Ewell

(1994a) states, "Times indeed are different. . . . visible particularly in the relationship between academic institutions and the wider society" (p. 26). Given the central role of higher education in the nation's future, educators need to expect continued scrutiny and to respond to this close examination. As Jerry Gaff notes, "Developing a quality educational program based on shared academic principles is one of the best ways to gain the public's trust and support" (1997, p. 689). Assessment plays an important role in establishing and improving quality and in building this trust. In fact, an institution's genuine commitment to assessment is a clear public statement of its desire to offer quality programs and improve student learning and development.

Pressures on institutions to reexamine their priorities and to place greater value on student learning will certainly continue. In Gaff's view, the future is likely to include more prominence for "the interests of students and learning" and more integrity in the curriculum (p. 703). Robert B. Barr and John Tagg have made a strong case for a new view of colleges and universities as institutions that "produce learning" rather than "provide instruction," a view that "necessarily incorporates the perspectives of the assessment movement" (1995, p. 16). In their view, assessment is the "key structure for changing the rest of the system" (p. 20). By its very nature, assessment puts students at the center of higher education. Educators need to tap the potential of assessment to improve existing academic and cocurricular programs and to help shape innovations such as interdisciplinary studies and learning communities. The dual nature of assessment to both improve programs and communicate with the public should be utilized.

2

Developing Definitions, Goals, and Plans

DEVELOP (*v.*): to bring into reality

Successful assessment requires carefully laid groundwork. This includes identifying purposes, making choices about how to organize for assessment, articulating goals and objectives for learning, and developing meaningful assessment plans. In this chapter, we address each of these issues.

Establishing Purposes, Defining Terms, and Developing Guidelines

Faculty and staff involved in assessment must allow time for themselves and others to reach understanding and consensus about the meaning of and purposes for assessment, or they will find little support for its use. Campus newsletters, round tables, and informal discussions about the aims of assessment can pay great dividends. At Truman State University, the campus culture only gradually embraced assessment as a way to "provide basic evidence for discussions on university interests and issues" (Magruder, McManis, and Young, 1997, p. 20). A. Michael Williford (1997) indicates that the greatest challenge in implementing department-based, faculty-involved assessment at Ohio University has been "to develop a common language about the meaning of and uses for student assessment."

Williford found faculty were used to thinking about assessment of individual student learning and dealing with curriculum issues, but were much less familiar with using assessment "for the purpose of improving programs." Because the absence of a common language has been a continuing obstacle, Williford has called for a continuing campus dialogue about the purposes of assessment (p. 52).

At Alverno College, focus has always been on "the individual student learner in action." Faculty look at not only *what* students are learning, but *how* they are learning as a result of participating in the assessment process itself. Alverno calls its approach "assessment as learning" (Sharkey, 1992, p. 164).

At Sinclair Community College, faculty define assessment as a process that "asks important questions about student learning, gathers some meaningful information on these questions, and uses the information for academic improvement" (Denney, 1996, p. 3). In their view, assessment's greatest benefit is fostering academic introspection—making the institution more self-conscious about what its programs are accomplishing. Other benefits include providing information for recruitment, planning, and accreditation, and generating improvements in teaching and learning. At other campuses, faculty explicitly recognize the role assessment can play in improving institutional image, enhancing funding opportunities, and attracting better students.

Along with a definition, it is helpful to have a description of the subject matter for assessment. Ball State University's assessment program collects information about what students know and can do when they enter the university, at the completion of their general education program, and in their major. It looks at issues of program completion, student satisfaction, and success after graduation. These basic avenues of investigation were clearly described in fall 1991 when the provost of the university, Warren Vander Hill, issued his statement in support of assessment (C. Palomba, 1997).

Many campuses find it helpful to develop a set of operating principles or guidelines that clarify the purposes and intended uses of assessment information. Guidelines may include statements like the following:

1. The purpose of assessment is improvement of educational programs.

2. Assessment of student learning and development will be a collaborative process involving faculty, staff, and students.

3. Assessment will be guided by the institution's mission.

4. Assessment results will not be used for faculty or staff evaluation.

5. The assessment process will itself be evaluated.

The specific list will vary by institution but should address potential problem areas. For example, at both Western Carolina University (Gray, 1995b) and Sinclair Community College guidelines explicitly state that assessment information will not be used for faculty evaluation. Sinclair's guidelines also include a commitment to provide benefits for students rather than use results in punitive ways (Denney, 1996).

Organizing for Assessment

A basic assessment issue is that of organization. Key players, committees, and structures must be identified before assessment can begin. The choices made at this point determine who will take significant responsibilities for assessment.

Assessment Leaders

One or more key individuals must step forward to foster the campuswide assessment process by communicating the institutional priority of assessment, committing resources to support assessment initiatives, and including assessment results in public statements (Nichols, 1995b; Peterson and Einarson, 1998). In some cases, the president of the institution is eager and willing to take this role. In others, the academic vice president or the vice president for planning becomes the person most identified with nurturing the assessment process. An individual faculty member can also be selected (or may seek responsibility) to lead assessment efforts.

Truman State University's assessment program was initiated soon after new president Charles McClain, who believed the campus should be able to "measure its positive impact on students," took office in 1970. This president, his new dean of instruction, Darrell Krueger, and faculty worked together to develop a strong "university-wide emphasis on student learning" (Magruder, McManis, and Young, 1997, pp. 17–18). McClain and Krueger kept faculty attention focused on assessment by routinely using data in conversations and speeches about campus strengths and weaknesses, new program initiatives, and goals for the future.

The president or other key leader will need to assign day-to-day responsibility for coordinating the assessment program to a respected member of the faculty or professional staff. Selecting a faculty member as coordinator may increase the credibility of the assessment process with other faculty on campus (Nichols, 1995b). However, in order to draw on professional expertise, the director of an institutional research or planning office may be asked to assume operational responsibility for assessment, or an assessment director may be appointed. The coordinator facilitates the assessment work of faculty and staff in various campus units and may serve as a regular or ex-officio member on a campuswide assessment committee.

Assessment Committees

Assessment must not be seen as the exclusive concern of administrators or experts (Ferren, 1993). In order to reflect a variety of interests, most institutions identify a committee or task force of faculty, staff, and students that assumes assessment responsibilities. Some institutions utilize an existing senate, curriculum, or planning committee for this purpose. Chaffee and Jacobson note that planners sometimes "underutilize existing structures," establishing new groups when an existing one with "a rich history of working together" could handle the task (1997, p. 242). Linking assessment to existing structures should increase the likelihood that assessment information will be used (Ewell, 1997e). However, because assessment is a substantial undertaking requiring focused attention, many institutions create a new committee to facilitate the assessment process. Creating a new committee provides an opportunity to include a variety of constituencies such as students, parents, and faculty who may have had limited opportunities to participate in campuswide planning processes in the past (Terenzini, 1993).

Assessment committees contribute in a variety of ways in helping to plan and carry out the assessment process. For example, the committee may create definitions, issue guidelines, and develop goals and objectives for learning. It may create a campuswide assessment plan that focuses on general education and the major and is submitted to the institution's governance procedures for approval. In some cases, the assessment committee acts as an oversight body that receives assessment information from campus units and issues summary and evaluative reports. The University Assessment Committee (UAC) at the University of Wisconsin–Whitewater provides feedback to departments about four areas of their required assessment reports. The UAC determines whether reports contain specific measurable objectives, multiple measures and thorough data collection, documentation for changes (or no changes), and evidence of feedback to students and faculty. Each criterion is judged as "needs improvement" or "meets the standard" (Friedman, 1995, p. 8).

At the University of Southern Indiana, the Faculty Senate has charged the University Assessment Committee to (a) facilitate the review and evaluation of student learning outcomes; (b) review existing assessment practices and measures, monitor their effectiveness, and suggest their modification as appropriate; and (c) recommend plans, policies, and review mechanisms for assessment activities (C. Harrington and T. Schibik, personal communication, Sept. 3, 1997).

At some institutions, the assessment committee's role is primarily to gather and share information. Committee members become familiar with factors that lead to successful assessment and with specific assessment practices. Then they help other faculty and staff become knowledgeable about the assessment process. At Pennsylvania State University, for example, a university-wide assessment team, chaired by the dean for undergraduate education, has been established to provide a forum for promoting and sharing assessment techniques and accomplishments (M. J. Dooris, personal communication, Sept. 10, 1997). The associate dean for undergraduate education from every Penn State college is a member of the team and other interested faculty participate on a voluntary basis.

Leadership in Units

Assessment at the division or department level also needs key players, committees, and structures. A department chair, assessment program coordinator, or faculty member may take this responsibility. The dean of Ball State University's College of Business sees his role as helping develop the general framework for assessment, providing momentum, and maintaining flexibility, while encouraging faculty to develop the specifics of the program. The college's undergraduate and graduate program coordinators provide administrative support for faculty who serve on the unit's undergraduate and graduate curriculum/assessment committees. Faculty were given the choice of creating separate assessment committees, but chose instead to incorporate assessment into already existing curriculum committees. They thought combining assessment issues with curriculum issues would lead to better decision making.

Central Assessment Offices

Some institutions have created central offices that provide continuity and support for the assessment process. Although some central offices require divisions and departments to report assessment information to them, most do not. More typically, office staff act as facilitators and consultants rather than as monitors of assessment. Office staff may coordinate large-scale assessment projects, such as senior surveys or standardized testing, that require extensive logistical support and are beyond the scope of individual divisions and departments.

The existence of a central assessment office makes a clear statement about the institution's continuing commitment to assessment, but it may increase the risk that assessment will be seen as "something the administration does." Although Truman State University uses its testing office to administer examinations, no central assessment office has been established. Assessment leaders at Truman State felt such an office "would actually reduce faculty ownership and analysis of the data." Instead, the dean of instruction's office became "the primary facilitator of data distribution and use" (Magruder, McManis, and Young, 1997, p. 20). Assessment leaders felt it was important to incorporate assessment into the culture and to use it as the "conscious foundation for many institutional decisions" rather than to institutionalize assessment through a compliance model (p. 27).

Central offices can combat the view that assessment is strictly an administrative concern by encouraging and supporting assessment in the disciplines. For example, staff can provide consulting services to faculty who are designing their own assessment projects. Making the results of campuswide assessment projects widely available and useful to colleges and departments is another helpful strategy. Southern Illinois University Edwardsville (SIUE) and Eastern New Mexico University are two of a growing number of institutions that make use of the World Wide Web to disseminate campus assessment findings. The Office of Undergraduate Assessment at SIUE regularly prepares one-page bulletins on studies of student satisfaction in the residence halls, parent feedback at freshman orientation, and other assessment topics, which find their way to the Assessment Web Page (D. J. Eder, personal communication, Sept. 23, 1997). The Assessment Resource Office at Eastern also publishes a newsletter and posts departmental and campuswide assessment plans and progress to its Web page (A. M. Testa, personal communication, Sept. 8, 1997).

Articulating Goals and Objectives for Learning

Once the key individuals, committees, and structures that provide the foundation for implementing assessment have been identified, it is time to develop the learning goals and objectives that guide assessment activities. Articulating goals and objectives for learning provides direction for other assessment choices.

Defining Terms

Statements about the intended results of educational activities provide the basis for assessment. In addition, they enhance communication with current and future students and among faculty and staff about expectations for graduates. Writing clear statements about what students should know and be able to do is sometimes made more difficult by a lack of agreement about language.

Although the terms are often used interchangeably, many educators draw a distinction between *goals* for learning and *objectives* for learning. Both can be used to describe the intended results of educational activities and both provide direction for assessment. The difference between the two is their level of precision. Goals are used to express intended results in general terms. Objectives are used to express intended results in precise terms. The term goals is used to describe broad learning concepts such as clear communication, problem solving, and ethical awareness. The term objectives is used to describe specific behaviors students should exhibit. For example, graduates in speech communication should be able to interpret nonverbal behavior and to support arguments with credible evidence. Objectives tell us more specifically what needs to be assessed, and thus are a more accurate guide to suitable assessment tools (Erwin, 1991).

References to general education learning goals are often found in the institution's mission statement and are generally developed through consensus of a cross section of the campus community. In contrast, any list of learning objectives for a specific academic program must come from the faculty who teach and assess that program. For example, nursing faculty at Southern Connecticut State University have defined the generic skill of communicating for their graduates (C. Thompson, personal communication, Nov. 11, 1997). Nurses communicate with clients to achieve mutual goals and with peers to promote changes in health policy and provide client advocacy. Thus upon completion of the nursing program graduates should be able to do the following:

1. Use effective verbal communication skills

2. Effectively document clinical data

3. Communicate clearly through scholarly papers

4. Use communication technology

By using language that is more comfortable to them, many faculty sidestep the distinction between goals and objectives. Some refer instead to indicators or competences, and others refer to learning skills and subskills. The exact language faculty use is not important. It is important that faculty reach agreement about what graduates of their programs are expected to know and be able to do and express these intended results with enough precision to guide the selection of assessment instruments.

Goals and Objectives for Learning

Educators identify cognitive, affective, and skill learning objectives. Faculty who are asked to write cognitive objectives may find it useful to refer to Bloom's taxonomy, which is discussed in many books and articles devoted to test construction, teaching, designing curricula, and assessment (Diamond, 1998; Freeman and Lewis, 1998;

Nilson, 1998; Jacobs and Chase, 1992; Bogue and Saunders, 1992; Banta, 1996b). Bloom's taxonomy of cognitive objectives contains six levels arranged in order of increasing complexity (Bloom, 1956):

1. *Knowledge* involves recalling or remembering information without necessarily understanding it and includes behaviors such as describing, listing, identifying, and labeling.

2. *Comprehension* involves understanding learned material and includes behaviors such as explaining, discussing, and interpreting.

3. *Application* is the ability to put ideas and concepts to work in solving problems. It includes behaviors such as demonstrating, showing, and making use of information.

4. *Analysis* involves breaking down information into its component parts to see interrelationships and ideas. Related behaviors include differentiating, comparing, and categorizing.

5. *Synthesis* is the ability to put parts together to form something original. It involves using creativity to compose or design something new.

6. *Evaluation* involves judging the value of evidence based on definite criteria. Behaviors related to evaluation include concluding, criticizing, prioritizing, and recommending.

Because application, analysis, synthesis, and evaluation require students to use information in various ways, they are sometimes called "higher order" thinking skills. For example, graduates of an economics program may be expected to apply time series analysis to current income trends, or to analyze the impact of various monetary policies on the economy. Assessing higher-order thinking skills may call for the use of performance measures (discussed in Chapter Five.)

Whereas cognitive objectives refer to thinking skills, affective objectives refer to attitudes and values. Attitudes capture feelings toward people, ideas, and institutions. Values reflect deeply held beliefs, ideas, and assumptions about life goals and ways of living (Erwin, 1991). Affective dimensions are directed toward a person (including oneself), object, place, or idea and predispose individuals to behave in certain ways. Examples of intended outcomes for affective dimensions include being sensitive to the values of others, becoming aware of one's own talents and abilities, and developing an appreciation for lifelong learning. Practicing ethical behavior, exhibiting personal discipline, and providing leadership are other examples of intended outcomes that address attitudes and values. Whether students are achieving intended results with respect to affective dimensions can be examined by actually observing behavior that occurs, for example, in group work or simulations, monitoring participation rates in activities related to the attitude, and asking students to report on their own behavior or attitudes. Both surveys and focus groups can be used to obtain self-reports (Gainen and Locatelli, 1995).

A third major category of intended learning outcomes is the area of skill and performance. A skilled individual is one who has developed expertise based on training and practice. Many vocational, technical, and professional education programs require students to develop psychomotor skills that involve perception, dexterity, and coordination. Areas such as the performing arts, health professions, physical education, and architecture emphasize psychomotor skills that should be assessed using performance measures that include direct observation (Kinnick and Walleri, 1995).

In addition to psychomotor skills, thinking skills, affective skills, and communication skills are identified in assessment programs and are, in fact, often interrelated. Communication skills, for example, include both cognitive and psychomotor elements. The curriculum at Alverno College is based on integrated developmental abilities that are assessed through individual performances. Among others, these abilities include communication, problem solving, valuing, social interaction, and aesthetic response—abilities that combine cognitive, affective, and skill outcomes (Loacker and Mentkowski, 1993; Hutcheson, 1997).

With respect to their associate degree students, the nursing faculty at the University of South Carolina–Aiken, have identified eleven program objectives, including some that are cognitive (knowing the subject), affective (appreciating the need for thought and reflection), and psychomotor (demonstrating abilities or skills to process information). Nursing students are required to weave these objectives together through critical thinking. The latter is applied as students examine issues, make decisions, and construct care plans (Cullen and Cook, 1998).

According to the Accounting Education Change Commission, graduates of accounting programs are expected to display competence with respect to intellectual skills such as thinking critically, interpersonal skills such as teamwork and interacting with diverse groups of people, and communication skills such as listening effectively (Gainen and Locatelli, 1995, p. 47).

T. Dary Erwin (1991) draws a distinction between subject matter objectives and more permanent and lasting developmental objectives. The former require students "to learn the vocabulary, principles, and theories associated with the discipline" (p. 37). The latter are concerned with "the ways in which people express their mode of thinking and feeling" (p. 39). Cognitive developmental objectives refer to higher-order thinking skills, whereas affective objectives include personal and social aspects involved in "developing the whole person" (p. 39). For example, Chickering's (1969) developmental model includes affective outcomes such as managing emotions, establishing identity, clarifying purposes, and developing integrity (Chickering and Reisser, 1993).

Most programs will identify some intended outcomes for their graduates in each of the categories just described. At the Virginia Military Institute, the measurement of outcomes such as written and oral communication, problem solving, critical thinking, and computing is supplemented with the assessment of intellectual and metacognitive development, including locus of control, learning style, and approach to processing information (Z. Zhang and R. S. RiCharde, personal communication, Sept. 18, 1997). The types of intended outcomes faculty choose have implications for appropriate assessment methods. For example, survey instruments can be quite helpful in obtaining information about affective outcomes, but less helpful in determining whether students have mastered appropriate skills.

Other Types of Intended Outcomes

In addition to intended outcomes concerned with knowledge, skills, attitudes, and values, many assessment programs are concerned with those that reflect on the success of their students. A recent taxonomy of outcomes developed by the National Postsecondary Education Cooperative (NPEC) working group (U.S. Department of Education, 1997) explicitly includes educational success as one of its elements. This refers to retention, persistence, educational attainment, time to degree, and satisfaction. Other elements of the NPEC taxonomy are occupational preparation including job placement, licensure, and job satisfaction; the development of workplace skills such as dependability, initiative, and leadership; and quality of life attainment such as sense of well-being, savings and investment behaviors, and leisure activity. Assessment programs at several institutions include the examination of factors involved in program completion, as well as determination of the satisfaction and success of their graduates. If important, statements about expectations in these areas should accompany those about expected knowledge, skills, and attitudes.

Engineering faculty at the New Jersey Institute of Technology have defined four types of outcomes considered essential for comprehensively evaluating the effectiveness of their curriculum: student, course, program, and professional (McGourty, Sebastian, and Swart, 1997). At the student level assessment focuses on knowledge and ability of individuals and groups to apply that knowledge in real or simulated settings. Courses are evaluated in terms of content coverage and quality of delivery as viewed by multiple raters, including students. Completion and retention rates are one criterion for judging effectiveness at the program level. Assessment criteria at the professional level include placement and promotion rates, income, employer satisfaction, and performance in postbaccalaureate education.

Developing Statements of Expectations

Developing statements about intended outcomes is clearly an area where faculty need to reach consensus. In fact, it is one of the most challenging aspects of assessment. To begin, faculty should check to see whether statements of intended outcomes are already available. Perhaps faculty have reached general agreement about expectations for their students and only need to update or disseminate the objectives. More likely, learning objectives exist for individual courses but not for the program as a whole. In this case, some departments begin by examining what is currently being taught in each of their courses. Examining course syllabi, classroom assignments, and other materials can help in developing statements of intended outcomes. Many faculty include learning objectives in their syllabi, although the language may describe what the instructor intends to cover rather than what students are expected to know and be able to do. Looking at current assignments for students, as well as the performance of students on these assignments, can help clarify expectations. These materials, and the discussion that takes place about them, can help faculty get started on preparing statements of expectations for the program.

In many disciplines, the standards and guidelines for learning developed by professional associations or accrediting bodies are key sources of information. Statements of expected outcomes developed by colleagues at other campuses can also be helpful. Informal or formal descriptions from employers about their expectations for graduates need to be considered. At Spartanburg Technical College, for instance, every five years faculty in each academic program ask technicians in the field to help them identify the skills, knowledge, attitudes and other characteristics needed for successful entry-level employees (J. Cantrell, personal communication, Sept. 15, 1997). Drawing on the advice of current and former students and involving them in developing statements is recommended as well (Banta, 1996b).

Faculty discussion about what is expected of students is necessary. As a group, faculty can consider such issues as the characteristics of an "ideal" graduate, expectations of alumni five years after graduation, characteristics necessary for graduates to succeed in the workplace or in advanced programs of study, and current aspects of the program that seem to be working best (Moore, 1992). These discussions can pay great dividends, not only in terms of creating written statements about intended learning outcomes but also in terms of the process of communication in which faculty engage. In fact, faculty who participate in such discussions often comment on how rewarding they are (Hill, 1996).

Chris Rust (1997) recently reported on his assessment experiences at the Oxford Brookes University in England. Faculty teaching each subject major were required to develop a graduate profile including explicit statements about what the graduates of a particular major should be able to do in terms of intended outcomes. According to Rust, this activity "had the great benefit of getting faculty to talk to one another about what they are trying to achieve in teaching their respective subjects" (p. 6). The graduate profiles also benefit students by making expectations for the major clear.

Using Matrices and Other Tools

In a recent column, "The Power of a Matrix," Banta (1996a) described the advantages of using matrices to address various aspects of assessment. A matrix is a rectangle divided into rows and columns that can be used to organize information. In defining learning objectives for their program, nursing faculty at the Indiana University

School of Nursing started with a simple list of five or six broad skills and then used a matrix to break each of these into subskills. Faculty conceptualized the broad area of time management as a set of subskills including managing the student's own time, managing one patient's care in a specified time, and managing care of several patients in a specified time. The matrix was then expanded to include the specific courses and experiences where these skills were addressed (see Exhibit 2.1).

A matrix displaying the methods used to provide evidence that the subskills were being learned was also created (see Exhibit 2.2).

The task of stating learning objectives can be greatly enhanced by asking faculty to complete a matrix that has possible levels of process skills (such as know, analyze, synthesize) as column headings and space to enter content areas as row headings. Faculty can use the matrix to link content areas and skill levels. Completing this kind of matrix can help faculty think through and then state the objectives they have for learning in their classrooms. See Exhibit 2.3 for an example of a learning objectives matrix.

After faculty develop statements of intended learning outcomes in their courses, a process of review and refinement can take place, building from the level of individual courses to the level of the program. At one college, the development of statements about expected outcomes for students began with individual faculty, but also included department chairs and the curriculum committee. Each group made important contributions to the final statements (Hill,

Exhibit 2.1. Subskills by Activities Matrix

Skill	Subskills		
Time Management	Manages own time	Manages one patient's care in specified time	Manages care of several patients in specified time
	Courses 101, 120	Clinical experience	Hospital setting

1996). We made the point earlier that it does not matter what language the faculty adopt as they proceed, but it is helpful if statements are written at a similar level of precision. For example, applying concepts of accounting is a broader level of accomplishment than identifying the tools typically used for monetary and fiscal policy. The latter is only one of several concepts students would be expected to master in economics. Faculty also should expect that programmatic objectives will be broader than those taught in individual courses.

Exhibit 2.2. Subskills by Measures Matrix

Subskills	*Measures*				
	Student Self Assessment	Faculty Rating Scale	Supervisor Observation	Written Exam	Patient Questionnaire
Manages own time	✔	✔			
Manages one patient's care in specified time	✔		✔		
Manages care of several patients in specified time	✔		✔	✔	✔

Exhibit 2.3. Learning Objectives Matrix

Content Areas	*Know*	*Analyze*	*Synthesize*	*Evaluate*
Monetary System	✔			
Monetary Policy		✔		✔
International Trade		✔	✔	

Objective: Students will be able to evaluate the impact of monetary policy on the economy.

Besides using matrices, another helpful approach is to have individual faculty members complete a goals inventory about one or more of the courses they teach. The Teaching Goals Inventory (TGI) developed by Tom Angelo and K. Patricia Cross (1993) can be used for this purpose. The TGI includes fifty-two goals divided into six categories, including higher-order thinking skills, basic academic success skills, discipline-specific knowledge and skills, liberal arts and values, work and career preparation, and personal development. Each of the goals within these areas is rated either essential, very important, important, unimportant, or not applicable. Completing the TGI and discussing the results can be used as an initial step in stating programmatic objectives.

A Delphi technique can also be used for reaching consensus about intended learning outcomes. In this technique, faculty complete a series of questionnaires designed to identify important skills. At each step in the process, responses from the previous administration of the questionnaire are provided to participants so they can revise their responses on subsequent forms. Peter A. Facione (1990) and a group of experts used a Delphi technique to define critical thinking.

Writing Good Outcomes Statements

To be most useful, outcomes statements should describe, using action verbs, student learning or behavior rather than teacher behavior; use simple language when possible; and describe an intended outcome rather than subject matter coverage (Erwin, 1991; Diamond, 1998). Care should be used to choose words that are not open to interpretation. Words like identify, solve, and construct are better than vague words such as understand and appreciate (Diamond, 1998; Freeman and Lewis, 1998). Ratcliff (1994) cautions faculty to make sure their goals are assessable. It may not make sense to claim that a program develops the whole person if there is no way to demonstrate this.

Some statements of learning objectives include performance criteria and frequency of performance. For example, in political science students may be expected to communicate *effectively* with three types of audiences. The aim should be enough specificity to guide assessment without requiring such precision that it becomes difficult to reach consensus about what is important. Some disciplines may find the behavioral approach of disaggregating goals into small steps in order to measure performance against standards quite unappealing. As Ratcliff (1997a) notes, some faculty are not comfortable with any framework that subordinates thought and imagination to "slavish consistency" (p. 147). Assessment approaches need to allow for "that messy discourse labeled as the advancement of knowledge" (p. 148) and to foster creativity and expression.

Assessment Planning

Although articulating learning objectives is vital, planning is required if assessment is to succeed. Planning is the establishment of a "readiness to act" on the basis of shared understanding (Chaffee and Jacobson, 1997, p. 233). A representative committee or task force must design a useful approach to assessment. The existence of an explicit and useful assessment plan helps support the assessment process (Peterson and Einarson, 1998). A written assessment plan is a statement of agreement about the measures and processes to be used in examining educational programs. However, emphasis should be on developing a workable design for assessment rather than on the quality of the written plan.

Planning Levels

In addition to institutional planning for assessment, on most campuses planning also occurs at the unit level. At large universities, planning may occur at the division level (units that may be called colleges or schools) as well as at the department (or program) level. Generally, institutional planning will be concerned with developing the process for assessing general education, selecting campuswide assessment activities, and establishing requirements for unit plans. The institutional plan may call for specific actions on the part of units or may allow each unit to develop its own assessment approach.

At SIUE, for example, faculty in all thirty-three academic majors were asked to develop Senior Assignments, which demonstrate that baccalaureate candidates have met learning expectations in their majors and in general education (Eder, 1996). On some campuses, departments are asked to write assessment plans but are given little specific direction about content. Most often faculty are given a generic outline to use as they develop plans to assess the major. The outline may ask for a description of learning goals, assessment techniques, and provisions for administering the plan.

If faculty are concerned about the contribution individual courses are making to an academic program, the institution or unit plan may call for the collection of assessment information at the course level. The assessment plan for Ball State University's MBA program asks instructors to provide evidence from their courses that students are achieving the overall learning goals of the MBA program. Course instructors design their own approaches for data collection.

Assessment activities tend to be broad and inclusive at the institutional level and increasingly specific at lower levels. A campuswide senior survey may ask students to rate their ability to communicate orally. In contrast, marketing students taking a capstone course may be asked to give oral presentations that are evaluated on several specific criteria, including the ability to hold an audience's attention. Whereas requirements for assessment planning and activities may flow from the top to the bottom, assessment results may flow from the bottom to the top (Nichols, 1995b). Assessment results generated in individual courses may flow upward to a committee assessing the program, and results from program-level assessment may be shared with a campuswide committee.

The basic organizational structure of the institution can have a direct impact on the assessment program that is implemented. For example, a large university is more likely to have a decentralized assessment program with each division creating its own assessment plan. Overall, private institutions are less likely to have assessment programs than public, and research and doctoral institutions report less comprehensive assessment programs than other institutional types (Peterson, 1998). Compared to four-year institutions, two-year institutions are more likely to assess basic college skills and to examine program completion, continuing education, and employer satisfaction (Peterson and Einarson, 1998).

Based on an extensive literature review, Peterson and Einarson report several decision-making patterns. In some cases, decision making for assessment is centralized at high administrative and governance levels, in others it is decentralized across units, and in some cases decision making is centralized with respect to strategies and planning but decentralized with respect to implementing results. The College of Arts and Sciences of the University of New England offers an example of the latter approach. The dean established an interdisciplinary committee to create a college assessment program. The committee required each department to design and implement its own assessment plan, but results of assessment were for department use only and did not need to be shared across the college. The committee's role was to make sure that department plans were implemented, not to monitor results (St. Ours and Corsello, 1998).

Elements of an Assessment Plan

Several aspects of the assessment process need to be described when writing an assessment plan, including the purposes for assessment, methods that will be used, the timeline for administration, the framework for using assessment information, and provisions for administering the plan. However, having a well-written plan does not guarantee successful assessment. The plan must reflect discussion and consensus among those charged with developing the plan and must be seen as a starting point for conducting the assessment program, not the final word. The following sections describe aspects of assessment that should be of continuing concern and should be regularly revisited throughout the assessment process.

Subject Matter of Assessment

This section of the plan (or aspect of planning) establishes why the program is being implemented and its scope. In addition to internal goals for improvement, an institutional plan must recognize the needs of relevant external audiences for assessment information, including regional accrediting bodies, state initiatives, and community interests. Whether the assessment program is aimed at improving and/or documenting the achievement of individual students should also be acknowledged. Unit plans should recognize needs of discipline-specific bodies, as well as any institutional guidelines that must be followed. The needs of internal and external audiences help establish the purposes for assessment and the relative mix between accountability efforts and initiatives for improvement. Although regional accreditation has been a strong influence in increasing campus assessment efforts (El-Khawas, 1995), all regional accreditors assert that the main intent of their policies is to promote institutional improvement (Peterson and Einarson, 1998).

The institution's mission needs to be considered in establishing the subject matter for assessment. At Spartanburg Technical College, for example, a mission-related goal is to equip students with "the knowledge, skills, and attitudes necessary to successfully secure a job, pursue a career, or transfer to a four-year college or university" (J. Cantrell, personal communication, Sept. 15, 1997). Each department defines competence in knowledge, skills, and attitudes and expects that at least 85 percent of its students will master each competence.

Units within an institution may establish their own mission statements that provide direction for assessment. In addition to undergraduate programs, the unit may have minor or graduate programs that need to be assessed and may also need to participate in programs to assess general education or computer competence.

Goals and objectives for learning must be identified as a basis for assessing all of these educational programs. These should be completed, or at least in working form, when the assessment plan or design is developed.

Methodology

This section of the plan describes the activities that will be used to examine whether or not learning objectives are being met. An institutional assessment plan should describe any assessment activities that will be carried out at the campuswide level, such as surveying alumni who graduated five years previously or administering a standardized test to a sample of sophomores. These activities generally concentrate on learning goals that cut across discipline lines, such as computer competence, clear communication, and ability to work in groups. General education learning goals may be addressed by, for example, asking all students to complete a common critical thinking instrument. Large-scale projects such as senior or alumni surveys can also address common aspects of the major, such as opportunities to learn computer applications related to the field or to participate in internships. Results can be disaggregated and provided to individual departments. However, information about specific learning in the major can only be obtained at the program level.

In deciding what instruments to use, faculty need to establish and consider various selection criteria (discussed further in Chapter Four). For example, they should consider the ability of various instruments to provide information that is relevant and useful for their purposes (U.S. Department of Education, 1998). Both institutional and unit plans should demonstrate a relationship between the learning goals that have been articulated and the methods that will be used. If faculty are concerned about developing an appreciation for lifelong learning, for instance, they need to demonstrate how one or more of the methods they have selected will demonstrate student achievement in this area. Perhaps students will develop portfolios that include an essay about their personal learning goals.

The methodology section of the plan should provide specifics about the target groups for assessment. Faculty who are going to conduct focus groups need to describe the characteristics of participants, such as employers in the local community or graduating seniors. If students are the target group, the plan should describe how the results will affect them. Will methods be used to document or improve their performance? Perhaps an entry-level assessment of writing will determine the placement of students in initial writing courses. The plan should also describe the approach for data collection. Although campuswide activities ordinarily occur outside the classroom, faculty at the program level can draw on what is going on in the classroom for assessment purposes.

Time Line

The time line addresses major steps in the assessment process, such as developing goals and objectives (if they are not yet available), collecting information, issuing reports, making decisions, and reviewing progress. Both external and internal needs should be considered when the time line is developed. The schedule of reviews by regional or professional agencies or state reporting requirements generally will have a major impact on the time line, as will an institutional schedule for internal program review. Because curriculum modifications frequently need approval by time-consuming campus governance processes, established deadlines for including academic program changes in the institution's catalogue may be a factor. Time lines for unit assessment plans must reflect reporting requirements established by campuswide committees, and certainly the unit's own timetable of internal needs for information should not be overlooked.

Use of Assessment Information

The assessment plan (or design) should describe how assessment information will be used, including likely analysis of data, types of reports that will be prepared, and intended audiences. It is particularly important to describe any internal processes for discussion, review, and decision making.

A key issue is how assessment results will be linked to other important processes. Often, recommendations for improvements and new initiatives will be prepared by an assessment committee and forwarded to more than one organizational unit for action. For example, a curriculum committee may act on suggestions with respect to course content and structure, whereas a faculty development group may act on suggestions for workshops about writing across the curriculum. Ewell (1994b) argues for development of an organizational map that shows which results will be used by which units.

Some colleges and departments specifically require assessment information before changes in curricula and programs can be considered or approved. Others explicitly link the assessment process to their internal budgeting process, setting aside a block of funds for initiatives to improve student learning based on recommendations from assessment activities. Several institutions have been successful in using assessment results to make their case for additional funding from state government. Both Ohio University and Truman State University have been particularly successful in this effort, as has the University of Tennessee, Knoxville, as it has pursued the Tennessee Higher Education Commission's performance funding plan (Magruder, McManis, and Young, 1997; Williford, 1997; Banta, Rudolph, Van Dyke, and Fisher, 1996). Based on its assessment information, Ohio University has received numerous academic challenge and program excellence awards from the Ohio Board of Regents for programs such as telecommunications, creative writing, film, and general education (Williford and Moden, 1993).

Many institutions have established program review processes that serve important external and internal needs for information. If assessment is going to be viewed as a meaningful undertaking, the information it generates must be included in program review. At Indiana University–Purdue University Indianapolis (IUPUI), program review reflects a commitment to continuous improvement of programs and services and draws on assessment information provided by the Information Management and Institutional Research Office, as well as from departments and programs themselves.

At the University of Scranton, the departmental annual report (DAR) was intentionally used as a vehicle to encourage assessment. Reflecting the importance of the DAR in charting progress and identifying budget needs, departments were asked to identify in their DARs any student outcome information that had been collected or discussed in the past year. After three years using this approach, nearly all departments now include references to assessment activity in their annual reports (Hogan and Stamford, 1997).

Provisions for Administering the Plan

Decisions about administration are decisions about roles and responsibilities. Institutions differ both in who writes the plan and who carries it out. If an ad hoc task force is charged with responsibility for designing a campuswide assessment plan, provisions must be made for administering the plan after it is approved. An existing senate committee may take on this role or a new committee may be created. In most cases, the committee that creates the plan will have continued responsibility for its administration. This campuswide committee may review reports submitted by units and make (or approve) recommendations for improvements to educational programs.

Separate provisions may be made for carrying out activities described in the plan. An existing campus office may assume this role or a new staff person may be identified. For example, a director of writing competence may be appointed to administer campuswide writing examinations or a faculty member may receive release time for this purpose. Likewise, a committee member or professional staff may need to support assessment by analyzing data, particularly for large-scale projects. Report writing may fall to committee members or to staff. The best plans call for involvement of several individuals and groups (Ewell, 1994b). Ewell points out that the faculty-staff committees responsible for assessment too often "see their job only as establishing a program, not developing and communicating its implications on an ongoing basis" (1997e, p. 377). He also warns against the syndrome of "administrative isolation" (p. 376) that can occur when assessment becomes too focused on external reporting and is not built into regular academic planning processes.

Assessing Assessment

A thorough plan will include provisions for evaluating the assessment program itself. In fact, the goal of refining the assessment program should be established from the start of planning and clear means to evaluate the program should be identified (Peterson, Einarson, Trice, and Nichols, 1997). The most important consideration is whether or not the assessment process is leading to improvements in academic and cocurricular programs. Although a key factor is whether or not assessment methods are closely linked to learning objectives, evaluating assessment requires more than monitoring the effectiveness of methods. It involves examining if appropriate constituencies including faculty, students, and staff are represented in the assessment process and if the institution's or unit's needs are being served. The assessment plan should include specific opportunities to reflect on the assessment process. For example, the plan may call for the assessment committee to devote a regular meeting to this discussion each year, asking if any problems have been identified, whether activities need to be modified or expanded, and whether information is being made available to appropriate audiences (Nichols, 1995a, 1995b). However, any issues about the assessment process should be considered as they arise, not postponed to an annual meeting. Voices other than those on the assessment committee also need to be heard. Students should be given opportunities to critique assessment projects as they participate in them and focus groups of assessment audiences can be held at any time.

At some institutions, the campuswide assessment committee reviews annual reports of assessment activities submitted by campus units, critiquing progress and offering suggestions for improvement. At IUPUI the plan states that the assessment program itself will be the subject of an external peer review at least once in ten years. Although evaluation of the assessment process is very important, recent studies of practices at several institutions have found few that evaluate the effectiveness of their assessment instruments and activities (Patton, Dasher-Alston, Ratteray, and Kait, 1996; Peterson, Einarson, Trice, and Nichols, 1997).

Formatting a Plan

Several possibilities exist for formatting an assessment plan. Most plans consist of a narrative describing assessment purposes and processes. In some cases, a campus committee will provide departments with a specific outline containing a series of topics that becomes the blueprint for the plan. See Exhibit 2.4 for an example.

Occasionally, the outline will be in a table format with a series of column headings to guide the narrative. Headings might ask for the following information about each of the program's learning goals: instructional activities addressing the goal, anticipated outcomes, assessment methods, time line, and processes for reviewing the information.

Another formatting approach is to organize the plan around a time line of activities and actions. This may include such things as establishing goals and objectives for learning, engaging in assessment activities, reviewing information, and making recommendations. Although it must reflect a great deal of thought, an assessment plan need not be lengthy. It needs to be sufficiently specific that all those involved know who is going to do what, when they will do it, and how they will use the information that is generated.

Helping Departments Plan

The job of planning at the unit level can be greatly enhanced if appropriate materials are provided to those who have been requested to write a plan. The undergraduate curriculum and assessment committee of Ball State's College of Business developed several "Char-

Exhibit 2.4. Assessment Plan Outline

1. Departmental Goals: Describe what the department intends to accomplish, how the department's goals relate to campus mission, and purposes for assessment.
2. Learning Objectives: Describe what students must know, do, and value.
3. Techniques and Target Groups: Indicate how you will determine whether learning objectives have been met, including methods, target groups, and any impact on students.
4. Time Line: Indicate when data will be collected and analyzed, when reports will be available, and when recommendations will be made.
5. Provisions for Administration: Indicate who has responsibility for seeing the plan is carried out, who will collect and analyze data, and who will summarize and report results.
6. Use of Information: Describe provisions for sharing information with internal and external audiences, and for making recommendations and decisions.
7. Assessment Evaluation: Indicate how the assessment program itself will be evaluated.

acteristics of an Assessment Plan" for faculty who were designing assessment plans for their programs. The characteristics identified by the committee included the following:

- All learning goals are identified and addressed by assessment procedures.

- Multiple assessment measures are used.

- Procedures are efficient.

- The plan includes a description of people, committees, and processes involved.

- The plan "closes the loop" (that is, uses the assessment information).

To achieve efficiency, the committee recommended the use of samples of student work and university-wide data where appropriate. The list of characteristics proved very useful when the committee critiqued program assessment plans.

At the end of its first year of department-based assessment activities, a committee of faculty members at Ohio University created what it calls a "list of best practices," including "a clear statement of department-specific goals that matches reported assessment activities" and "a focus on student outcomes with emphasis on both benchmarks and value-added measures" (Williford, 1997, p. 54).

Most regional accrediting bodies have developed a set of characteristics that must be reflected in institutional assessment plans. The North Central Association *Handbook of Accreditation* (1994) includes five guidelines for plans submitted by their members. Plans must be linked to the institution's mission, goals, and objectives for academic achievement, including learning in general education and the major. They must show evidence of faculty involvement. Plans need to incorporate an appropriate time line and provisions for administration. They also need to demonstrate likelihood that the assessment program will lead to institutional improvement (p. 156).

Evaluating Plans

Committee members or others who will be reviewing assessment plans should have a set of established evaluation criteria. Sometimes, a list of desirable characteristics or best practices similar to those just described can be used to evaluate plans. In other cases, a separate list of criteria is provided. In order to encourage carefully developed plans, North Carolina State University developed twenty-six standards for use in evaluating plans. In addition to appropriate statements of mission and program purposes, plans must provide precise statements of what students are expected to learn. The standards call for a reasonable number (three to five) of outcomes, including at least one that is cognitive- or knowledge-based. Plans must identify processes for communicating results to faculty and for using results to improve programs (Green, 1993, pp. 4–5). To be most helpful, the set of criteria for evaluating plans should be distributed in advance to those who will be writing plans. Identification of the committees and individuals who will be responsible for evaluating unit plans is also important and should be clearly spelled out in the institutional or divisional plan. Similar provisions must be in place for evaluating assessment reports that may be required from campus units after the assessment program is implemented.

Anticipating Costs

Although specific figures ordinarily do not appear in the assessment plan itself, it is impossible to do meaningful planning without some consideration of cost. Assessment takes a great deal of effort by many individuals. Occasionally, new positions are created in order to carry out assessment, but most frequently, faculty and staff time is reallocated from other efforts. Thus, rather than separately budgeted new funds, the greatest cost of assessment is generally the opportunity cost of using faculty time on assessment rather than something else.

Some tangible costs will occur. Faculty may receive stipends for participating in faculty development activities related to assessment or small grants for carrying out assessment projects. There may be initial costs for background materials and consultants hired to train faculty and staff. There also will be costs for the materials needed to carry out projects. Surveys need to be printed and mailed. Data must be entered. Reports have to be reproduced and shared. Funds for these purposes may have to be reallocated from dollars previously used for other activities.

No established figures or guidelines exist for the financial costs of assessment. Expenditures vary greatly across institutions. Some campuses keep costs quite low by using locally developed instruments and classroom assignments as sources of assessment information. Others, particularly those using combinations of locally developed and commercial instruments, incur higher costs. At

Washington State University some assessment costs are transferred directly to students, who pay a $9 fee to take a locally developed entry-level writing examination (Haswell and Wyche-Smith, 1996). Some institutions have been successful in securing external funding from businesses or government agencies to support assessment projects. The Fund for the Improvement of Postsecondary Education (FIPSE) has supported many assessment projects.

The commitment of campus leaders to assessment is visibly demonstrated in the area of resources. Providing funds for materials, faculty stipends, and faculty-staff development efforts demonstrates support of assessment, as does providing resources for recommended changes in educational programs based on assessment results.

Stretching Resources

Faculty faced with limited resources can adopt a number of strategies. First, they need to set priorities and concentrate on the most important questions. Perhaps they are most concerned about internships or study abroad experiences. Second, they may be able to alternate their activities. Everything does not need to be done every year. Collecting information from a sample of students may be sufficient to answer programmatic assessment questions. Using existing information and taking advantage of campuswide assessment or institutional research information can help conserve resources. Using naturally occurring data collection points such as orientation, required courses, or application for graduation is an additional strategy.

SIUE, the University of Maryland College Park, and Winthrop University are three of many institutions that take advantage of existing points of contact with students to collect data in cost-effective ways. SIUE and Maryland conduct surveys on graduation day. Each student must hand in a card containing his or her name so that it can be read by a faculty marshal during commencement. SIUE simply places a couple of questions on the card and asks graduates to respond as they are waiting in line (D. J. Eder, personal communication, Sept. 23, 1997). At Maryland this same strategy is designed to yield responses that can be compared across colleges and schools (D. Moore, personal communication, Sept. 15, 1997). Winthrop University incorporates its senior survey into an exit conference conducted with each graduating senior by the Office of Records and Registration (Prus and Tebo-Messina, 1996).

Picking a Starting Point

A very practical question about timing is where to start the process of assessment. Some schools start by identifying their most pressing question, perhaps examining their learning objectives or conducting a curriculum review. If a department has recently introduced a new program such as one to improve writing competence, it may wish to concentrate initial efforts on determining the value of this program. Sometimes the best approach is to enhance an activity already in use, such as an alumni questionnaire. The latter may be expanded from a short survey concentrating on employment questions to a longer survey asking about preparation in important areas of learning. Some units begin by doing a pilot study, thus helping to decide which direction is best. For example, portfolios may be tried out with a sample of students before being widely used. The overall assessment questions and needs of the department provide the best direction about where to start (Wolff and Harris, 1994). Tom Angelo (1998) recommends that departments start by examining their strengths, rather than focusing on their problems. The latter can cause contention; the former can build on what the program does well.

A Word of Caution

Writing assessment plans and articulating goals and objectives for learning are necessary components of successful assessment programs. Unfortunately, these activities can sometimes become so labor intensive that they get in the way of moving forward. To a large extent assessment has to be viewed as a work in progress. Thus, it is possible to make plans without having goals and objectives perfectly articulated. It is also possible to engage in assessment activities without having a beautifully written plan. Sometimes, a general consensus about direction is all that is needed to get started. And, if the choice is between plans without activities or activities without plans, the latter is sometimes the better of the two. Remember, plans are often written and rewritten based on experience, so getting started with a less-than-perfect plan in place is sometimes a good choice. In fact, Peter Ewell (1997e) explicitly cautions against "excessive rigidity in planning and carrying out assessment activities" (p. 377). Instead, he recommends an approach where goals and hypotheses are continually reformulated based on emerging data.

3

Encouraging Involvement
in Assessment

INVOLVE (*v.*): to include or occupy

Of all the important factors in creating a successful assessment program, none matters more than widespread involvement of those who are affected by it. For this reason, it is vital that faculty have a strong role in the assessment process. Indeed, as one observer has said, "If administrators want faculty to shape the assessment process, then they need to turn assessment over to faculty" (Pitts, Lowe, Ranieri, and Palomba, 1997). Students, too, need to be valued participants in the assessment process. In this chapter, we discuss several approaches for involving faculty and students in assessment. (Many of our suggestions apply equally well to involving professional staff who have responsibilities for educating students.)

Involving Faculty in Assessment

In this section of the chapter, we consider ways to ensure that faculty take the lead in carrying out assessment programs. We have organized our discussion around three Rs of faculty involvement: responsibility, resources, and rewards. Faculty need to have clearly defined roles, they need to have resources to learn about and understand assessment, and they need to receive rewards for their efforts such as recognition, stipends, or funds for assessment-related

travel. If these three Rs are used wisely, they will help overcome another R of assessment, faculty resistance.

Faculty Responsibility

To ensure assessment is a faculty-driven activity, faculty must have
responsibility for carrying it out. Initially, faculty should articulate
the purposes of assessment for the campus or unit, select a comfortable definition of assessment, and identify the central questions or
areas of inquiry that will drive assessment activities. Further, they
should develop learning objectives, create assessment plans, select
and design assessment tools, interpret results, and develop recommendations based on assessment findings. In other words, faculty
need to be involved in all steps of the assessment process.

Carrying out these responsibilities will take several forms and
will differ from individual to individual. Some faculty will serve as
assessment coordinators in their departments. Some will serve on
department, division, or campuswide committees that provide direction for assessment. Serving on assessment committees puts faculty in leadership roles with respect to assessment and often
becomes a major responsibility for them. Committee members generally are more knowledgeable about assessment matters and more
involved in making decisions about assessment. Although the number of faculty members serving on assessment committees may be
small, other faculty will participate in assessment by attending meetings, administering assessment instruments in their classes, providing comments, and responding to other requests with respect to
assessment. Some faculty will have responsibility for analyzing data
or writing reports. Where possible, their interests should drive how
they contribute. For example, those who enjoy planning should
plan, and those who enjoy working with data should conduct analysis. Ann Ferren warns assessment leaders to "set realistic goals for
faculty involvement" (1993, p. 3) and to expect involvement to be
"episodic" with faculty moving in and out of active roles (p. 5).

Certain approaches to assessment lead to more involvement
than others. On some campuses, faculty who are teaching general

studies courses are asked to demonstrate that these courses are meeting the learning goals of the program. Thus course instructors must work together as they develop and carry out a plan for assessing the course. In this approach, the responsibility for assessment is placed directly on individual classroom teachers, usually with a campuswide committee that acts as a review body for the reports it receives from faculty.

An explicit list of expectations about the roles of various groups involved in the assessment process can help clarify and establish responsibilities. After faculty on the graduate curriculum and assessment committee (GCAC) of Ball State's College of Business developed a draft assessment plan for the MBA program, they created a statement of responsibilities for all parties, including individual faculty members, students, and the GCAC. The plan and statement were then presented to the entire graduate faculty for approval. Sharing the statement with all faculty made it clear what was expected of them, as well as what they could expect of others (N. Palomba, 1997). Exhibit 3.1 displays this statement.

Assessment Resources for Faculty

The resources provided for faculty must mirror faculty responsibilities. Information about the reasons for undertaking assessment, strategies for formulating learning outcomes, and possible approaches for writing assessment plans are all important topics and well worth any time spent on them. Only after faculty are comfortable with the basics of assessment should time be spent on learning about methods. Here, we describe some of the assessment resources available to faculty.

Written Materials Developed on Campus

Many institutions have developed assessment materials for internal use. Some of these are meant for all faculty regardless of their disciplines; others have been developed within departments or colleges and are discipline specific. Examples include pamphlets describing assessment, question and answer documents, and loose-leaf binders

Exhibit 3.1. Participation in Assessment of the MBA Program

Faculty, Students, and the Graduate Curriculum
and Assessment Committee (GCAC)

MBA faculty are expected to provide the GCAC with

A checklist of course coverage vis-à-vis MBA program objectives
A copy of the course syllabus
An assessment plan that indicates how program objectives addressed
in the course will be assessed
An assessment report with results and conclusions
Exam questions for the MBA Core Competency examination

MBA students are expected to

Participate in written assessment projects
Maintain examples of their classroom assignments
Complete a Core Competency Exam

The GCAC will

Review faculty checklists to determine if program objectives are
being met
Review course assessment plans and reports
Review selected examples of student work
Review the results of the Core Competency Exam
Provide faculty with feedback and opportunities for discussion at each
stage of the assessment process

---

containing assessment materials that can be supplemented as time passes. Several campuses use assessment newsletters that keep faculty up to date on what is happening locally as well as in the overall field of assessment. At Southern Illinois University Edwardsville (SIUE), assessment office staff have placed a number of faculty development resources on the Assessment Web Page (D. J. Eder, personal communication, Sept. 22, 1997). Some campuses have developed workbooks that contain comprehensive information about assessment (Rogers and Sando, 1996; Wolf, 1993; Palomba and others, 1992). Eastern Michigan University has created both a "Questions and Answers About Assessment in the Academic Major at EMU" brochure and a monthly newsletter with the title "Assessment Matters" (Bennion, Collins, and Work, 1994).

There are specific points in the assessment process where it is particularly helpful to provide faculty with resource materials that can facilitate their tasks. For example, the work of faculty who are asked to create plans to assess their programs can be greatly enhanced if they have an outline to follow. Other helpful materials include a list of characteristics of good assessment plans or a list of criteria that will be used to critique plans after they are submitted. At Ohio University such criteria include a clear statement of goals, faculty involvement, use of multiple measures from entry to exit, use of data collected centrally, and evidence that data are used to direct improvements (A. M. Williford, personal communication, Sept. 19, 1997). If faculty are expected to submit annual assessment reports, providing them with a report outline is helpful. Criteria for evaluating reports about assessment activities can also be developed and shared with faculty.

Written Materials from Other Sources

Several helpful books have been written about assessment (Banta and Associates, 1993; Banta, Lund, Black, and Oblander, 1996; Gainen and Locatelli, 1995; Nichols, 1995a, 1995b) that provide overviews of the process and specific examples about the experiences of many institutions and departments. *Assessment Update*, a bimonthly publication, is another valuable source, not only for examples of assessment in practice but also for more general discussions of assessment trends. The American Association for Higher Education Assessment Forum has published a helpful resource guide, *Learning Through Assessment* (Gardiner, Anderson, and Cambridge, 1997), that contains annotated bibliographies as well as descriptions of several assessment instruments. Another useful way to obtain written assessment materials is to request them from other institutions. The practice of assessment has been marked by a tremendous willingness of institutions to share with one another. For example, many campuses have developed Web sites containing assessment materials, including Montana State University and George Mason University (Connolly and Lambert, 1997).

National, Regional, and State Conferences

The American Association for Higher Education (AAHE) began its annual assessment conference more than a decade ago and continues to draw more than a thousand participants each year. This conference provides sessions that cover many areas of assessment, including examples from individual campuses and discussions of assessment issues. The annual assessment conference in Indianapolis is now in its eighth year, and for six years prior to the move to its present site it was held in Knoxville, Tennessee. Alverno College regularly conducts one-day sessions that provide participants with information about ability-based curriculum design. Participants are invited to spend "A Day at Alverno College" focused on teaching and assessing student abilities. For more than a decade, a number of states, such as Virginia and South Carolina, have convened assessment practitioners from within their boundaries and beyond for annual conferences. The Virginia Community College System Group has presented workshops on assessment design and techniques through interactive video teleconferencing (Banks, 1996). Many discipline-specific conferences such as speech communication and physical education also highlight assessment issues.

These conferences give faculty a tremendous opportunity to learn about assessment. At the AAHE conference the sessions are tracked by subject matter and by level of expertise so that attendees can make good choices about which sessions to attend. At the Indianapolis conference, all participants have several opportunities to hear from national assessment leaders. Both of these conferences are preceded and followed by workshops that allow participants to study specific aspects of assessment in more detail. It is impossible to attend these conferences without becoming significantly more knowledgeable about assessment.

Campus Gatherings

In addition to sending faculty to national or regional conferences, strategies are available for faculty to learn about assessment on their own campuses. Many departments regularly offer lectures or symposia for faculty. External assessment experts can be invited to share general or specific information at these gatherings. Alternatively, experts on campus can share their knowledge with others, providing a real source of expertise. For example, faculty in teachers' colleges or English departments may have experience with portfolios or with developing learning goals and objectives they are willing to share with faculty in other units. Faculty at Ferris State University were invited to a series of sessions led by members of their own faculty and staff who are experienced in aspects of assessment. Each session included an overview of a particular topic followed by a question-and-answer period. The program was called the "This-Is-How-We-Do-It Series" and was well received by faculty (Outcomes Assessment Council, 1994, p. 49). Workshops can serve similar purposes but are usually designed to give participants a chance to actually work with the information they are receiving. For example, faculty can complete worksheets designed to help them state learning objectives.

At Northern Illinois University, several departments have scheduled full-day retreats to launch assessment planning. Faculty are asked to bring any materials developed by disciplinary associations and to think about desired student outcomes. At the retreat the campus assessment coordinator provides some background information about assessment and writing program-level objectives. Then faculty work in subject area groups to develop drafts of student learning objectives (R. Gold, M. Pritchard, and S. Miller, personal communication, Oct. 29, 1997).

Rather than conducting workshops that tend to last no longer than a day or two, another strategy is to create a "working group." Working groups tend to meet over a period of several weeks, generally with the goal of completing some task. This strategy has been used with classroom assessment where faculty meet once a week for two or three weeks to learn techniques and then meet several additional times to report on their experiences using these techniques in the classroom. Discussion groups are a similar strategy but tend to be more open-ended and less focused on completing a particular task.

Other ways to gather faculty together to learn about assessment include brown-bag lunches, round tables, town-hall style meetings, and development days. The latter might involve several presentations on a particular topic. The University of Indianapolis recently devoted its annual fall Faculty/Staff Institute to the topic of assessment, inviting faculty to present posters describing their assessment activities. Twenty-three faculty participated by creating posters and preparing abstracts that were included in a descriptive booklet. The poster session was well received by attendees who found it helpful in learning about assessment (Domholdt, 1996). Faculty at Eastern Michigan University and surrounding campuses were invited to display posters describing their assessment work at a one-day Assessment Expo held in spring 1998. In addition to professional colleagues, students were also invited to come and learn about assessment (Bennion and Work, 1998).

Institutional Support

Appropriate institutional and administrative support for assessment greatly enhances faculty efforts. Secretarial support is necessary for activities such as letter writing, data entry, logging surveys, and other tasks. Support from professional staff and administrators is also important. Some divisions have an undergraduate or graduate program coordinator who can facilitate the activities of the faculty and maintain an overall view of how assessment is proceeding. At campuses where there is no assessment office, there may be an institutional research office with responsibility for facilitating assessment. An alumni, career services, or student affairs office may engage in assessment-related activities or have expertise that can support assessment in other units. For example, career services may be collecting useful information about the short-term placement of graduates. At many campuses, computing center staff have expertise in designing research projects or in survey or test construction that can facilitate assessment.

Faculty Rewards

Faculty who participate in assessment should be rewarded for their efforts. Some of the rewards are intrinsic. A well-designed assessment program will result in interaction with other faculty that may have been lacking in the past. It will lead to improved clarity with respect to goals and objectives for learning and ultimately to improved teaching and learning. Faculty may also see a link between assessment and other important processes such as internal program review, planning, and budgeting. The latter is particularly rewarding if additional funding is made available to achieve departmental objectives. Faculty in units that are accredited by professional organizations often show strong support for assessment, reflecting the increased interest of accreditors.

What about more explicit rewards? In some units, faculty may receive release time to serve as assessment coordinators or to undertake projects. At Northern Illinois University, faculty involvement has been encouraged initially through release time for a single faculty member for one course for one semester (R. Gold, M. Pritchard, and S. Miller, personal communication, Oct. 29, 1997). This has provided time for the individual to study assessment, attend campus workshops and national conferences, and prepare to lead colleagues in identifying course and curriculum outcomes and selecting or designing assessment instruments.

Promotion and tenure processes should also recognize assessment efforts. In some units, faculty are encouraged to report assessment activities on their annual reports under the heading of teaching and teaching-related activities. Assessment may also be recognized as service to the department, division, or campus.

Recognition

At many institutions, participation in assessment leads to recognition on the local campus. Presenting posters, writing reviews of activities for local newsletters, or giving on-campus presentations provide recognition for assessment efforts. Faculty also have opportunities to publish articles about their assessment activities in journals that are related to the disciplines. Accounting, mathematics, economics, journalism, and other fields have journals that publish assessment-related studies. The bimonthly *Assessment Update* provides an opportunity for faculty to publish their work. These activities can be supported through release time for faculty research and should be recognized in the promotion and tenure process.

Grant Programs

These programs can take several forms. Some institutions provide substantial grants to a small number of faculty who are undertaking major projects. In this model, a team of faculty might receive release time to accomplish a large-scale assessment project during the academic year. At Ohio University $200,000 annually is set aside for awards to six units that propose to improve undergraduate education using assessment data to establish need and chart progress (A. M. Williford, personal communication, Sept. 19, 1997). At Northern Illinois University (NIU), four to six proposals are funded annually to accomplish substantial assessment projects. Initially the NIU Assessment Committee awarded grants to faculty who were interested in student outcomes as a research area and had innovative project ideas. As departments became more involved, faculty proposals were required to demonstrate a relationship to the assessment plan for a degree program. Grants often fund the work of teams composed of faculty and graduate students (Gold and Hewitt, 1996).

Another approach is to give smaller grants for work that can be accomplished during the summer. Summer grants give faculty the opportunity to focus their energies on specific projects in a concentrated time frame. Rather than conducting routine assessment business, the summer can be used to undertake a task that is quite focused, such as developing an alumni survey. It is often easier to create faculty teams in the summer, when schedules are more flexible. The usual approach to awarding summer grants is to ask for proposals that are reviewed by a committee of peers. Guidelines for grants generally ask for a description of the project and a statement of how the project fits into department assessment plans. The proposal should also include a description of how results will be used.

Faculty may need some guidance in applying for assessment grants because they are not quite sure what a credible assessment project involves. To ensure that proposals focus on important tasks needed to move a department's overall assessment program forward, faculty should be encouraged to consult with deans, chairs, or assessment committee members about what might be included in a proposal.

Ball State University has had a very successful summer grant program in place for several years. Each summer, as many as forty faculty members work individually or on teams to undertake assessment projects. Stipends range from $300 to a maximum of $1,200 depending on the focus of the project and the number of individuals involved. Although many proposals arise from faculty members, the director of the Office of Academic Assessment also visits with deans and department chairs early in the spring semester to discuss assessment needs. After a plan for summer activities is developed, faculty are invited to work on the projects. This approach has brought more focus to summer activities and has helped colleges and departments make great strides in assessment.

Travel Funds

Because there are several conferences that focus on assessment, faculty have opportunities to give presentations about their assessment activities to audiences beyond their own campuses. Funding this travel is a way to reward faculty for their assessment activities. Providing funds for faculty who are new to assessment to attend conferences, perhaps with colleagues who are presenting there, is an effective way to encourage additional faculty involvement in assessment.

Maximizing the Role of Faculty and Faculty Acceptance

At most institutions there is a desire to maximize the role of faculty in assessment—to involve as many individuals as possible and to engage them in meaningful ways. In this section we share some hints about maximizing the role of faculty in assessment. These observations come from our own experiences working with faculty from many different disciplines. And because faculty can play a role in assessment without necessarily valuing it, we also address the issue of faculty acceptance.

Share Tasks Wisely

A number of strategies can increase the likelihood that many faculty will assume responsibility for assessment. First, involvement is maximized if each faculty member is given at least some role in the process. That role may be something easy to accomplish, such as reviewing a plan developed by a committee or ranking the importance of program goals. It may be much more extensive, such as developing an assessment plan to reflect the contributions of an individual course to an overall academic program or designing an assessment instrument. The important point is that faculty cannot be involved in assessment if they have no responsibility for its undertaking.

A second strategy is to put in place a plan that divides the assessment process into specific assignments. It is easier to involve faculty if they know the specific task at hand and if they can approach the assessment program as a series of steps rather than an overwhelming burden. As Ann Ferren states, "Assessment can be made up of many small projects, which, when integrated, give a fuller picture " (1993, p. 7). Taking an incremental approach is greatly facilitated by a plan with a clearly developed time line. For example, the initial step of developing statements about goals and objectives for learning can be followed by a careful consideration of assessment techniques that address them.

Next, make sure that faculty are involved in every step of the process. Too often, faculty are asked to articulate learning objectives for their courses, but the department chair writes the assessment plan. The assessment committee should be responsible for actually creating the assessment plan, not for providing comments on approaches proposed by administrators (Chaffee and Jacobson, 1997). A different pitfall occurs when a small committee takes so much control of the process that the typical faculty member has little role. Thus, broadly representative committees and shared tasks are preferred.

Use at Least Some Local Instruments

Assessment practitioners have learned from experience that the role of faculty can be maximized if local instruments are used rather than nationally available instruments. As John Muffo recently observed on the basis of his decade of experience in assessment, "faculty, like many others, will accept the results of studies most readily if they gather the data themselves. . . . It's far better to have less-than-perfect data gathered by departmental faculty than perfect data from some other source" (Muffo, 1996, p. 1). Integrating assessment activities into the classroom and drawing on what faculty are already doing increases faculty involvement.

Encourage Teamwork and Team Building

Educators understand the value of teamwork for students and frequently give group assignments in the classroom. Similarly, assessment flourishes when faculty, staff, and students work together. Not only the assessment committee but additional faculty members should have opportunities to work in teams. For instance, several faculty can be invited to design a portfolio project. One of the benefits of grant programs is the ability to get several individuals together to collaborate on specific projects.

Chaffee and Jacobson (1997) recommend team-building activities for groups that will be working together on planning. Strategies include brainstorming—that is, getting all the ideas out on the table for careful attention—and consensus taking to see if there is substantial agreement on essential points. Senge (1990) distinguishes between dialogue, where a group openly examines previously held assumptions and explores complex issues from many perspectives, and discussion, where different points of view are presented and defended. Teams that work well must use both as they seek to reach agreement. Brookfield (1995) suggests having ground rules for group conversations that might include such things as providing evidence for assertions; taking periodic breaks to allow those who have not spoken to do so; limiting the time any one person can speak; and including periods of mandated silence for reflection (allowing participants to think about their own thinking) at some point in each meeting. To be meaningful, each group must set up its own ground rules and, of course, follow them. Occasionally, inviting an outsider to help facilitate meetings is a good idea. An assessment specialist may be able to help faculty keep focused at meetings and make the progress needed to keep everyone engaged.

Meetings should be held only when there is a specific agenda. Although it is often helpful for faculty to get together, especially if they are trying to accomplish a specific task, they can contribute to assessment in many ways without attending meetings. Reactions, suggestions, and ideas can be solicited through campus mail or e-mail.

Foster Acceptance of Assessment

Maximizing the role of faculty may contribute to faculty acceptance, but it is only one of several ingredients. At the most basic level, it helps to concentrate on important questions—questions that faculty care about. Start with what matters most and, rather than trying to assess every possible program goal, concentrate on three or four major learning objectives.

Faculty often have concerns about the methods and instruments used to collect assessment data. They are not likely to accept results generated with instruments that are not of high quality, and they will not support decisions based on this information. Issues of reliability and validity need to be addressed, and campus experts on instrument design should review data collection instruments and procedures. Faculty acceptance of assessment is also enhanced if assessment information is used in appropriate ways. If information is collected but not acted on, faculty soon lose interest in continued participation.

Helpful Administrative Actions

Key administrators have an important role in the assessment process. The actions they take can hinder assessment or foster it. If administrators view assessment as an unpleasant burden, many faculty will as well. Likewise, administrators can impose unnecessary restrictions on how the program is carried out. For example, they may insist on a particular method, such as standardized testing.

Administrators need to be willing to express as well as reiterate a sincere commitment to assessment; allow adequate time for faculty to understand, accept, and carry out assessment; encourage and support use of assessment information; and be flexible in their approach. A college dean recently summarized some of the lessons he has learned after working with assessment for several years. In his view, faculty must design the assessment program themselves. However, "You have to let faculty know that assessment is a serious endeavor, and you have to be willing to repeat yourself." He also feels that, "While being flexible about time schedules helps faculty make progress, faculty need to see annual progress if they are to maintain interest" (N. Palomba, 1997).

View Faculty Development as a Continuing Process

Just as the student body changes from year to year, so do at least some members of the faculty. Thus faculty development related to assessment must be seen as a continuous process. On many campuses new faculty receive an introduction to outcomes assessment during the annual orientation for newcomers. According to D. Eder (personal communication, Sept. 22, 1997), new faculty at SIUE "are beginning to ask their departments to become more engaged in assessment."

Some Stumbling Blocks in Understanding Assessment

For assessment to be successful it must build on shared values. Some points of confusion create stumbling blocks in the way faculty view assessment and these are areas in which clarification is particularly important.

Entry-Level Placement

Many programs collect and use information about potential students to determine their qualifications for entering a program. In some cases, information is also used to select the appropriate level for students to begin their studies. Educators are comfortable making these decisions. They realize how important it is to select students who are qualified for their programs and to place new students at appropriate levels for learning. The information collected for entry-level decisions about individual students often provides a good starting point for assessing academic programs. Reviewing initial papers, performances, and portfolios provides valuable information about where students begin. Programmatic assessment requires faculty to collect information about the curriculum as a whole. Faculty need to know where students end up, as well as where they begin, and something about what happens along the way. Thus, although entry-level data collection might be part of an overall program of assessment, it can only be a beginning. Additional information needs to be collected during the time students are on campus.

Course Grades

Confusion often arises about the role of course grades in assessment. One of the primary functions of teachers is to grade individual students in their classes. Course grades tell students how they did in the class relative to other students and convey to students how well they have met their teachers' expectations. Grades also allow educators to compare groups of students across courses and over time using a common (although inconsistently applied) measure. Some faculty believe their grade distributions tell all there is to know about the performance of students in their classes. This belief is one of the biggest stumbling blocks in getting individual faculty involved in and excited about assessment.

Why aren't course grades enough? The assignment of a grade to an individual student provides a summary measure about the student's performance in the class and, perhaps, tells something about the standards of the teacher. It does not usually convey direct information about which of the course's goals and objectives for learning have been met or how well they have been met by the student. Likewise, the grade distribution for the class as a whole tells about the relative performance of the group of students but not about what or how much they have learned. Course grades alone do not necessarily help students improve. To be meaningful, assessment should provide both students and faculty with information for improvement at both course and program levels. A recent article by Barbara Wright (1997) contains a discussion of these issues. She notes the supportive and respectful spirit of assessment as compared to the often judgmental nature of assigning course grades. As Leon Gardiner (1994) reminds us, rather than generating improvement, the preeminent use of grades is for those outside the institution, such as employers and graduate schools, to use when selecting among graduates.

In a move that is all too rare in higher education, faculty at Rivier College are working to integrate goals described in the institution's mission statement and the standards on which grades are based (P. F. Cunningham, personal communication, Aug. 27, 1997). That is, individual course grades should reflect that a student has achieved specific course objectives and collegewide general education goals and competences at a level considered appropriate for the course and subject matter.

Tests and activities on which grades are based can be useful for assessment. But educators must find ways to take what they have learned from these activities and make it meaningful for assessment purposes.

Faculty Evaluation

Many faculty fear the relationship between assessment and faculty evaluation, often thinking the two processes are the same. Thus it is important to make a clear distinction between them. The information collected through assessment strategies is collected for the purpose of evaluating programs, not faculty members. Yet many times assessment activities generate results that may reflect on individuals. This information can be made available to these instructors for purposes of improvement, but should not be included in their personnel folders nor used for making tenure, promotion, or salary decisions. An essential factor in making assessment work is building trust among faculty that the information collected through assessment activities will not be used for inappropriate purposes. A clear distinction must be made between rewarding assessment activities and using assessment findings. As we noted earlier, faculty should be rewarded for the time and energy they invest in assessment-related activities. Institutions should encourage the recognition of assessment activities in faculty review processes.

The Nature of Resistance

At least two recent national surveys have identified faculty resistance as among the most important challenges facing assessment

(Ewell, 1996; Steele, 1996). Although we saved a description of the last R, faculty resistance, until the end of our discussion about faculty involvement, it is important to be aware of its nature. Some faculty, as well as administrators, resist assessment for a number of reasons. Some continue to believe that assessment is primarily for external audiences and fail to see its potential to improve programs. Some resent the cost of assessment in terms of time and resources. Others question the quality of the data collected. Some fear their efforts will be for naught if the information is not used; others fear that the information will actually be used but in some way that is harmful to their interests.

Some faculty view assessment as a threat to academic freedom. As several observers have pointed out, many faculty consider teaching to be a very private activity and they do not want to open themselves to judgment on the results of this endeavor. Assessment requires a sharing of information and a commonality of goals that can cause individuals to be uncomfortable at times. Assessment is a group activity that requires a great deal of openness.

Because of these issues, some faculty question the value of assessment. Fortunately, many who initially fear assessment come to accept it over time. This chapter has considered a variety of ways to support the role of faculty in assessment. If faculty have responsibility, resources, and rewards for participating in assessment, the chance they will come to appreciate its value greatly increases.

Involving Students in Assessment

Assessment must be seen as an activity done with and for students, rather than to them. Students need to be active partners in assessment. Here we discuss several ways to involve students in the assessment process. As with our discussion of involving faculty, we refer to three areas of importance: responsibility, resources, and rewards. Students need to know what is expected of them, have appropriate support and information to live up to these expectations, and have some incentive or reward for their participation. If educators are thoughtful about how they include students in the assessment process, they can help overcome motivation problems that can hinder assessment.

Student Responsibility

In order for assessment to work, students must be active participants. Questionnaires and focus groups can obtain information from other interested parties, but assessment information that directly demonstrates the learning of students originates with students themselves. Thus, the most basic responsibility of students is to participate in direct assessment activities such as tests, performance measures, and portfolios as well as indirect assessment activities such as interviews and focus groups. In addition to participating in activities, students can play a number of other roles in the assessment process.

Serving on Committees

Several campuses or units include students on their assessment committees. In this capacity, students play a very important role, helping to conceptualize and design the overall program. In addition, students may serve on task forces that are concerned with developing specific assessment instruments. For example, students can help plan activities such as portfolios or other performance projects. Some colleges or departments have student advisory boards that contribute advice on a variety of topics. Asking these boards to provide feedback and suggestions about the assessment process makes sense.

Providing Comments

Whether or not they are serving in an official advisory capacity, students should be encouraged to provide their comments about the activities in which they participate. This can happen in both formal and informal ways. Many assessment instruments ask students about the usefulness of what they are doing. For example, students who are completing portfolios are often asked to provide comments

about what they have learned from their experiences and how valuable the activities have been for them. Students can also be asked
to participate in focus groups that are concerned with various aspects of the assessment process, such as examining the value of a
capstone experience.

Even without a specific request for comments, students can be
quite vocal about an assessment activity that they do not feel is
worthwhile. Educators need to consider these opinions very carefully. Students will ordinarily have great insight into the value of
what they are asked to do. Listening to them does not mean faculty
have to abandon what they are doing every time students voice
criticisms. It may mean they need to make some modifications in
their approach. For example, one university modified its writing
competence examination for juniors after receiving a steady stream
of negative comments from students. Many students felt the test du-
plicated assessment in their writing classes and was too general in
the topics provided. The examination was changed so that students
now sign up for specific test sessions in which they receive essay topics related to their majors. They also receive their writing topics at
the test sessions rather than in advance. These changes have helped
increase the motivation of students to do well on their essays.

Facilitating Assessment

At some institutions, students play yet another role with respect to
assessment: acting as assessors themselves. One fairly common example of this is with respect to group work. Many group work projects ask students to evaluate the functioning of the group and the
contributions of other students, as well as themselves, to the group.
In fact, Jack McGourty (McGourty, Sebastian, and Swart, 1997) at
the New Jersey Institute of Technology has designed software called
Student Developer to enable these assessments to be recorded and
summarized electronically. Students can also be asked to critique
class projects or presentations of other students. They will need
some instructions and practice to do this well.

At Alverno College, professional communication students in a junior-level course work in teams to devise a campaign theme and rationale, design a logo and other visual materials, and create an outline for a promotional event for a local nonprofit agency. In addition to evaluations by the instructor and the agency representative, students receive peer assessments of their contributions to their team's culminating presentation (A. J. Johnson, personal communication, Sept. 26, 1997).

Students can be trained to conduct telephone interviews or to take notes for focus groups. The University of Minnesota uses work-study students called "pulsers" to conduct regularly scheduled telephone surveys of undergraduate students. Project Pulse surveys are used to investigate needs of the institution and are requested by various units on campus including colleges, departments, and student affairs offices. Approximately twenty surveys are conducted each year (Upcraft and Schuh, 1996, p. 42).

Students can help interpret results from completed assessment projects. For example, focus groups of students can be useful if faculty want to gain insight about test or survey results that are surprising. Students can also help the assessment process by acting as mentors for other students. Juniors and seniors can be asked to help freshmen get started on portfolios. Students can be asked to work together or be available to help each other prepare for assessment activities that involve performances or products.

Resources for Students

Universities, colleges, and departments can provide information for students to help them fulfill their assessment responsibilities. These approaches include catalogue statements, flyers, brochures, project instructions, and examples of completed assessment activities. All of these approaches can help students understand what assessment is about, why they are asked to participate, what is expected of them, and how they will be evaluated. In particular, students must be made aware of the goals and objectives for learning that drive programs. If students are aware of what faculty want them to know, do, and value, they have a much better likelihood of achieving these objectives.

Catalogue Statements

A Web search reveals that many institutions include statements about assessment in their catalogues. Generally, these statements are relatively short but nevertheless describe the basic responsibility of students. Whereas many statements indicate that participation in assessment is *required* of all students, other statements indicate that participation in assessment is *expected*.

The 1995–97 catalogue at Bloomsburg University of Pennsylvania includes the following statement of expectations about student participation in assessment activities: "The university routinely conducts campus-based studies of student attitudes, student achievement, student satisfaction, and personal, professional and career development. These studies are grouped under the heading of student outcomes assessment. Participation in outcomes assessment activities is expected of all students. While every student is not selected for participation in every activity, it is likely that an individual student will be involved in one or more assessment activities during the college years. It is only through cooperative participation in the assessment process that the university can better understand itself and better serve its students" (p. 58).

In contrast, Jacksonville State University's 1996–97 catalogue includes the following statement requiring students to participate in assessment activities: "To assess and improve its academic programs, the University must obtain periodic measurements of student perceptions and intellectual growth. As a requirement for graduation, all seniors must take a general education achievement test (currently, the College BASE Examination) and complete a Graduating Senior Questionnaire. Additionally, some programs require that their majors take a comprehensive test of achievement in the discipline. Students may also be required to participate in other evaluations of University programs and services. The information obtained through these assessment procedures is used solely to improve the quality of the educational experience for future generations of JSU students" (p. 38).

Both of these catalogue statements are concerned with obtaining information for programmatic assessment. The first statement sets out an expectation, the second a requirement. Although participation in the same assessment activities is required of every student at JSU, graduation is not tied to any performance level. If students are required to achieve a satisfactory level of performance on an assessment activity as a condition for graduation or advancement within a program, they should be made aware of this in the catalogue. For example, a particular performance level on a test of writing or computer competence may be required. If this is the case, students need to know.

Statements such as those just reproduced contain information that is applicable to all students, but catalogues can also contain statements about assessment activities in particular majors. Several programs require students to complete standardized assessment tests such as the Educational Testing Service Major Field Tests prior to graduation. Some colleges require students to pass the general knowledge and communication skills sections of the National Teachers Examination prior to participation in student teaching. If so, the catalogue needs to include these requirements.

Brochures and Flyers

In addition to catalogue statements, some campuses have developed other materials to convey information about assessment activities. Truman State University has developed a small but effective brochure for students called "Assessment at Truman." Although the brochure is sixteen pages long, it is only four inches wide and six inches tall. The brochure opens with a letter from the university president expressing the hope that students will use assessment activities as tools for self-improvement as well as a means to provide feedback to faculty and staff at the university. It contains descriptions of the tests, surveys, writing experiences, and other assessment activities in which students at Truman State University participate. It estimates the amount of time students will spend on each activity and indicates that students will spend an average of sixteen total hours on assessment while at the university. The brochure ends with an invitation for students to help assess the assessment program. Students are told they can participate in this process by serving on the advisory panel, participating in focus groups and interviews, or simply providing their comments.

Some schools provide flyers or brochures when students begin classes; others provide them earlier, perhaps at orientation. In fact, some campuses provide flyers to both parents and students at orientation. This is particularly helpful if students are being asked to participate in testing at that time. These flyers can be used to describe the purposes of testing, how it will affect grades and placement in courses, how much time it and other assessment activities will take, and who will see results.

Brochures and flyers about assessment in particular programs can often be more specific than those provided to all students. For example, a brochure designed for majors can provide a rationale for each of the programs' learning goals, explain how goals are addressed in various courses, and describe how assessment activities will be used to determine if these goals are being achieved.

Project Instructions

Students need to have specific directions for all the assessment activities in which they participate. Instructions are particularly important with respect to comprehensive projects such as portfolios, where students are asked to accumulate materials for an extended time. As they begin their portfolios, students need to have enough information to understand the overall dimensions of the project. They need to know what is currently expected of them, as well as what they will be asked to provide in subsequent classes or time periods. They also need to be aware of the specific criteria that will be used to judge their portfolios. This is true for other types of performance assessment as well. Students need to know what is expected of them and how their performance will be scored. Some institutions provide written guidelines for creating portfolios and participating in performance assessment. Others ask their students to attend orientation sessions so any questions they have can be addressed. It is important as part of any instructions to indicate how information will be used and to assure students that their results will be treated confidentially. Almost all institutions have policies regarding the use of human subjects in research that may be applicable for assessment projects.

Examples

Another helpful approach for providing assessment information to students is to let them examine past examples. Students who are being asked to develop portfolios can be provided examples that represent a range of work. Opportunities to examine average work as well as excellent work can be very useful. Such material can be helpful with respect to other performance projects as well, such as essays or art objects. Versions of assessment tests that are no longer in use can also be made available.

Student Rewards

Just as some faculty rewards from assessment are intrinsic and others extrinsic, the same is true for student rewards. Students can and should benefit from the assessment process in a variety of ways.

Improved Programs

Assessment frequently leads to changes in academic programs (Banta and Associates, 1993; Banta, Lund, Black, and Oblander, 1996). Although some improvements may be introduced after current students have left campus, many faculty have been able to introduce changes rather quickly so current students benefit as well. Improvements such as clearer syllabi, more fully articulated goals and objectives for learning, and more explicit evaluation standards are often introduced soon after assessment programs are initiated. In addition, improvements to instruction based on classroom assessment activities may occur immediately. Nevertheless, some change is slower in coming. Fortunately, as evidenced by their thankful comments on student surveys, we have observed that current students often welcome the opportunity to provide feedback about what they have experienced, even if it is future students who may benefit.

Feedback

Direct feedback to students about their own performances is an additional benefit of many assessment projects. Although some tests provide only group results, many assessment instruments provide results at the individual level. In these cases, it is recommended that students be given their scores. One of the primary advantages of performance assessment is the opportunity to give direct and immediate feedback to students. In some cases, feedback will be provided by professionals in the field as well as by departmental faculty. Peer review is also included in several assessment projects.

Grant Wiggins (1997) has argued strongly for the appropriate use of feedback. He notes, "You can't learn without feedback" (p. 33). Useful feedback lets students know what they did or did not do, without expressing approval or disapproval. It is "rich, clear, and direct enough to enable students and teachers to self-assess accurately and self-correct their own performances increasingly over time" (Wiggins, 1998, p. 12). Helpful feedback causes students to think about what they have or haven't done, and how they can improve. Wiggins argues for assessment strategies that "include the student's ability to use the feedback" (1997, p. 35). Because self-adjustment is more important than self-assessment, students learn best if they can respond to feedback, if they can decide which feedback to take and why, and if they can explain their choices. In Wiggins' view, the best assessment allows faculty to see if students can deal with feedback.

Survey projects can also be structured to provide feedback to students. In many cases, students are asked if they would like to receive a summary of results. Those who answer "yes" can be sent a short summary of highlights from the project. Alternatively, a page or two of results can be sent to all participants. Results can also be made available through department, college, or university Web pages.

Some schools have developed survey projects that provide individualized results for participants. These reports can be created using word-merge software. Ball State University's Making Achievement Possible Survey (MAP) is administered to entering freshmen each fall semester. Soon after they complete the survey, respondents receive a personalized report with specific messages based on their own responses to the survey. For example, students who indicate they plan to study only a few hours per week are reminded that faculty will expect them to study approximately two hours for each hour spent in class. Many students report that they find this feedback very valuable. The MAP project is a collaboration between the Learning Center, Academic Assessment, Housing and Residence Life, and Academic Advising.

Opportunities for Reflection and Self-Assessment

Although students often need time to develop self-assessment skills, among the greatest benefits from many assessment projects is the opportunity they provide students to reflect on their own learning and development. Kramp and Humphreys describe self-assessment as "a complex, multidimensional activity in which students observe and judge their own performances in ways that influence and inform future learning and performance" (1995, p. 10). In their view, self-assessment provides a valuable opportunity for students to think carefully about their learning activities.

Most portfolio projects include specific requests for expressions of self-reflection. In fact, the very act of creating portfolios requires students to think carefully about the materials they have developed and their performance on these items. In addition, students are generally asked to justify their choices explicitly and to reflect on their growth through written statements or essays contained in their portfolios. Other direct assessment methods can also be used for self-reflection, including journal entries and oral presentations. Several classroom assessment techniques provide opportunities for self-assessment as well.

Nona Lyons believes that reflection should include "making connections" through critical, collaborative conversations rather than be conducted as a "solitary, individual enterprise" (1998b, p. 254). Reflection benefits from a listener who participates in the dialogue. In this view, as in Wiggins' view, feedback and reflection need to occur together.

Indirect assessment methods provide additional opportunities for self-assessment. Many surveys include blocks of questions asking students to reflect on their learning and development. Students often comment on surveys that they appreciate the chance to think about what they have experienced and to provide their reactions. Focus groups, too, provide an opportunity for students to consider and react to various aspects of their education.

Self-assessment is one of the hallmarks of the master's-level program for practicing professionals at the School of New Learning at DePaul University. Marienau and Fiddler (1997) report the results of research conducted with students in the master's program on the role of self-assessment in their professional development. Almost two-thirds of a group of eighty adult students said they had become more goal oriented as a result of engaging in self-assessment; more than half reported that they were taking more responsibility for their own work. The greatest impact of self-assessment appears to be on interpersonal skills: 75 percent of the participants in the study said they had become more active listeners, more adept at giving and receiving constructive feedback. Self-acceptance, self-confidence, autonomy, and self-direction in one's career were other attributes influenced by experience in self-assessment.

Tangible Rewards

Some campuses provide incentives for students to participate in assessment projects. Rewards such as passes to movies, coupons for free food, or small payments of money are sometimes used to increase participation in projects. In some cases, coupons are included in mailings to all eligible students. In other cases, respondents are sent a coupon after they have returned their assessment instruments. Students who participate in focus groups may be treated to pizza and sodas.

Rather than providing all participating students with small tokens, some campuses use raffles for institution-wide projects. For example, the cover letter for a survey may tell all students who are invited to participate that a small number of respondents will be randomly selected to win prizes. Prizes can include such things as cash awards or free semesters of books. Local bookstores are often willing to cooperate in providing free books or books at cost. These raffles can increase the motivation of students to participate in assessment projects. As one respondent optimistically wrote with respect to a possible cash prize for completing a survey, "Show me the money!"

Maximizing Student Acceptance of Assessment

The most important element in enhancing student acceptance of assessment is the commitment shown by faculty to assessment. The messages given by faculty with regard to assessment are very powerful motivators. If faculty care about assessment, students are much more likely to care too. Alternatively, if students perceive from the way faculty introduce an assessment project that they are not interested or actually resent the time the project is taking from other activities, students will be resentful as well. Even the most enthusiastic faculty need to share information with students about the purposes of assessment and the way the information will be used.

Tying assessment to classroom activities is also helpful. If assessment is seen as a natural part of the teaching and learning process, students are motivated to do well. Drawing on already existing classroom activities for assessment provides a way to utilize information that is tied to important consequences for students. Other consequences may exist as well; for example, at some institutions, participation in assessment has an impact on students' priority in registering for classes (Hyman, Beeler, and Benedict, 1994). Practical concerns are also important. In cases where students are required to attend testing sessions, provisions should be made for their convenience. Offering alternate test days may be necessary. At the University of Wisconsin–Superior, no classes are scheduled on testing days. In addition, a temporary day-care center is set up to accommodate students with child care responsibilities (Katz, 1996).

Acting Ethically

M. Lee Upcraft and John H. Schuh (1996, pp. 298–305) provide several suggestions for ethical conduct with respect to all assessment activities. Among others, ethical behavior includes the following considerations.

1. Where possible, give students the right to decide whether they will participate in an assessment. For example, students who are tested in orientation should be excused if they object. Assessment done in classes is often required, but should be an important factor in course grades only if it is a natural part of class assignments.

2. Ensure that participation in assessment does no harm. Information that is collected should be treated confidentially. No information should be released publicly in such a way that individual students are identified. Notes or tapes from focus

groups or interviews should never identify participants by name.

3. Explain the purposes of assessment projects to students and carry out projects as described. Researchers need to honor all promises for reports, feedback, and rewards. Overall, students need to be treated with respect, as valuable partners in assessment.

4

Selecting Methods and Approaches

METHOD (n.): a way of accomplishing something

Once faculty have completed the challenging work of articulating learning goals and objectives, it is time for them to examine, select, and, in many cases, develop the methods that will be used for assessment. As Reid Johnson and his coauthors point out, "There is no more critical juncture in implementing a successful assessment of the major than the moment of methods selection" (Johnson, McCormick, Prus, and Rogers, 1993, p. 153). This statement applies to assessment of general education programs as well. Appropriate and effective assessment methods are necessary for success.

An extensive array of possible assessment techniques exists, but some strategies are available to help in choosing among them. We begin by discussing the use of inventories to help identify methods already in place that can be used for assessment. We also discuss the importance of developing selection criteria—the characteristics of methods that are important. Central among these characteristics are validity and reliability, the hallmarks of technical quality. Others include timeliness, cost and benefit, and student motivation. Once faculty become familiar with assessment techniques, they can compare them with the selection criteria they have developed. We discuss them sequentially, but in reality many of the steps we suggest will occur simultaneously. For example, faculty often develop their criteria for good assessment methods at the same time they become familiar with various instruments. This chapter includes a brief overview of several assessment methods and concludes with some suggestions about developing local instruments.

Completing an Inventory of Existing Activities

Completing an inventory of current data collection methods may uncover several activities that, though not necessarily designed for programmatic assessment, can help to accomplish its purposes. An inventory may be undertaken at the campus level to identify departmental activities that provide information about student learning. Examples include capstone projects or exit interviews with graduating seniors. Alternatively, an inventory may be undertaken in an academic department to identify assignments or projects carried out by faculty in their classrooms. Faculty are often pleased to find that some of these activities can be used to assess their programs at the same time they assess the learning of individual students. Faculty at Ohio University found this to be true (Williford, 1997).

Members of a campuswide assessment committee can make personal visits to department chairs or faculty members to discuss current activities. Talking in person is particularly helpful when individuals are new to assessment and need some help in determining which activities could be useful for assessment. Another strategy is to obtain information through a written questionnaire about assessment practices. At Ferris State University these approaches were combined. The director of assessment first developed a questionnaire about assessment activities, then interviewed department heads and program coordinators to obtain responses. The survey collected information about the use of such activities as tracking performance on state, national, or professional licensing exams; surveying alumni; and administering locally developed competence assessments in the major. In addition to gathering information about activities, the survey and visits also provided information about the larger aims of outcomes assessment (Outcomes Assessment Council, 1994, p. 32). Thus the value of an inventory is greater than the benefit derived from counting who is doing what; it also serves an important educational function. On a more practical level, an inventory can be used to create a database for future reference by those who are considering a technique that has been tried elsewhere.

Developing Criteria for Choosing Methods

A useful strategy for selecting assessment instruments is to ask faculty to identify the qualities they consider most important in the instruments they will use. Discussing criteria and creating a list of characteristics that matter is a productive use of time. Faculty concerns about the quality of instruments will quickly become apparent. They will likely raise issues of reliability and validity—essential criteria for selecting instruments. Both faculty and administrators will be concerned with the cost of various methods. Here we examine some of the criteria that are most important in selecting assessment methods.

Relationship to Assessment Questions

The most important consideration in choosing among assessment methods is the ability of these methods to address assessment questions, issues of relevance and utility (U.S. Department of Education, 1998). Many methods have potential to answer several assessment questions, but are stronger for some purposes than others. For example, objective tests are quite useful in measuring knowledge and recall but less useful in determining skills, particularly as compared to performance measures. Surveys and focus groups are very helpful for determining student satisfaction and can also be used to determine the success of students who have graduated. They are less useful in determining whether students possess appropriate skills. The relative advantages of various methods need to be examined in light of specific assessment questions and the way the information will be used.

Reliability

Reliable measures are ones that can be counted on to produce consistent responses over time. Technically, reliability is a property of the scores or assessment data derived from using an instrument rather than of the instrument itself. An instrument yields reliable data to the extent that the variance in scores is attributable to actual differences in what is being measured, such as knowledge, performance, or attitudes. Data are unreliable to the extent that score variance is due to measurement error.

Cherry and Meyer (1993) describe three sources of measurement error: the individuals (students, faculty, alumni, or others) responding to the instrument, the administration and scoring of the instrument, and the instrument itself. Therefore faculty need to look at both the assessment instrument and the conditions under which it will be administered. The instrument must be well constructed—items must be worded clearly, words must be unambiguous, and possible responses to test or survey items must be developed appropriately. The length of the instrument must be consistent with the time available to administer it. If raters are involved, they must agree on the meaning of items in a well-designed scale.

Information about the internal consistency of items on an assessment instrument is important. That is, all the items on a scale designed to measure test anxiety should actually measure it. Techniques to determine internal consistency are available for both tests and survey instruments and provide information about how well the items on the instrument are related to one another. For example, surveys can be examined to see if responses to similar questions are genuinely similar. Screening questions can be included to see if respondents choose consistent answers.

With respect to instrument administration, the instructions given and the time allowed for completion must be consistent across administrations. The use of well-developed standards to train those who will be rating or scoring student responses is an additional concern. Measures of interrater reliability for instruments that involve rating scales are commonly used to compare ratings assigned by two or more raters. Coefficients of 0.70 or higher are recommended (Erwin, 1991), with 1.0 being perfect reliability and 0.0 representing total unreliability.

Reliability can be a troublesome issue in performance-based assessment. Delandshere and Petrosky (1994) suggest thinking differently about interrater reliability in this context, that "consistency . . . could be thought of as a process of confirmation rather than one of independent replication" (p. 16). Cherry and Meyer report that "at least eight different statistics—and probably more—have been used to compute the interrater reliability (or agreement) of holistic scoring" (1993, pp. 119–120). The irony of inconsistent methodology used to report a consistency statistic is not lost on practitioners. However, a review of the literature on reliability in performance assessment reveals consensus on these two issues: that interrater reliability can be significantly improved by careful training of evaluators, and that reliability and validity are enhanced by the development of clear, articulate scoring rubrics. Further, there appears to be emerging agreement on appropriate methods for calculating interrater reliability (Cherry and Meyer, 1993; Erwin, 1991; Linn and Baker, 1996).

An additional issue related to the reliability of performance-based assessment deals with the trade-off between reliability and validity. As the performance task increases in complexity and authenticity, which serves to increase validity, the lack of standardization serves to decrease reliability. Traditional measurement standards dictate that an instrument cannot be valid if it is not reliable. The challenge becomes to design or select assessment methods and instruments that achieve the most effective balance between these two concerns (Wiggins, 1993).

Validity

Once faculty have determined that an instrument is reliable, that it will provide dependable information time after time, they need to determine if it is appropriate for the use to which it will be put. This is an issue of validity, the most fundamental aspect of technical quality. Validity demands asking, "Does an instrument measure what we want it to measure?" Although the importance of validity cannot be overemphasized in theory, it is often given insufficient attention in practice, perhaps because it is a very complex concept. Gathering evidence to support an instrument's validity in a particular context is often a time-consuming and challenging task.

Technically speaking, as with reliability, validity is not a property of the instrument itself, although the term is commonly used in this way. Messick describes validity as "an overall evaluative judgment, founded on empirical evidence and theoretical rationales, of the adequacy and appropriateness of the inferences and actions based on test scores" (1988, p. 33). The program evaluation standards of the Joint Committee on Standards for Educational Evaluation (1994) stress that validity demands compiling evidence to support the interpretation and use of test or survey data for a particular purpose. The standards further recommend using multiple sources of data in order to make valid judgments about the quality of a program. As Linn and Baker (1996) point out, clarity about purposes, intended interpretations, and likely uses provide the "essential starting place for determining priorities" when evaluating the technical quality of an assessment instrument (p. 100). The term *validity* means scores on a test permit "appropriate inferences to be made about a specific group of people for specific purposes" (Crowl, 1996, p. 102). In White's words (1994, p. 32), "Validity means honesty, that we are measuring what we say we are measuring and that we know and can show what it is we are measuring."

Validity has many aspects; the most common are construct, criterion, and content. Construct-related validity, which undergirds all aspects of validity (Messick, 1988), refers to the congruence between the meaning of the underlying construct and the items on the test or survey. To support a claim of congruence, Crowl suggests asking: Do results correlate with other instruments examining the same construct? Do results differ for groups of individuals expected to exhibit differences? Do results change in expected ways as a function of factors that should affect the construct? For example, do scores on an instrument measuring anxiety increase prior to taking examinations?

Criterion-related validity includes predictive validity: How dependable is the relationship between the scores or answers on an instrument and a particular future outcome? It also includes concurrent validity: How well do scores estimate students' current standing on the characteristic of interest? Content-related validity refers to the match between the content of the instrument and the content of the curriculum or other domain of interest. In program assessment, the most important considerations are whether a given instrument contains items related to the curriculum being assessed and whether it provides evidence that learning was successful (Wiggins, 1998).

Other validity issues include the following: Is the instrument thorough in covering the objectives of the curriculum? Does it address desired levels of cognitive complexity? To what extent can results be generalized? Are tasks credible to those who will use the results? Will results provide useful information for improving programs? Linn and Baker (1996), as well as Herman, Aschbacher, and Winters (1992), raise these and other important issues associated with high-quality assessment. Whether or not the instrument provides information that relates to the success of students after completing their programs is particularly important when assessing achievement in the major. Most faculty care greatly whether their graduates are prepared for careers and for continuing education.

Timeliness and Cost

When confronted with the need to assess program effectiveness, faculty always ask how much time it will take. One great concern is that working on assessment projects will take time from other important tasks and will not be worth the effort. Thus the likely time demands of developing, administering, and evaluating various instruments should be examined. Even if exact estimates are unavailable, rough comparisons can be made. For example, commercial instruments require time for selection but not for development. Portfolio projects can require a great deal of time both for development and implementation. Campuses that administer writing competence exams need to allocate time for training of raters, as well as for scoring sessions for them to evaluate papers. To help faculty choose among classroom assessment techniques, Angelo and Cross (1993) rate each as low, medium, or high with respect to preparation time, response time for students in class, and analysis time.

Cost is also important and is related to time. That is, using faculty time on assessment rather than other activities involves a true opportunity cost. Tangible costs of various methods need to be considered. Commercial instruments can involve substantial costs for materials and scoring. Costing procedures differ by company and instrument. For purposes of test security, campuses that administer the Educational Testing Service Major Field Tests are sent test books that are numbered and sealed and must be returned. Test books must be paid for when they are ordered; campuses are only partially reimbursed for those they return unused. Surveys may involve considerable costs for mailing or telephone charges as well as for materials.

Motivation

It is important to choose instruments that will be valuable for students and that will elicit their cooperation. One of the strongest arguments in favor of course-embedded assessment techniques is their ability to draw on existing classroom activities and to overcome motivation problems associated with large-scale testing projects unrelated to the natural flow of teaching and learning (Ewell, 1991). Some assessment activities provide students with opportunities for active learning. In contrast to traditional classroom styles where teachers do the bulk of the work while students remain passive, active learning "provides opportunities for students to *talk and listen, read, write, and reflect*" about an academic subject (Meyers and Jones, 1993, p. xi). Case studies, simulations, role-playing, and problem-solving exercises require students to apply what they have learned, and if results of these activities are evaluated carefully they can be used as very effective assessment instruments. They also provide opportunities for people who learn in different ways to demonstrate their accomplishments, a concern voiced particularly by culturally diverse and nontraditional-age students (Meyers and Jones, 1993). In addition to using assessment techniques that are associated with active learning, some campuses administer instruments designed to determine preferred learning styles. Faculty choosing assessment techniques can consider results from these instruments when choosing assessment methods.

Assessment practitioners often seek information from individuals who are not current students, such as alumni or employers. Whether an assessment project will be successful in motivating these participants needs to be considered. Much as educators might like them to, alumni generally are unwilling to return to the campus for further testing. However, they are often willing to participate in surveys or focus groups or to write about their experiences.

Other Considerations

Additional questions can be raised about potential assessment instruments. Will results be easy to understand and interpret? Will fluctuations in results reflect changes in academic programs rather than something else? Will instruments provide information valuable for programmatic assessment as well as for documenting the achievement of individual students (Hatfield, Krueger, and Hatfield, 1998)? Assessment requires that educators look at their programs in a holistic way. This can be more difficult if individual faculty members are using a wide variety of techniques.

Whether information can be used for external reporting is another important question. Experts are divided about whether an instrument designed for improvement can also be used to demonstrate accountability. Furthermore, consequential validity—the consequences of using a particular instrument in a particular setting—has been heavily debated at conferences and on listservs devoted to educational measurement. For example, critics of standardized tests point to their unintended consequences in terms of narrowing the curriculum and reinforcing the use of instructional techniques inconsistent with active learning. Herman and her coauthors (1992) recommend asking whether an assessment represents an enduring problem that students are likely to face in their future lives. Fairness to individuals is an additional consideration. An assessment instrument should not be biased in favor of particular groups. Results should not reflect characteristics such as culture, gender, or socioeconomic background (Linn and Baker, 1996; U.S. Department of Education, 1998; Herman, Aschbacher, and Winters, 1992). Applying this criterion to performance assessment means looking at the traits that are chosen for measurement and the way they are scored in order to ensure there is no bias.

The criteria that are important to faculty in one program may differ from those that are important to faculty in other programs. When planning the evaluation of a recently funded program for freshmen, a newly appointed assessment and evaluation committee at one university developed a set of operating guidelines that included the following principles: use existing measures that are appropriate and available, avoid overlap or duplication of measures, and avoid overmeasuring in an effort to preclude being intrusive with students.

Becoming Acquainted with Possible Methods

After (or while) faculty develop criteria for selecting methods, they need to become familiar with the methods that are available and to consider how they might adapt these methods to their own use. In addition, because no list is exhaustive, they should have the opportunity to consider methods that may be completely new. Written materials and campus gatherings can be particularly useful in this process of familiarization. One important distinction is between techniques that directly determine whether students have mastered the content of their academic programs and those that ask students to reflect on their learning. Examiners for the North Central Association, one of six regional accreditors, have used this distinction as they evaluate the merits of assessment plans submitted by member institutions in their region (Lopez, 1996), and the New England Association of Colleges and Schools has also adopted this approach.

An Overview of Methods

Among direct assessment methods, most familiar are exams of all kinds, including multiple-choice and true-false tests where students select a response as well as essays and problems where students produce an answer. Both locally developed and nationally available instruments are widely used. Oral exams provide an alternative to pencil and paper tests and allow for extensive probing of student learning.

Direct measures include performance assessments that require students to demonstrate their competence in one or more skills. Many kinds of performance measures are in use, including oral presentations, projects, demonstrations, case studies, and simulations. Simulations are used when it is not feasible to demonstrate a skill in a real-world setting. Several medical programs now use "standardized patients" to assess their students' capabilities. Essentially, these patients are actors who have been carefully trained to describe particular illnesses to medical students who are then evaluated on their diagnostic skills (Barrows, 1997).

Portfolios constitute an important kind of performance assessment in which student work is collected over time. Their appeal is their ability to provide longitudinal information and opportunities for student reflection. Courts and McInerney (1993) point out that portfolios are powerful tools for guiding as well as assessing student learning, for encouraging students to take responsibility for their own learning, and for giving students a voice in assessment. In their view, "assessments inviting interaction, dialogue, reflection, and learning offer us a way to evaluate, respond, and promote learning" (pp. 49–50).

Additional direct measures include juried activities with outside panels who rate student work, evaluations of performance in internships or other field work, and scores on national licensure or professional exams. Many times direct measures of learning will be embedded in a capstone course or referred to as a capstone experience.

Indirect methods ask students to reflect on what they have learned and experienced rather than to demonstrate their knowledge and skills, providing proxy information about student learning. Methods such as questionnaires, interviews, and focus groups fall in this category. Each of these methods allows faculty to listen to their students' voices, to hear from them about what they have learned and experienced in academic programs.

Mailed questionnaires and telephone surveys are very popular assessment methods. Part of the appeal of surveys is the wide variety of information that can be collected. Students can be asked about their attitudes, opinions, experiences, expectations, perceptions, and needs. They can provide their reactions and reflections. Surveys are frequently used to address issues of student satisfaction and success. Questions may also ask students to reflect on what they have learned. Self-ratings of learning obtained from surveys can be compared to direct measures of learning to see if results are consistent.

Surveys can be quite comprehensive in the topics they cover. Surveys administered to freshmen at the end of their first year often ask students to reflect on several aspects of their experiences, including academic plans and programs, use of student services, campus involvement, study behaviors, class attendance, personal reflections, and academic progress. In contrast, some surveys are focused on specific topics and can be used to ascertain or investigate issues with respect to those topics. Surveys about computer competence, advising, writing experiences, or out-of-class learning are a few possibilities.

Besides allowing for a wide range of subject matter, surveys and focus groups have the advantage of reaching many different target groups. Thus, as part of its assessment plan, a department could design and administer surveys to such groups as entering students, current students, graduating seniors, alumni, faculty, or employers. These methods represent the main approaches for collecting information from students after they have graduated.

During the past several years, practitioners have shown increasing interest in qualitative approaches to assessment that provide descriptions of learning rather than assign numbers to tests or performances (Wright, 1997). Qualitative methods can yield direct as well as indirect evidence of learning. For example, faculty can examine materials in students' portfolios for evidence of critical or creative thinking and then provide a narrative summary of how students have grown in college.

Use of Existing Data Sources

One of the remarkable things about assessment is the degree to which educators can learn from each other. Thus departments or programs that are embarking on assessment can benefit from finding out about what others on the campus are doing. Units can start by checking with the assessment committee to see if an inventory of activities is available. Because all regional accreditors ask their members to undertake assessment, an individual unit can also benefit from being aware of the institutional assessment plan and any campuswide activities that currently are in place. At several institutions, survey extracts are made available to departments so these units can see how their own graduates compare to campuswide averages. At Winthrop University, academic departments receive customized reports of alumni survey results that provide information about employers and job titles of graduates (Prus and Tebo-Messina, 1996).

Institutional research offices often have data that can help a unit interpret the results of their assessment projects. Data about the characteristics of students in the program and how these characteristics have changed over time can be important when looking at the results of assessment projects. Institutional data may be available to help track particular groups of individuals such as nontraditional students, students who transfer from other institutions, or those who change from one major to another. Sometimes information about course-taking patterns can be obtained and can help in interpreting assessment results.

Choosing Between Nationally Available and Locally Developed Instruments

One of the most important choices that must be made when selecting assessment instruments is whether to purchase and use nationally available standardized instruments or to use instruments that are developed locally. Several commercial assessment instruments cover a broad range of general education outcomes; others address specific learning skills such as writing or critical thinking. Some instruments examine learning in specific disciplines and are appropriate for graduating seniors. A number of commercial survey instruments address issues of student satisfaction with college and success after college. Other surveys focus on student motivation and potential success while in college. *The Mental Measurements Yearbook* (Impara and Plake, 1998), published by the Buros Institute at the University of Nebraska–Lincoln, contains a bibliography of hundreds of commercially available instruments on a wide variety of topics designed for many purposes and includes reviews by qualified professionals—a valuable aid to busy assessment practitioners. One important advantage of nationally available instruments is that reliability and validity have already been addressed, and these efforts should be described in supporting documents. Another advantage is that national norms for comparison purposes have been developed. Generally, materials that accompany tests tell the percentage of a reference group that scored at or below each possible test score, and those for survey instruments tell the proportion of students selecting each response to survey items. In addition to providing overall norms, norms for subgroups such as students by class level or gender may be available. Some companies provide norms by institutional type, such as public and private universities. These norms allow faculty to examine how their own students are performing or responding on the instrument compared to similar students elsewhere. In contrast, locally developed instruments can only provide norms for local test or survey takers over time or for subgroups of local students.

Some important considerations govern the assessment of norms. In many cases, norms are based on results obtained from institutions that have previously purchased and used the instrument. In these cases, although they may provide results for a large body of users, the norms do not necessarily provide results for a representative national sample of possible test or survey takers. For this reason, it is important to be aware of the types of institutions that have used the instrument and to determine whether results for these institutions are meaningful locally. Most test developers will provide information about users if it is requested. Awareness of the time period over which norms were developed is important. Norms that are not routinely updated may fail to reflect changes in demographics of the student body or changes in the curriculum.

Besides their national norms, commercial instruments have the advantage of being readily available. It does take time to become familiar with these instruments, including their content and properties, and to choose among competing alternatives, but virtually no time is spent on instrument development.

In contrast, locally developed instruments can take a great deal of time to construct and may provide results that are difficult to interpret. Quite often, local tests are criterion-referenced examinations. In these tests, faculty determine absolute levels of mastery or proficiency that denote competence in the subject matter, providing a yardstick for helping them judge whether students are reaching the level of competence established as appropriate. Although very helpful, such absolute standards leave faculty unable to answer questions about how local students compare to students elsewhere. In addition, some faculty are skeptical of locally developed instruments because they are most often designed, administered, and scored by the same individuals who use the results to assess their programs.

The principal advantages of locally developed instruments are the opportunities they provide for involving faculty in the assessment process and the likely result that the instruments they develop will closely match the local curriculum as well as local issues and concerns. If the purpose of using the instrument is to assess the extent to which students are mastering the content of the institution's curricula, well-designed locally developed methods should yield the most valid inferences about student learning. Locally developed tests and surveys can easily be modified to reflect changes in the curriculum and can be analyzed according to local needs. In contrast, it is sometimes difficult or costly to obtain a particular desired analysis from a commercial company.

In addition to nationally available or locally developed instruments, faculty can contact their peers at other institutions to see what they are doing. In many cases, faculty elsewhere are willing to share their assessment instruments and may welcome the opportunity to compare results across campuses.

In the final analysis, many faculty adopt assessment plans that include a combination of nationally normed and locally developed instruments. At Rivier College, for instance, the Academic Profile purchased from the Educational Testing Service is used for freshmen and seniors to study gains in generic knowledge and skills, but locally developed writing and math tests have been given at the sophomore level (P. F. Cunningham, personal communication, Aug. 27, 1997). Faculty at the University of Wisconsin–Oshkosh use the ACT-COMP to assess growth by comparing results to the ACT scores of entering freshmen. In addition, they have developed local measures of information literacy and global awareness. Information literacy is examined by looking at senior papers written in classes and global awareness is measured through an objective test that includes discussion questions (Wresch, 1998).

Comparing Potential Methods to Criteria

Once faculty have had the opportunity to discuss the criteria they want to apply and to decide on the relative importance of these characteristics, they can consider how well various assessment techniques match the criteria. This step in the assessment process can be enhanced if faculty complete a matrix comparing possible methods to selection criteria. In this matrix, the potential methods are used to create the column headings and the row headings are made up of the selection criteria. One such matrix included the following characteristics (row headings) for consideration: curriculum match, cost, preparation time, analysis time, value to students, privacy issues, and programmatic information. Clearly, the row headings for this type of matrix should be based on the criteria that are important to the unit doing the assessment. Interestingly, it does not always matter if the matrix is completely filled out; what matters is that it provides a good basis for generating a focused discussion. Exhibit 4.1 provides an example of this kind of matrix.

Exhibit 4.1. Selection Criteria Matrix

Criteria	Measures				
	Objective Tests	Performances	Portfolios	Surveys	Classroom Assignments
Match to curriculum					
Technical quality					
Preparation time					
Value to students					
Programmatic information					

Another type of useful matrix is shown in Exhibit 4.2. The column headings are, again, the possible techniques being considered and the row headings are the learning objectives for the program. This type of matrix is particularly useful in helping determine whether the methods that are selected will match the curriculum goals of the program.

As part of a summer grant project, faculty at Ball State University's College of Business were asked to do some thinking about assessment techniques that would help assess the undergraduate business core. Although the learning goals of the program were still under discussion, these faculty were able to work from a tentative list and create a matrix comparing possible methods to goals. They were particularly creative with respect to the methods they considered. Among others, they proposed a test to be given midway through the business core—a test that is now in place (Hill, Hoban, Stone, and Zivney, 1993). In addition to learning objectives, this kind of matrix can be used to consider the relative merits of assessment techniques in addressing other kinds of objectives, such as determining the satisfaction of students and their success after graduation.

Exhibit 4.2. Objectives by Measures Matrix

Objectives	Measures		
	Term Paper	Questionnaire	Speech
Write at a scholarly level	✔		
Adapt verbal messages to a specific audience			✔
Value lifelong learning		✔	

Designing Instruments

In this section we share a few suggestions about designing assessment instruments locally, including recognizing the uniqueness of the task, drawing on campus experts, and taking steps to enhance the reliability and validity of instruments.

Recognizing the Uniqueness of Designing Instruments for Assessment

As practitioners gain experience with assessment it becomes clear that the methods chosen and techniques used are often quite similar to activities in which they have engaged previously. Faculty routinely use tests and assignments in the classroom. Performances such as speeches and writing are part of normal classroom activities. Even surveys are sometimes used in collecting information from students in classrooms or on a larger scale. So why does assessment seem so different from the normal routine of things? *The principal difference is the group effort that is necessary to undertake assessment activities.* Faculty who have traditionally worked independently to develop and administer assessment instruments in their classrooms now find that decisions need to be made in concert with others. Some individuals need a little time to get used to this group effort. The second difference is the way results are used. Typically classroom activities are used to find out about individual students. With assessment the emphasis is on group performance. Even in those cases where individual students receive results from assessment activities, programmatic assessment requires that faculty summarize the results across students and across courses and ask what the results imply about the program as a whole. Thus the uniqueness of assessment comes not so much in the type of instruments that are chosen, but in the ways they are developed and used.

Enlisting Help from Campus Experts

Faculty need support as they embark on assessment activities, particularly with respect to designing instruments. Measurement specialists either in administrative units or in other departments or divisions can provide valuable advice in designing and using tests and assignments for assessment purposes, and can also help with survey construction. Designing surveys is not a routine part of the job for most faculty. In fact, faculty sometimes approach survey construction the same way they approach the construction of a multiple-choice test creating possible answers that overlap. Designing good questions and response options is at the heart of survey construction and needs to be done with care in order to obtain valid and reliable results. Campus experts in social sciences, institutional research, or elsewhere should review any surveys that are constructed for assessment purposes.

Enhancing Instrument Reliability and Validity

Drawing on the advice of campus experts is one way to help enhance reliability and validity of measures, as is asking peers on and off the campus to review instruments. Combining data from several years is helpful when dealing with programs that have a small number of students to assess in any one year. Using item analysis for objective tests and surveys is very valuable. Most campuses have computer programs that can be used to analyze items on tests or surveys. For test items these packages will indicate the item difficulty—the proportion of students answering the item correctly. High scores mean the item is easy rather than difficult. Item discrimination scores show how well the item distinguishes between students with good performances and those with poor performances. If those with low overall scores perform better on an item than those with high overall scores, the item will have a negative discrimination score and may need to be rewritten or dropped from the exam.

Barbara Walvoord (1996) cautions faculty to watch for evidence from students. If they consistently complain about an exam, if their performances do not match what would be expected based on their other work, or if students perform in other unanticipated ways, faculty may have evidence that the instrument they are using is not doing what it was designed to do. The ability to rule out alternative explanations for measured outcomes is the hallmark of construct validity. Taking the opportunity to pilot items before they are used on a large scale is also very important. For example, rating scales designed for assessment projects should always be tried on a small number of students and then revised if necessary.

Using a test blueprint as an aid in constructing a test is another helpful strategy. A test blueprint is a matrix that is used to plan a test. The content areas to be covered by the test make up the row headings. Column headings represent skill levels, such as recall, comprehension, and application, that are to be addressed by the items. This kind of blueprint helps ensure that the test items will cover the appropriate material and that the items will be sufficiently challenging. The cells of the matrix can include the number of items that will address the particular content area at a given skill level or the percentage of the test that will address the content-skill combination. Many instructors create test blueprints either formally or informally when they develop classroom exams. Because consensus in the design of instruments is so important in assessment, a test blueprint can help faculty reach agreement as a group on appropriate test content. An outline, similar to a blueprint, can also help in creating surveys (Erwin, 1991). However, because performance-based tasks generally involve multiple processes and integrated content, faculty may find that these tasks "do not fit neatly into the cells of a traditional content-by-process matrix" (Linn and Baker, 1996, p. 91).

Determining Approaches for Implementation

In Chapter Two, we discussed the importance of developing an assessment plan. Here we focus on some of the planning questions that need to be addressed when deciding on methods to use and ways to implement them.

Levels for Data Collection

A small number of colleges and universities may collect all the information they need through one or more campuswide activities, but in most cases information will be collected at the program level as well. With respect to assessment of the major, almost all assessment programs recognize the uniqueness of individual academic programs and therefore encourage collection of information at that level. Although campuswide information can help in assessing the major, it ordinarily needs to be enriched with program specific information.

Within programs, faculty must decide the mix between data collection methods focused at the programmatic level and those focused at the course level. In some departments, graduating seniors are asked to take a standardized test that covers all subjects addressed in the major or to complete a comprehensive senior project or thesis. In other departments, students who are completing portfolios that address their entire programs may be asked to include some information from each of their courses, thereby combining programmatic level data collection with information from specific courses.

An additional possibility is to have classroom instructors utilize their own assignments and tests to demonstrate the way their courses are contributing to the program. Materials used to assign grades in individual classes can be reexamined to see what they imply about the overall process of teaching and learning in the program. This "course-embedded" assessment has the advantage of being based on what is going on in the classroom already. Designing and administering common instruments in multiple section courses or including a set of common objective or essay questions on otherwise different exams are other possibilities for collecting assessment information in classrooms (Wright, 1997; Ewell, 1991, 1997e).

Research Strategies

Some assessment studies use a cross-sectional approach, comparing different groups of students at a common point in time—a useful strategy if faculty are focusing on groups of students rather than individual students. For example, entering students and junior students may be asked to complete writing competence examinations, and their respective performances can be compared. However, it is difficult to attribute any differences in ratings to academic experiences if characteristics of the students differ greatly. Thus it is very important to describe any characteristics of the two groups of students that are likely to affect their performances. Information about high school class rank or test scores on entry-level assessment instruments is often helpful in this connection.

Many campuses are interested in tracking and comparing successive cohorts of students. If characteristics of the student body stay relatively constant over time, this approach can help faculty understand how programs are working. For example, faculty can use results from successive senior surveys to see if attitude and satisfaction ratings improve after various program changes are introduced. Ewell (1995) offers insights into a variety of approaches to study changes in important variables over a period of time.

Some assessment studies are purely descriptive, collecting information about a group of students at a particular point in time to answer a relatively focused question. Krueger (1994) recommends using focus groups to gather rich, descriptive data on complex issues or as a prelude to designing a questionnaire. Many teachers use classroom assessment techniques to find out about learning as it occurs and to make immediate adjustments.

Longitudinal designs involve the collection of pre- and post-information, and are often used with respect to general education assessment. Students are asked to take the same test, survey, or performance assessment when they enter the university and again two, three, or four years later. Because the same students participate in both assessments, it is possible to calculate changes in their scores or ratings between the two time periods. However, researchers need to be cautious about attributing changes in scores, ratings, or opinions strictly to academic programs. Students mature and change in many ways over time. In addition, comparisons made between beginning and end points provide little information about why changes have occurred and thus little information about what is working or not working with respect to academic programs (Terenzini, 1989). Alexander Astin's work has been very helpful in pointing out the pitfalls of drawing conclusions without sufficient information about students' experiences (Astin, 1991).

On a practical note, this approach can be difficult to implement in terms of tracking students. Because some students drop out over a period of years, researchers need to be aware of how this affects results. When reporting conclusions, they must indicate the number of students who are still in the study and describe how characteristics of students who have remained in the study compare to those who have left. If using sampling techniques, Peter Ewell (1994b) recommends beginning a study with more students than will be needed for making reliable generalizations to allow for expected attrition.

Faculty who conduct course-level assessment often develop pre-post measures for in-class use. Because these are usually focused on course content and application and are administered within a relatively short time frame, they suffer less from the limitations just mentioned. Many in-class instruments are administered only after instruction. In these cases, interest is usually in the overall competence of the group rather than in the way the group has changed. Alternatively, the use of normed tests provides data for external comparisons. C. Robert Pace (1985) argues that pre-post testing need not always be used. "Giving the final exam to students on the first day of a course would be of little use if the content of the course was highly specific and if it was very unlikely that the student would have encountered it elsewhere" (p. 16). He questions whether both tests would be measuring the same thing in terms of thinking skills. Simple difference scores have other limitations. For example, they are subject to ceiling effects because students with high pretest scores have little room for improvement (Terenzini, 1989).

One of the great values of portfolios is the opportunity they provide to collect longitudinal information about individual students. Rather than looking only at the beginning and end points in terms of students' programs, portfolios provide information about what happens along the way. They can yield rich information about students' experiences and the learning process, as well as about their knowledge and skills (Schilling and Schilling, 1998).

Occasionally, as new programs are introduced, educators have a chance to design a true experiment. In these studies, students are randomly assigned to experimental and control groups. Thus, improvements in student learning can be more readily attributed to the treatment that is introduced. Unfortunately, it is usually difficult to introduce random assignment of students to treatment and nontreatment groups because it is not ethical to withhold treatment from students who are eligible for programs.

When random assignment is not possible, statistical analysis may be used to control for differences in important characteristics that exist between students who are in a treatment group and those who are not. A group comparison involving intact groups is known as a quasi-experiment (Crowl, 1993). Regression and analysis of variance are two methods that can be quite helpful in this regard. However, researchers always need to be aware of selection bias. If students have volunteered to be in the treatment group, they may differ greatly from another group of students in motivation and interest, even if matched on demographic characteristics. In practice, it is extremely difficult to control for differences in motivation.

The specific approach faculty use will often be limited by circumstances. Ewell warns against "excessive methodological purity" when generating decision-related information (1997e, p. 377). Terenzini (1989) urges educators to use the criterion of reasonableness with respect to research design. The most important consideration is that information be valid and useful for decision making and improvement. Although there are few opportunities for true experiments in assessment, there are possibilities to engage in interesting and valuable research projects. In fact, faculty at the University of Colorado College of Business and Administration are specifically encouraged to view assessment issues as issues appropriate for research. This has increased the commitment of college faculty to the assessment process (Singell and Palmer, 1998).

Identifying Eligible Participants

Practitioners must develop clear criteria to identify individuals who will be required or invited to participate in assessment projects. For example, all entering freshmen may be expected to participate in an assessment of achievement in general education. In contrast, assessment may be restricted to degree-seeking students only. Perhaps part-time students or transfer students will be excluded as well. At the upper-division level, general education assessment may include only those from a particular entering cohort, or it may include all those who have currently achieved a certain level of classification, such as sophomore or junior. The selection of participants depends upon the inferences that will be made and the population to which educators wish to generalize after data are collected and analyzed.

Initial assessment in academic disciplines may include all students who intend to major in a program, or it may be limited to those who pass specific entry requirements. Most often, all graduating seniors will be eligible for assessment that occurs at the completion of the major. Even here there may be conditions for eligibility, such as a minimum number of courses taken on campus. Specifications about who is eligible should reflect decisions about the overall purposes of assessment and specific assessment questions.

Sampling

After determining who is eligible, faculty need to decide whether they will assess every student or only a sample. Assessing a sample is less costly and is feasible if results for each individual student are not needed. However, to ensure student motivation, the same data may be collected from every student and assessed to give individual feedback; then only a sample of student work can be selected for program assessment.

If sampling will be used, an approach needs to be chosen. One possibility is to identify a random sample of students and invite them to participate. When drawing a random sample, every individual must have the same chance of being selected. Simple computer programs can generate a list of individuals for the sample. Rather than random sampling, stratified sampling is often used when researchers want to make sure they have adequate numbers of individuals in some subgroups. With this approach, the overall group of interest is divided into subgroups or strata based on a categorical variable such as race, class standing (freshman, sophomore, and so on), or declared major. Individuals are then randomly selected within the subgroups. Proportions of various subgroups in a stratified sample ordinarily differ from their proportions in the population. Some groups are over- or undersampled based on particular characteristics in order to have a subgroup large enough to detect differences in an outcome variable. Conclusions about the population are based on weights that represent the proportion of each subgroup in the population.

Many times information is collected from a "convenience" sample. This essentially means that researchers cannot comply with the rules for appropriate sampling and have simply done the best they can in locating individuals to participate in the assessment. For example, tests are often given in class. However, unless attendance or participation is required, tests given during class periods will include only those attending the day the exam is administered. The characteristics of these students may not be representative of the group as a whole. Practitioners need to be aware of any limitations introduced into results because of differences between the group of students included in the sample and the overall population of eligible students. Reports of results should include a comparison of characteristics between those in the actual study group and those who were eligible.

Sample Size

If sampling is appropriate, one of the important decisions to make is the number of cases to study. Considerations include costs of materials, printing, mailings, interviews, and data processing and the time available to carry out the project.

Project results based on samples are usually reported with a "sampling error"—the possible difference between project findings and true results. For example, faculty may report that 80 percent of students are satisfied with their majors with a sampling error of plus or minus 3 percent. (Almost all national poll results are reported this way.) Sampling error primarily depends on the desired confidence level (typically 95 percent), the error in the overall population, and the sample size. The larger the sample size the smaller the sampling error, and therefore the more accurate are project results (Suskie, 1992; Fink and Kosecoff, 1998). Statistical textbooks often include tables to help estimate sample size.

Another factor in determining sample size is the likely response rate of those invited to participate in the project. If a 50 percent response rate is expected, researchers need to double the number of people invited to achieve a desired number of cases. Sample size also has to be large enough to disaggregate results if data will be reported for subgroups of the population. Thirty cases per subgroup is considered a minimal number. However, if results are going to be reported for subgroups using percentages it is desirable to have as many as one hundred cases per subgroup. M. Lee Upcraft and John H. Schuh (1996) raise the issue of credibility. In their view, a project with fewer than three hundred cases overall lacks credibility with a collegiate audience. Although important, the size of the sample cannot make up for a project that is not otherwise well designed.

Putting Everything Together

Once faculty determine criteria for instrument selection, think through implementation strategies, and evaluate the various possible instruments, they will be ready to make choices about what to do. At this point, it is a good idea to look at choices as a whole to make sure that assessment activities have the characteristics that are important to a successful assessment program. Activities must make sense overall, tell about student experiences along the way, and provide information that can direct actions. Although various instruments will differ in their strengths and weaknesses, the totality of selections must provide the needed information. This is, of course, part of the argument for using multiple methods. Truman State University's assessment program, with its concept of triangulation, is an excellent example of the strength of multiple methods (Magruder, McManis, and Young, 1997; Young, 1996).

5

Using Performance Measures and Portfolios for Assessment

PERFORMANCE (*n.*): the act of carrying out

In addition to asking about what students know when they finish college, most assessment programs address questions about what students can do. During the past several years, there has been "an explosion of interest" in alternative forms of assessment that go beyond objective tests in how they measure student achievement (Herman, Aschbacher, and Winters, 1992, p. 1). Performance assessment draws on the understanding that students learn best when they are engaged in active tasks. In this chapter, we review the use of performance assessment methods, including portfolios, to obtain information about the accomplishments of students.

Using Performance Measures

We begin with an overview of the diverse selection of approaches that is referred to collectively as performance assessment.

Definition and Description

Performance assessment is the process of using student activities or products, as opposed to tests or surveys, to evaluate students' knowledge, skills, and development. As part of this process, the performances generated by students are usually rated or scored by faculty or other qualified observers who also provide feedback to students.

Performance assessment is described as "authentic" if it is based on examining genuine or real examples of students' work—work that closely reflects goals and objectives for learning (Wiggins, 1989, 1990). As Wiggins notes, authentic assessment reveals something about the standards that are at the heart of a subject asking students to use judgment and innovation as they "do" and explore the subject (1998, p. 22). At their best, these measures reflect the knowledge and skills that will be expected of graduates when they become professionals in their fields. Using the broadest definition, performance assessment includes any technique that requires students to generate their own responses rather than to select among responses that have been provided for them. By this definition, almost all direct assessment methods, with the exception of multiple-choice and other objective examinations, fall under the broad heading of performance assessment. Among others, these methods include essays, oral presentations, exhibitions, and demonstrations. In Wiggins' view, not all performance assessments are authentic. He reserves this label for tasks that "closely simulate or actually replicate challenges faced by adults or professionals" (1998, p. 141). Although still of value, not all performance assessments meet this standard.

The potential for performance assessment is greatest in those instances where it can be readily linked to the curriculum. If the focus of an academic program is on the creation of products or performances, then assessment should draw on these natural results of the educational process. In academic programs that develop complex, integrated skills, faculty often find performance assessment appealing because it asks students to display their skills in a way that is more direct and thorough than that provided by traditional paper and pencil tests. Typically performance measures require students to demonstrate skills such as critical thinking, creative thinking, and problem solving by using information within a meaningful context.

Advantages and Disadvantages

Because teachers can observe many aspects of learning, performance assessment allows faculty to obtain valuable insight about their students' skills and abilities. Compared to other assessment methods, the opportunity to observe performances enables faculty to provide more comprehensive feedback to individual students. In this role, faculty often act more like coaches than like judges. An important side effect of performance assessment is increased communication between faculty and students. Indeed, some performance assessment projects involve joint research conducted by students with faculty guidance.

Compared to other methods, performance assessment provides students with more information to use in improving their skills. By receiving and responding to feedback and by observing the performances of other individuals as well as their own, students are in a better position to evaluate their own competence. Opportunities and abilities for self-assessment are enhanced. Because students are asked to demonstrate skills that are integral to their programs, student motivation is often stronger with respect to performance assessment than for other kinds of assessment. Unlike standardized tests that are applied to students in uniform fashion, many performance assessment projects appeal to students because they allow latitude in the choice of tasks (Linn and Baker, 1996).

As with all assessment methods, good performance assessment requires clear statements about desired learning outcomes. The act of creating and implementing performance assessment leads faculty to think carefully about what they want their students to know and be able to do, and about the methods they use for teaching and assessing their students. Because performance assessment techniques are, by necessity, closely related to curriculum and course content, faculty see an immediate connection between the two. The processes of teaching and assessing become integrated, rather than separate. As Linn and Baker point out, "performance-based assessments are expected to be indistinguishable from the goals of instruction" (p. 86). Teaching to these assessments is considered not only acceptable but exemplary.

What are possible limitations? Performance assessment is a labor-intensive undertaking. Time is needed to develop instruments as well as to use them. In fact, a great deal of care has to go into planning for the use of any performance assessment (Herman, Aschbacher, and Winters, 1992). At a minimum, considerations include the following:

1. Articulating the skills to be examined

2. Designing appropriate tasks to demonstrate the skills

3. Specifying the criteria for evaluating performances

4. Developing a reliable process for rating performances

5. Training raters

6. Evaluating results

Validity issues are also important (Herman, Aschbacher, and Winters, 1992). Faculty need to ask several questions: Does the particular assessment cover the appropriate content? Does it reflect the best understanding of the subject matter? Is it assessing the appropriate level of cognitive complexity? Are students asked to reason and to engage in real problem solving? Are tasks meaningful for students? Will there be enough replications to make results generalizable? Faculty who teach writing often warn about the limitations of judging a student's work by the quality of one essay (Belanoff, 1994; White, 1994). Linn and Baker (1996) identify generalizability, the degree to which performance on one task provides the basis for generalization to similar tasks, as a major issue for performance-based assessment. Low levels of generalizability limit the validity of inferences about performances and may pose problems with respect to fairness when individuals are judged on a small number of tasks.

In addition to generalizability, Linn and Baker raise a number of other issues concerning "external" validity criteria—criteria that relate to the impact of assessment. Issues include consequences such as the amount of instructional time devoted to various content areas, the impact on individual students of decisions about program eligibility and advancement, and the fairness of tasks in reflecting cultural diversity and differences in instructional experiences. Whether an assessment method is sensitive to instructional effort rather than to general intellectual ability is also important. Originally published in 1995, the Conference on College Composition and Communication Committee on Assessment has addressed some of these concerns in their position statement on good practice for assessment of writing. Sheila C. Ewing reviews several aspects of performance assessment in a recent *Assessment Update* article (1998). In spite of possible reservations, a rich variety of performance assessment is available for use. Several of these methods are described next.

Oral Examinations

An oral examination is a traditional assessment method that can be used as an alternative to paper-and-pencil tests. Orals usually involve one or more examiners who pose several questions to individual students about their understanding of and ability to apply what they have learned. Often these examinations are intended to cover the cumulative impact of college on students. Thus questions generally encompass the broad range of content covered in students' programs. However, an oral examination may focus on a particular course or a particular subject area. Although examiners may start with a series of planned questions, they are generally given plenty of latitude to explore the knowledge of individual students. In addition to covering a broad range of topics, oral examinations provide an excellent chance to examine students' knowledge in depth.

Faculty in the Department of Chemical Engineering at West Virginia University ask their students to participate in oral exams. Seniors are assigned three projects of increasing difficulty. Each student's work must be submitted as a written report and must also be presented orally before two faculty members. Joseph A. Shaeiwitz (1996) describes the project presentations as one-hour tutorials with questions focused on areas in which students appear to need help.

The tradition of oral examinations is quite old. Prior to the 1880s, when expansion in the number of students forced colleges to assign credit hours and grades to courses, seniors graduating from college were required to complete oral examinations, often in front of external examiners. As Hutchings and Marchese (1990) point out, the current emphasis on assessment—looking at the overall impact of college on student learning—is a return to a tradition of long ago.

Products

In contrast to oral examinations that can be given in any field of study, some examples of performance assessment are specific to particular majors. As a basis for evaluation, students may be asked to create and exhibit products that are representative of work done by professionals in the discipline. Art students can produce paintings or drawings, journalism students may write newspaper articles, geography students can be asked to create maps, and computer science students may generate computer programs. In each of these cases, the products created by students should reflect their mastery of various aspects of the major and should be carefully evaluated by appropriate individuals. Disciplines such as journalism and art have long traditions of examining these products to assess individual students. The current challenge is to use this information for purposes of programmatic assessment.

Performances

In addition to physical products, performance assessment, as the name implies, can be used to evaluate actual demonstrations of student work. Examples include acting in a theatrical production, playing an instrument, conducting an interview, and completing a physical exercise. In many cases, the assessment of students' performances is conducted in a naturalistic setting. For example, nursing students may be observed interviewing a patient, and counseling students may be observed conducting a therapy session. Observing a student teacher managing a classroom is a well-known example of conducting performance assessment in a realistic setting. In other cases, performances may be simulated. Simulations allow faculty to assess the ability of students to perform in lifelike situations. Students majoring in organizational behavior can conduct mock interviews of job candidates, nursing students can provide care for model patients, and law students can conduct trials in moot court. Computers can also be used for simulations such as designing buildings or planning landscapes. Whether in a naturalistic or simulated situation, these performances usually provide more direct information about learning than do objective tests.

A unique approach to performance assessment is the development of an assessment center. This method, which originated in industry and government, involves several carefully planned steps, including identifying key aspects of learning, using simulations and other techniques to generate student behaviors, and having two or more trained assessors independently observe and assess these behaviors. Assessors can then share and debate their insights about what they have observed. Some programs include in-basket exercises where students play the role of a newly appointed supervisor. In this role, they are asked to handle the letters, memos, and reports contained in the in-basket. Information from these tasks allows assessors to evaluate decision making, initiative, and ability to delegate (Byham, 1988, p. 260).

Working with consultants from Development Dimensions International, faculty at Indiana University of Pennsylvania (IUP) developed a center to assess teacher skills. One simulation involves watching videotapes and responding to focused questions about how to handle problems illustrated on the tapes. Students also plan presentations that they can use for teaching. Although it takes a great deal of time to administer and score simulations, faculty at IUP feel the approach is valuable in preparing successful teachers (Millward, 1993).

Faculty at the Baylor College of Dentistry have developed fifty-six competences for dental hygiene graduates that cover knowledge and attitudes as well as communication and psychomotor skills (A. L. McCann, P. R. Campbell, and P. A. Cohen, personal communication, Oct. 24, 1997). Because they do not perceive that all fifty-six are assessed in the Baylor curriculum or on national board or state licensing exams, McCann, Campbell, and Cohen have developed a five-hour performance assessment for seniors. In an objective structured clinical exam, students interpret radiographs and health histories, measure vital signs, describe intra-oral lesions, and communicate with standardized patients. Next students design and explain a community oral health program for a given setting. And finally they interpret a research article and solve an ethical dilemma (a confidentiality issue for an HIV-positive patient) in a written section. Students' performance in general has convinced faculty to include more patient assessment exercises in senior courses, devote more effort to describing intra-oral lesions, and conduct a performance assessment on taking vital signs every quarter.

Western Carolina University has a particularly thorough and comprehensive Oral Communication Assessment and Curriculum program (P. A. Cutspec, personal communication, Sept. 12, 1997). All 1,300-plus incoming freshmen are assessed in three ways during summer orientation. Students complete self-report instruments, parents complete an assessment of their offspring's communication skills, and trained observers use an eight-item rating scale to assess oral skills as students take part in small-group (fifteen members) discussions focused on a particular topic. Aggregated assessment results are used to advise students to take one of four sections of a basic communication course: honors, standard, high communication apprehensive, or remedial. Upon completion of the appropriate section of the course, which fulfills a general education requirement, each student is posttested with both of the student instruments given during orientation. A follow-up course has been designed for any student who needs additional training after completing the basic course.

Other Examples of Performance Assessment

Just as oral examinations can be conducted in any discipline, other traditional performance measures have applicability across many subjects. Essay examinations are administered to many majors, as are research papers, poster presentations, oral presentations, and problem sets. Many times these techniques are used to assess learning of specific skills required in the major, but the acquisition of general competences such as critical thinking, problem solving, writing, listening, and speaking can also be assessed through performance measures. Some faculty ask students to keep journals containing daily or weekly entries reflecting on their learning.

At the University of South Florida, liberal arts requirements, including writing, are taught in learning communities that attempt to make connections across disciplines (T. Flateby and E. Metzger, personal communication, Sept. 16, 1997). Flateby, director of evaluation and testing, and Metzger, coordinator of learning communities, have developed an instrument to assess general writing skills, course content, and cognitive level. Writing skills such as purpose, tone, audience, unity, coherence, and mechanics can be evaluated. Bloom's *Taxonomy of Educational Objectives—Cognitive Domain* (1956) has been adapted to assess writing level. Writing skills, cognitive level, or both can be assessed using students' papers from the learning communities courses.

Existing records such as supervisor reports from internships can also provide information about student performance. Evaluation sheets completed by internship supervisors constitute an example of performance assessment used to judge the behaviors of students over an extended time period.

Capstone Experiences

Many academic programs include capstone experiences for graduating seniors that are designed to demonstrate comprehensive learning in the major through some type of product or performance. Most capstone experiences draw on earlier activities providing students with a valuable chance to make important connections based on what they have learned. In some cases, the capstone experience is the final submission of a portfolio that has been developed across several years of study. Capstone experiences may also include written projects, case studies, research papers, or other kinds of performance. In addition to emphasizing work related to the major, capstone experiences can require students to demonstrate how well they have mastered important learning objectives from the institution's general studies program. For example, capstone experiences often require students to demonstrate attitudes and values, such as an appreciation of lifelong learning.

At St. Mary's University, seniors in business take a capstone course incorporating a comprehensive case study analysis (C. Olney and R. Menger, personal communication, Oct. 14, 1997). Instructor Richard Menger has developed a scoring rubric for the case that includes both generic skills and competence related to the major. Examples of the former include writing skills and cultural awareness; examples of the latter include knowledge of historic and current theory and practices in business and ability to integrate tools and techniques from business specialties when analyzing business cases.

Occasionally, completion of a capstone experience is a specific graduation requirement that exists outside of courses necessary for graduation. In most cases, capstone experiences are located within capstone courses. Capstone courses are usually relatively small classes designed to help students integrate their knowledge. However, requiring students to complete a capstone course does not, in itself, guarantee that students will have a capstone experience. A capstone experience is a well-thought-out project that is comprehensive in nature and allows students to demonstrate a range of abilities. Activities in capstone courses need to be carefully planned if they are to provide useful assessment information and bring appropriate closure to students' college experiences. For example, they need to be designed and evaluated by faculty responsible for the program, not just the instructor of the course (Ewell, 1991). In addition to the capstone experience, capstone courses provide an appropriate time and place to collect other assessment information that can be useful in evaluating programs. In some cases, the capstone course is used to administer nationally available or locally developed assessment tests that are focused on learning within the major. Surveys can also be administered in the capstone course.

One of the most outstanding examples of assessment using capstone experiences is that in place at Southern Illinois University Edwardsville. As a requirement for graduation, all seniors must complete departmental senior assignments that demonstrate student achievement in general education as well as in the major field. A typical senior assignment requires students to examine the research literature in their area of study, explain a topic in their discipline to a lay audience, and describe new developments in the field in terms of their ethical impact on society. In some departments, students complete a research paper and a poster that they defend orally. Since 1993, approximately a hundred undergraduates in psychology have presented their work at professional meetings (S. L. Thomas, personal communication, Sept. 22, 1997). In all departments, the senior assignment must measure the objectives for learning that have been chosen by the faculty (Eder, 1996).

The capstone experience provided at Portland State University requires students to participate in interdisciplinary teams that conduct community-based projects. Students work together to address problems in the metropolitan community, obtaining real-world experience related to the expertise they have acquired in their majors (Reardon and Ramaley, 1997). Because of the rich information they provide, capstone projects are valuable for assessment of both individual students and programs.

Evaluating Performances

One of the biggest challenges of performance assessment is developing a useful approach for evaluating the activities or products generated by students. Some performances can be evaluated by using checklists to indicate the presence or absence of various aspects of a performance. Did a student giving a speech make eye contact with the audience? Has a nursing student filled out the appropriate paperwork to admit a patient? Checklists are useful to address questions that can be answered "yes" or "no." Rather than checklists, in some cases observers use narrative reports to summarize strengths and weaknesses exhibited in students' performances. Because the variety of evidence students use to respond to performance tasks can vary greatly, Delandshere and Petrosky (1994) recommend that raters be required to make the reasoning behind their judgments explicit by writing interpretive summaries in response to critical questions about the student's performance.

In most cases, faculty want to examine several different aspects of a performance or product, such as accuracy of the work, frequency of various behaviors, and timeliness of response. If it is possible to evaluate these behaviors or attributes at several different levels, then a scoring rubric or rating sheet may be designed. When developing rating sheets, faculty first identify various aspects of the performance or product that are of importance, then develop a scale for use in scoring.

In some cases, a performance or product will be given a single overall score. This type of evaluation, which focuses on an overall impression, is called holistic scoring. Although several aspects of a performance may be of interest, one overall score is assigned. High scores mean students have performed well or satisfied all, or nearly all, aspects of the assignment. For example, students who receive the highest possible score on a critical thinking assignment may be expected to interpret evidence, identify and evaluate arguments, and draw appropriate conclusions. Low scores mean that few, if any, important aspects of the performance were met satisfactorily. In many cases, faculty will want to rate separately various characteristics of a performance or product. This is called analytical scoring. In these cases, characteristics such as organization and completeness receive individual scores. Ewell (1991) recommends rating scales that contain a sufficient number of dimensions to provide diagnostic information when ratings are aggregated.

For example, at Ball State University, students in a media writing and editing class are asked to submit hard-news and feature stories (M. H. Massé, personal communication, Sept. 16, 1997). These can be evaluated for headline writing, lead writing, clarity, accuracy, and grammar, among other aspects (see Exhibit 5.1). The rating scale used to judge the various aspects of performance might include 5 points, ranging from 1 for very poor to 5 for excellent. The scale can be further developed by describing what scores of 1 through 5 mean for clarity, as opposed to scores of 1 through 5 on grammar. In fact, a description of behavior should be available for each aspect of the performance and each point on the scale.

Many different scoring scales are in use. For example, each aspect of a performance can be rated from unsatisfactory to outstanding. In some cases, a scale including the categories "standard met," "standard partially met," and "standard not met" will provide the necessary information. Some rating scales ask for a narrative explanation justifying extreme scores. Barbara E. Walvoord and Virginia Johnson Anderson (1998) recommend primary trait analysis as a useful approach to developing rating scales (discussed in Chapter Six.)

According to Grant Wiggins (1998), the best guidelines for scoring performances concentrate on important aspects of the

Exhibit 5.1. Scoring Sheet for Media Writing

Characteristics	Rating				
	1	2	3	4	5
Headline writing					
Lead writing					
Clarity					
Accuracy					
Grammar					

Rating Scale: 1. Very Poor
2. Flawed
3. Average
4. Competent
5. Excellent

performance, not just those that are easy to see or count. They are based on analysis of many samples of work, rely on descriptive language about what the presence or absence of a quality looks like, and focus on the impact of the performance more than on its content or format.

If performance assessment is to be meaningful, it is important to achieve some consistency across different raters at any given time and by the same rater across time. Well-developed rating scales help minimize problems that contribute to interrater disagreement or unreliability. Careful training of raters is also important. T. Dary Erwin (1991) provides several helpful hints for reducing problems with the use of rating scales. The use of rating scales should ordinarily involve more than one rater, more than one performance or product, and several aspects of any given performance. Clearly, better judgments can be made if more information is gathered. Erwin recommends that the rating scale itself contain only three to seven reference points per item, because reliability does not improve beyond seven categories. Herman, Aschbacher, and Winters (1992) recommend that practitioners monitor the scoring patterns of raters during the actual scoring process. For example, raters can be asked to score the same piece more than once. This helps protect against shifting of standards that sometimes occur as raters drift away from formal criteria.

The circumstances under which performances will take place must be determined. Will they occur within specific courses and be graded by classroom teachers? Will there be a panel of faculty who review the work of students from multiple courses or sections? Another possibility is to invite professionals in the field to act as raters. In each case, the conditions under which performances will be examined need to be decided in advance and made clear both to those who will judge the performances and to the students who will generate them.

If rating scales are going to be used to generate programmatic information, there should be discussion and agreement among faculty about which aspects of a product or performance to measure. Faculty must also agree on how these characteristics will be defined. In identifying important elements of a performance or product, faculty often benefit by considering current and past examples of students' work. Drawing on information about the performances of graduates who are successful in the workplace is also a helpful strategy. In addition to identifying important aspects of performances, faculty should also discuss and come to agreement about the exact scale they will use for scoring.

Usefulness for Programmatic Assessment

Many times performance assessment tasks are completed by students within individual courses and graded by individual instructors. Rather than creating a new layer of activities, faculty may find that existing classroom assignments can be used as the basis for looking at the program. Alternatively, a synthesizing activity such as a review of students' art work by external examiners may be designed.

All students in the College of Fine Arts at Eastern New Mexico University are assessed through portfolio review or auditions each semester by a panel comprised of faculty, students, community representatives, and staff or faculty from outside the college (A. M. Testa, personal communication, Sept. 8, 1997). As a result both of informing students about their performances and working together on changes to improve student learning, college faculty have noted improvements in students' conceptualization, creativity, and technique.

If information generated about individual students is to be used for improving a program, as in the example just given, faculty in the department need to look collectively at results coming from all, or an appropriate sample, of their students. They need to ask whether the collective results provide information that can be used to modify and enhance their programs. Are there areas where students seem to be particularly weak? Are there gaps in their ability to apply what they have learned? How does this year's class compare to previous classes?

When results from individual students are looked at in the aggregate, faculty can begin to see how their programs are working. The approach that is used need not be elaborate. It might be based on a summary of individual student scores generated with locally developed rating scales. Perhaps a department committee will reevaluate a sample of work from individual classes. Another strategy is to ask faculty to complete reflection sheets sharing their reactions about the performances of students they have observed and their conclusions about what these performances imply about the program. Results from reflection sheets can be summarized and shared at a faculty meeting. A summary of narrative responses can be a useful guide for generating faculty discussion. In many cases, simply providing regular opportunities for focused discussion can be the vehicle for summarizing and sharing results. Perhaps a regularly scheduled department meeting can be used for this purpose. Chapter Six discusses an approach for aggregating results from classroom assignments that has been suggested by Barbara E. Walvoord and Virginia Johnson Anderson (1998).

Using Portfolios of Students' Work for Assessment

Because many academic programs have come to value their use, we turn now to a discussion of portfolios as a particular approach to performance assessment.

Definition

Portfolios are a type of performance assessment in which students' work is systematically collected and carefully reviewed for evidence of learning and development. Generally, students create portfolios by entering items in some kind of collection device or container such as a folder, binder, or disk. Materials, sometimes called artifacts, are added to portfolios as students progress through their academic programs. Thus, constructing a portfolio involves "gathering a body of evidence of one's learning and competence" (Lyons, 1998a, p. 19). In addition to examples of their work, most portfolios include reflective statements prepared by students. Evaluators periodically examine the content of portfolios for evidence of student achievement with respect to established goals and objectives for learning. Because they contain longitudinal information, portfolios can be evaluated for degree of improvement as well as for overall quality. Often the focus of portfolios is on documenting a process of change and determining the effect of the curriculum and environment on student growth (Ewell, 1991). Both the selection of items for portfolios and the evaluation of portfolios are based on criteria established by faculty.

The use of portfolios by the Teacher Education Department at Samford University provides a good example (J. A. Box and C. Dean, personal communication, Sept. 11, 1997). The purpose of the portfolio is to assess preservice teachers' preparation for the classroom and to strengthen connectors between the campus and the education community. Students learn during their first education course that they are to prepare a portfolio that presents their understanding of *teacher*, demonstrates their knowledge and skills in practice and in writing, and can be used in seeking a teaching position. The portfolio is kept in a thirteen-by-sixteen-inch presentation case and includes a résumé, statement of philosophy, and photographs of teaching experiences. Other items might include teaching units, games, a reflective journal, or a teaching video.

Teachers and principals from schools in the community often serve as advisors and informal reviewers for individual Samford students as they build their portfolios. At the end of student teaching, a ten- to fifteen-minute PowerPoint presentation, as well as the portfolio, are evaluated by the instructor and an educator from the community.

Use of Portfolios

The general purpose of portfolios is to collect information about student learning. In practice, portfolios have been implemented for a variety of purposes: to assess learning in general education and the major, and to evaluate such varied aspects of learning as critical thinking, analysis, synthesis, evaluation, clarification of values, and integration of concepts across subject areas (Black, 1993). Valley City State University has joined a growing number of institutions using electronic portfolios to assess specified skills developed in general education courses. A computer literacy course in the first semester introduces students to the CD-ROM portfolio concept, and the portfolio is submitted to faculty upon completion of the general education core curriculum (R. Brown, personal communication, Aug. 28, 1997).

Portfolios have been used in many disciplines including music, art, and theater, as well as teacher preparation, English, architecture, computer science, and engineering. They have also been used in disciplines such as history, sociology, and other social sciences. Portfolios may focus on a single area of study such as writing, analytical skills, or computer competence. More often, portfolios encompass a range of complex skills and abilities that graduates are expected to master.

Portfolios can be linked to one or more specific courses and used to demonstrate achievement with respect to learning goals addressed in those courses. In most cases, portfolios are used to demonstrate learning across all of the courses that make up a program. Secondary education master's degree students at George Washington University are required to select for their portfolios two artifacts from each course and write an essay that describes how the items illustrate their growth and development as effective teachers (L. Hall, personal communication, Sept. 19, 1997). One of the greatest appeals of portfolios is the potential they provide for students to demonstrate that they can integrate what they have learned across a variety of courses.

Although most portfolios are concerned primarily with evidence of student learning, initial work on portfolios at Miami University in Ohio also examined information about students' assignments and experiences (Schilling and Schilling, 1993a). Satisfaction of students with their academic programs has also been addressed through reflective statements contained in portfolios.

Goal Setting for Portfolio Projects

Agreement about goals and objectives for learning should occur before other choices about portfolios are made. Once consensus has been reached, faculty need to consider carefully what they want to achieve through the portfolio process. Faculty need to ask themselves what they want to learn from portfolios, as well as what they want their students to learn. These goals provide the conceptual framework for portfolios (Vavrus, 1990).

Faculty from the Butler University Elementary/Early Childhood Team (1997) ask students in their teacher preparation programs to prepare and defend portfolios that are designed to achieve several distinct objectives—to assess learning over the course of professional development, to model "alternative assessment" for students through the use of professional portfolios, to provide a chance for students to practice interviewing and presenting themselves before other professionals during the portfolio defense, to provide a way for students to integrate what they have learned, and to provide a way for students to learn about and use the new standards for education developed by the Interstate New Teacher Assessment and Support Consortium.

Portfolios for English majors at the State University of New York College at Fredonia were developed to serve several purposes including empowering students to choose for themselves what is or is not important, make connections across both in-class and out-of-class learning experiences, and become aware that learning is a cumulative process (Courts and McInerney, 1993, pp. 100–101). Thinking through the specific purposes of portfolios in this way helps guide the many other decisions that must be made when portfolios are used.

Practical Considerations

Many practical questions need to be addressed in designing a workable portfolio project (Knight and Gallaro, 1994). Initially, decisions must be made about which students will be asked to participate in the project and how portfolios will affect them. Will portfolios be used to grade individual students, or will they be used for programmatic assessment only? Faculty must agree on the types of materials that will be collected, as well as how, where, and for how long materials will be stored. Although many portfolios are actual folders or binders filled with various items, software is now available to store materials electronically. Decisions must also be made about the way materials will be evaluated. How often will they be reviewed and by whom?

Faculty in the Mass Communication Department at Winona State University identified skill and knowledge outcomes for their majors several years ago and determined that student portfolios would provide the best vehicle for gathering evidence for review (D. H. Pack, personal communication, Sept. 15, 1997). But after considering the logistics of reviewing and storing portfolios for three hundred majors, faculty almost gave up on the idea. More recently faculty have discovered the *Skill View* template for creating electronic portfolios and can now encourage students to include photographs, graphics, audio and video clips, as well as text. Faculty can choose paths through the portfolios and decide how deeply they want to explore any given material.

Content

Using portfolios requires faculty to make many decisions about the kinds and quantities of work to be collected by students and the ways materials will be organized.

Reflection of Purposes

Agreements about content provide the blueprint or outline for the way portfolios will look—the physical structure of portfolios. As with other choices, decisions about content need to reflect the purposes for which portfolios are being developed—the conceptual framework (Vavrus, 1990). In addition to demonstrating and evaluating student learning and development, other important objectives may need to be considered. If students will be using their portfolios when they enter the job market, the types of items they include should reflect this. For example, photojournalism majors might be asked to include in their portfolios specific kinds of photographs that will be expected when they participate in job interviews. Portfolios that emphasize materials for the job market are often called professional portfolios.

Types of Items

In practice, the general content of portfolios is quite similar across applications. Almost all portfolios contain examples of students' work, as well as reflective statements written by students indicating why they selected the items and what the items reveal about their intellectual growth. Although the general content is similar, the specific items contained in portfolios vary widely, reflecting the diverse goals and objectives for learning that are taught in academic programs. As long as the items are representative examples of student learning and provide useful information, there is almost no limit to the kinds of items that can be placed in portfolios. Typical items include such things as research papers, essays, lab reports, and computer programs, as well as posters, photographs, drawings, exhibits, videos, and problem sets. Items may be drawn from in-class or out-of-class activities.

Selection Strategies

The leeway given to students in selecting content for their portfolios differs across projects. In some cases, students are asked to provide examples of specific types of work such as essays, projects, or photographs, and to indicate the significance of their selections. Nursing students may be asked to submit care plans; student teachers may be asked to submit lesson plans. Occasionally, direction about items is even more specific. For example, a writing portfolio may contain particular essays from identified courses. Alternatively, students might be asked to select and arrange their materials according to a specified time line, with little direction concerning the type of materials.

Most often faculty provide general directions for the content of portfolios and allow students to select the specific materials. Frequently students are asked to demonstrate through their selections that they have met the program's goals and objectives for learning. For example, students who are preparing to be nurses may be asked to demonstrate that they have mastered appropriate procedures for nursing intervention. Evidence of writing competence, team-building skills, or problem-solving abilities can also be requested.

Students will often need help in seeing the connection between learning goals and objectives, appropriate evidence that they have met these objectives, and specific items to include in their portfolios. For example, at East Carolina University, students who are preparing to be teachers are given information linking the standards for beginning teachers with key "indicators" that demonstrate these standards have been met, as well as suggestions for related items to include in their portfolios. Future teachers can illustrate they "understand how students differ in their approaches to learning" through key indicators such as designing instruction appropriate to students' stages of development, adjusting instruction to accommodate learning differences, and accessing appropriate services or resources to meet the needs of exceptional learners. Possible portfolio items include differentiated lesson plans illustrating a variety of teaching strategies, videos of student performances, scrapbooks, and bulletin boards (D. A. Powers and W. S. Thomson, personal communication, Sept. 25, 1997).

Although some portfolios are designed to include all of the assignments students have completed, other portfolios contain what students judge to be their best work. However, some strategies ask students to provide a range of work. For example, students can be asked to contrast their best work with weaker work indicating how their best work distinguishes itself. They can include examples that show their progress or how their thinking has changed about a subject. They can be asked to include what they consider an unsatisfactory item or to include a draft of a paper as well as the finished product. Faculty at the University of California–Santa Barbara added a "growth over time" criterion for portfolios in teacher education explicitly embedding opportunities for reflection on learning. As a result, students "no longer attempt to dazzle with perfection" but instead include a range of their work (Snyder, Lippincott, and Bower, 1998, p. 140).

Student Reflections

In almost all portfolio projects, students are asked to provide reflections on their work in addition to the individual items. They may be asked to justify each of their selections and to explain the reasons why they included the items. They may elaborate on what the items demonstrate about their learning and how they have grown over time. Because reflective statements often become the basis for valuable discussion between instructors and learners, Courts and McInerney urge that "students be required to write about why a given entry does or does not matter to them and about how it did or did not function in their growth and learning" (1993, p. 104).

Reflective statements about the portfolio as a whole may also be included. For example, students may write a statement of expectations about their portfolio at the beginning of the term and a reflective statement at the end of the term about how their expectations were met. Such self-reflection helps students reach a better understanding about what they have learned and how they have progressed. Students must be given specific directions about the need to provide reflective statements.

Frank J. Spicuzza (1996) describes the experience of seniors in social work at the University of Tennessee, Knoxville. Seniors who graduated in 1994, 1995, and 1996 were asked to provide written comments in their portfolios describing any benefits of the process in helping them understand themselves, prepare for employment or graduate school, understand social work, comprehend the curriculum, and enhance decision-making skills. Seniors were not required to address every one of these areas but were asked to provide accurate self-reports. In their comments, seniors consistently indicated that developing portfolios was "a challenging assignment, an integrating experience, and a confidence builder" (p. 4). Creating portfolios helped students learn "where they had been, what they had done, and where they were going" (p. 6).

Other Materials and Considerations

Portfolios often include materials that go beyond course assignments, such as letters of reference, information on conferences attended, and notations about recognition received. Portfolios may also contain standardized test results, advising reports, or other institutional information. The opportunity to create electronic portfolios greatly increases students' opportunities to include a variety of information.

In addition to decisions about the types of items to include, thought must also be given to the number of items and the schedule to be followed in selecting and entering the artifacts in portfolios. Experienced portfolio users generally recommend that the number of items be limited (Black, 1993, p. 142). If students have good directions, a relatively small number of representative items should be sufficient.

Scoring and Training

While faculty are deliberating about the content of portfolios, they must also decide how portfolios will be scored. These decisions should be made at approximately the same time, otherwise faculty run the risk of collecting a lot of information that they do not know how to evaluate. Unfortunately, this does happen in practice.

Many possibilities for scoring present themselves. Occasionally, portfolios are evaluated by using a simple checklist to indicate they contain all the required items. More often, students' portfolios are evaluated on the appropriateness and quality of the items they contain. In these cases, scoring protocols need to be developed.

Some portfolios are scored holistically. That is, rather than grading individual items in the portfolio, the collection of work it contains is examined and given one overall grade. For example, each portfolio may be scored excellent, average, or unsatisfactory based on how well it demonstrates that the student has mastered the goals and objectives of the program. The portfolio can also be scored separately on various criteria such as completeness, conciseness, organization, variety of materials, and professionalism.

A description of performance at several different levels can be developed and used for each of these criteria. For example, at one extreme, a well-organized portfolio would have a clear framework that was apparent to the evaluator; a poorly organized portfolio would lack this structure. See Exhibit 5.2 for an example of a (partial) portfolio scoring sheet.

Peter Elbow has noted that "Portfolios don't lend themselves to single numbers" (1996, p. 122). Holistic scores do not give feedback about what scorers consider strengths and weaknesses. He has recommended multiple-trait scoring that includes the subtle dimensions of what captures the essential quality of the work. For example, scorers of writing portfolios need to consider such things as "voice" and "effectiveness of examples" (p. 128).

Rather than just scoring the overall portfolio, another possibility is to examine and score each item or a sample of items it contains. Separate criteria can be developed for different types of items. Models of previous work, expectations about various levels of performance, and scoring guides developed elsewhere can be used to identify appropriate criteria for assessing various items (Herman, Aschbacher, and Winters, 1992). Regardless of the approach selected, there must be agreement among faculty about the methodology for evaluating portfolios.

As with all assessment methods, issues of reliability and validity remain important. Portfolios are generally viewed as valid in terms of being highly related to the curriculum content of academic programs. However, those who initiate a project may want to collect

Exhibit 5.2. Scoring Sheet for a Portfolio

Criteria		Rating Scale	Score
Organization	3	Has clear framework	
	2	Framework present, but lacks clarity	
	1	Framework not apparent	
Completeness	3	All elements present	
	2	Most items present	
	1	Several items missing	

some evidence relating scores on portfolios to other indicators of student performance. This will help users understand the kinds of inferences that can be made from portfolio results.

To achieve reliability, evaluators need to have procedures in place that will lead to accurate and consistent results. As with other assessment methods, these procedures should be precise enough to enable the same evaluators to make similar decisions at subsequent times. In addition, different evaluators should be able to agree with each other (Forrest, 1990; Herman, Aschbacher, and Winters, 1992). These issues are of great concern with respect to performance assessment where human judgment plays such an important role. In their review of research on student portfolios in public schools, Joan L. Herman and Lynn Winters optimistically conclude, "evidence suggests that one basic requisite for technical quality— interrater reliability—is achievable" (1994, p. 54).

Pamela A. Moss (1998) suggests that, rather than using a conventional approach where results from readers who work independently to score separate portfolio entries are averaged, an integrative approach to scoring can be used. Readers can "work together to construct a coherent interpretation, continually challenging and revising initial interpretations, until they account for all the available evidence about a candidate" (p. 203). Moss suggests that this kind of approach, allowing readers to engage in dialogue about the comprehensive evidence contained in portfolios, might result in sounder decisions. Faculty who are reviewing portfolios or other performance materials for purposes of examining the overall program, rather than individual students, often use this kind of deliberative approach.

In addition to the ability of evaluators to score portfolios reliably, the potential of users to provide external information in meaningful ways is often questioned. Care must be taken to provide at least some summary information that can be communicated easily to external audiences. As Johnson and his coauthors (1993) note, some observers view portfolios with suspicion because those who design, administer, and score them are usually the same faculty who are responsible for providing instruction. Using faculty from other programs or other campuses as evaluators can alleviate this concern. Some programs ask employers of their graduates to evaluate portfolios; others invite interested individuals from the community to undertake this responsibility.

The effective use of portfolios requires extensive training. Students who will complete portfolios, those who will assist students as coaches or mentors, and those who will evaluate portfolios need specific instructions. Identifying appropriate outcomes, collecting and organizing useful materials, formulating and applying scoring protocols, and evaluating and communicating results are areas where discussion, agreement, and training are essential. One helpful strategy with respect to providing information about portfolios is to maintain a library of examples of various levels of performance. This information should be available to students, faculty, and those who will assess portfolios. Faculty may be able to draw on other portfolio users on the campus to help with training. As with other aspects of assessment, those who have had some experience are usually ready to share what they have learned.

Review

The potential for portfolios to enhance the growth and development of students is more likely to be achieved if students get regular feedback on their work. Because the intent of portfolios is to help students with their learning and development, successful portfolio projects contain regular feedback to students in oral or written form. Based on their experience with writing portfolios, Crouch and Fontaine (1994) stress the value of allowing students to rework, rethink, and revise the contents of their portfolios as they work toward a level of mastery.

Opportunities for review can be arranged more easily for portfolios that are developed for a single course. For comprehensive portfolios, reviews should be completed periodically according to an established timetable and should be frequent enough to help students make necessary adjustments as they proceed with their portfolios. Reviews can occur at natural decision-making points in the academic program. For example, many programs have formal admission points that occur after entry to the university. Other natural points are before student teaching, prior to beginning a practicum or internship, and before graduation. Students may receive periodic advice from one or more members of the team reviewing their work. Some programs allow conferences with reviewers at the student's request. Faculty at the Bank Street College of Education have required their students to participate as a group in regularly scheduled sessions designed to promote discussion of their evolving portfolios (Freidus, 1998).

Ordinarily, more than one individual will be looking at portfolios. A team may include one or more faculty, an advisor, and perhaps student peers. Professional or other community representatives may be involved as well. In many cases, students are asked to participate in oral defenses of their portfolios conducted by the review team.

Potential Impact on Students

Portfolios provide an opportunity for active involvement of students—one of the most desirable characteristics of any assessment method—through making and justifying selections of items, evaluating their own work, and preparing reflections about their growth. Indeed, portfolios provide an important opportunity for students to view their own work as a whole (Crouch and Fontaine, 1994). Courts and McInerney (1993) believe portfolios "help the learners become integral and conscious participants in their learning processes, by having them recognize both individual responsibility and ownership within that process, and by having them become interactive partners with the teacher in shaping that learning process" (pp. 85–86).

Before portfolios are introduced, faculty must decide how they will affect the progress of students through the program. In some cases, decisions about a student's ability to continue or to graduate will be linked to the portfolio performance. Students must be told if this is the case, particularly if the portfolio is an activity that is completed outside traditional coursework. If portfolios are an additional requirement for graduation, students need to be informed, and they need to know the standards that will be used for decision making. Portfolio users may develop handbooks that help students understand the process, what is expected of them, and how it will affect them. Faculty at Truman State University have developed an appealing brochure for students describing the portfolio process on their campus. Students are encouraged to save materials that reflect their growth as active learners as they progress through Truman State. Portfolios form the basis for discussions with advisors, are reviewed at the sophomore level, and are submitted to faculty during the senior year. Majors in most areas are required to submit the portfolio in their capstone courses or at senior interviews. The Portfolio Task Force then reviews the portfolios looking for patterns in senior learning. In addition to a reflective cover letter, students are asked to include work in their portfolios that demonstrates interdisciplinary thinking, aesthetic analysis and evaluation, quantitative thinking, and other areas of thought.

The confidentiality of portfolio materials is an additional consideration. Students should be told how the materials in their portfolio will be used. Is the material the property of the student or of the program? If the material is being collected for programmatic evaluation, faculty need to let students know how they intend to use the information. If material will be shared with accreditors or others outside the department, students must be informed in advance. In fact, some programs ask students to sign a statement indicating that they give permission for this use.

One of the principal advantages of portfolios is their appeal to students. Many assessment methods suffer because students are reluctant to give their best effort, particularly if they are asked to participate in activities that seem unrelated to their learning. Because portfolios are usually created from materials that have been generated for classroom use, the issue of motivation is of less concern. Some new items may be generated for portfolios, but most will have been graded already. That portfolios are often useful when seeking work after graduation provides another incentive for students to do their best.

Use of Portfolios for Programmatic Assessment

Although portfolios have a long history of use in evaluating the progress of individual students in several disciplines, their use for programmatic assessment purposes is relatively recent. To be useful for programmatic improvement, faculty need to have some agreement about how portfolios will be viewed collectively. That is, how will results from individual portfolios be summarized in a meaningful way? How will conclusions be drawn from them about the overall program?

Faculty must also decide how many portfolios will be reviewed for programmatic purposes. Must all students participate, or will a sample be sufficient? It is not unusual to ask all students in a program to submit portfolios for decision making about their individual progress, but to review only a sample for programmatic assessment. Faculty can collectively review a reasonable number of portfolios, concentrating their discussions on what the portfolios imply about the program. Existing scores can be aggregated or an additional scoring tool can be developed for this use. Alternatively, faculty can discuss and answer a set of open-ended questions about programmatic strengths and weaknesses evidenced from student portfolios.

A useful variation on portfolios for programmatic assessment is one in which faculty rather than students prepare a collection of examples of course assignments and student essays and examinations. Usually, faculty collect examples that represent a wide range of students' work. These materials can be reviewed as one source of evidence of how the overall program is functioning and where it can be improved.

Appeal of Portfolios

Sixty-nine percent of college and university administrators who responded to a recent American Council on Education *Campus Trends* survey (El-Khawas, 1995) indicated their campuses were using portfolios as part of their assessment programs. In 1990, the figure was 27 percent (El-Khawas, 1990). Portfolios appear to have widespread appeal. Why is this so? Whereas faculty often see programmatic assessment activities as intrusive and irrelevant to the teaching-learning process, portfolio assessment is viewed as integrated with it. Because portfolios contain materials that have been generated by students as they progress through their programs, faculty see portfolios as linked to programmatic learning objectives. In White's view, "portfolios bring teaching, learning, and assessment together as mutually supportive activities (1994, p. 27).

Part of the appeal of portfolios is the rich and diverse information they provide about students. In contrast with simple before-and-after measures, portfolios provide a great deal of information about what students are experiencing, and therefore more information about what might need to be improved. Portfolios are also appealing because they call on students to undertake complex work, providing an opportunity for teachers to challenge students. Portfolios engage students in the active process of learning and prompt conversations (Hutchings, 1990). Peer mentoring sessions, for example, are particularly valuable for students engaged in the portfolio process (Freidus, 1998). In Lee Shulman's view, "portfolios institutionalize norms of collaboration, reflection, and discussion" (1998, p. 36).

There are criticisms, however. Some faculty consider portfolios to be intrusive, particularly those that involve collaborative grading. They fear that if students' grades are attached, their own judgment will be questioned by those who are evaluating portfolios. Some resist the redistribution of power inherent in portfolios and the loss of control that results from allowing students to select their own content (Belanoff, 1994). Other faculty raise security issues. Because students prepare their portfolios independently, it is not always possible to tell if they did all of the work. Allowing students to draft and revise items may be criticized as allowing too much support. Some faculty distrust the authenticity of revisions containing improvements suggested by the teacher. Issues of reliability and validity are frequently raised. Because topics addressed in portfolios often differ across students, validity problems become very complex. Although more representative of a range of work, the greater inclusiveness of portfolios increases scoring difficulties (White, 1994). Shulman (1998) mentions several possible dangers if portfolios are misused, including trivialization, documenting material that is not worth reflecting on, and misrepresentation, documenting only best work rather than typical work (p. 35).

Clearly, portfolios represent an assessment technique that requires a substantial amount of time from both students and faculty, both for planning the portfolio process and for carrying it out. And although the primary advantage of portfolios may be that they provide longitudinal information, this means that it may take several years before they produce sufficient evidence to direct program improvement. Exhibit 5.3 captures some planning issues that must be raised when designing a portfolio process.

In spite of any reservations, many faculty have been willing to try portfolios. By allowing faculty to link learning goals with rich evidence about learning, portfolios have much potential to strengthen academic programs.

Exhibit 5.3. Portfolio Planning Sheet

Establish purposes of portfolios for students
> Identify how portfolios will affect students (required? graded?)
> Identify what students should demonstrate/learn from portfolios
> Articulate particular learning goals that will be addressed

Determine content of portfolios
> Identify types of items (writing samples, exhibits, exercises, and so on)
> Establish selection criteria for items
> Describe reflective statements that need to be included

Provide opportunities for feedback to students
> Create review teams
> Establish review cycle
> Provide other opportunities for consultation

Establish scoring approach
> Develop specific scoring criteria and rating scale
> Develop a reliable process for examining and rating portfolios
> Provide for training of raters

Establish procedures for programmatic assessment
> Decide whether to review all portfolios or a sample
> Create process for summarizing results
> Allow for faculty discussion of results
> Provide opportunities for developing recommendations

Practical considerations
> Provide a timeline for portfolio activities and review
> Provide for storage of materials

6

Using Tests, Classroom Assignments, and Classroom Assessment

ASSIGNMENT (n.): a lesson or task

W hen assessment first began to filter into institutions of higher education, it was often through the use of commercially available objective tests that were administered to large groups of students. A decade ago, when discussing classroom assessment as an approach to improving teaching and learning, K. Patricia Cross noted, "Most people think of assessment as a *large-scale* testing program, conducted *periodically* at the *institutional or state level*, usually by measurement *experts*, to determine what students *have learned in college*" (1989, p. 4). Cross and Steadman's recent book about classroom research reiterates this view of mainstream assessment (1996, pp. 7–8). Their observation is an interesting one. It reminds us that some individuals still see assessment as an undertaking beyond the reach of many faculty.

At the beginning of the assessment movement, several campuses did purchase or develop standardized objective tests and administer them to large numbers of students. Although this type of information gathering is still in place, most institutional assessment programs now include additional techniques such as performance measures, surveys, focus groups, and other qualitative measures.

With the passage of time, assessment of academic efforts spread from the institutional level into individual departments and programs. Several of these units use either commercially available or locally developed examinations that focus on particular disciplines, but more recently there has been a realization that assessment can be enhanced if it draws on all kinds of activities that occur in the classroom. Barbara E. Walvoord and Virginia Johnson Anderson (1998) have been strong proponents of this point of view. In this chapter, we review the use of objective tests and classroom assignments for assessment purposes. We also discuss the classroom assessment techniques that have been developed and shared by K. Patricia Cross and Tom Angelo (1988; Angelo and Cross, 1993).

Using Objective Tests for Assessment

Objective tests are a normal and expected part of the classroom experience. In addition to their role in establishing individual grades, objective tests can make important contributions to programmatic assessment. Rather than addressing students' attitudes and opinions, these tests help answer assessment questions about cognitive outcomes.

Definition and Description

Although there are many possible formats, objective tests are usually made up of a series of questions that allow students to demonstrate both the knowledge they have acquired and their ability to process and use that knowledge. Students select a correct answer from a set of responses that have been provided for them. Multiple-choice, true-false, and matching items fit this description.

Commercially available norm-referenced tests report students' scores as a percentile or other standardized score, allowing faculty to compare the performance of their students with the performance of students elsewhere. Norms can also be developed for local tests, allowing comparisons across groups or over time. Criterion-referenced tests report students' scores on an absolute basis, permitting faculty to compare the performance of their students to a designated level of competence or preset standard. With this approach, faculty determine the minimum number of items that need to be answered correctly in order to demonstrate competence or mastery of the subject. Both types of tests are used for assessment, and both are available commercially.

Most assessment tests provide an individual score for each participant, providing faculty with options for reporting and using results. Several companies have developed test modules that contain questions about a single subject such as English, history, or science. Campuses can use several modules to obtain information about performance across subjects. Some commercial companies have used item-spiraling techniques to develop test instruments that report scores for groups of students rather than for individual students. With these instruments, each student answers only a subset of questions in the subject areas covered by the exam. When results are aggregated, a group picture of performance across all subject areas emerges.

Usage

Both commercially available and locally developed tests are used to examine knowledge and skills acquired through general education or to collect information about learning in particular disciplines. All four of the universities featured in the recent Gray and Banta monograph (1997) about campus-level assessment programs have included standardized testing among their methods. For example, Truman State University (Magruder, McManis, and Young, 1997) initiated the use of standardized examinations in the early 1970s. By 1980, all students were required to take a nationally normed general education test as freshmen and again as seniors. In addition, they were required to pass a local writing assessment and to take a nationally normed examination in their major. In contrast, faculty at the State University of New York (SUNY) College at Fredonia (Hurtgen, 1997) developed nine separate tests to examine areas such as writing, reading, quantitative problem solving, and reflective reasoning. The same students were tested at entry into the university and again two years later. Support for the project was received from the Fund for the Improvement of Postsecondary Education.

Although some colleges and universities use a pre-post testing format for general education examinations, discipline-specific examinations are more often administered on a one-time basis immediately prior to graduation to indicate how well students have mastered important aspects of learning in their majors.

Assessment tests can be focused at different levels of aggregation. Some tests cover all or most of the subjects addressed in general education or the major. In fact, assessment has renewed the interest of faculty in senior comprehensive examinations (Ewell, 1991, 1997e). Assessment tests can also be developed for use within course sequences to see if prerequisites have prepared students for further study. Some assessment tests cover content across multiple sections of a single course, others focus on learning within a particular section. The appropriate level of aggregation needs to be determined when assessment plans are being developed.

Consideration must also be given to when and where a test will be given to students. Large-scale testing of entering students is often done during orientation sessions. Testing of upper-division students may occur on designated testing days or during class periods. In the latter case, faculty must be willing to set aside time from regularly scheduled class work to accommodate testing. They must explain the purpose of testing to students and encourage them to give it their best efforts. Rather than occurring in a fixed time frame, some tests are now being designed for administration on computers at the students' convenience.

Advantages and Disadvantages

Objective tests appeal to many faculty because they require students to demonstrate their knowledge explicitly. They present an opportunity to test various levels of cognition, including application and synthesis. These tests are often included in assessment programs because they allow faculty to examine a wide range of content knowledge in a single instrument—one that is comparatively easy to score and summarize. They allow faculty to ask several questions about each area, contributing to precision in measurement and to the test's reliability. The fact that objective tests can be subjected readily to well-established measures of reliability and validity is an advantage.

Objective tests allow educators to examine a large number of individuals in a relatively short period of time. Although it may take considerable effort to develop (or select) an objective test, the biggest time investment usually occurs at the initial stages of development and implementation. Once developed, the time needed to administer and score objective tests is minimal compared with other measures. An appropriately developed test can often be used for several administrations, allowing faculty to create a longitudinal data set. The ability to collect information with a common instrument over an extended period of time is very helpful for assessment purposes. Objective tests can be used in a pre-post format to collect information about the same group of individuals at different points of time. Alternatively, different groups of students can be compared across time. Many assessment programs employ the same test for subsequent classes of entering freshmen so they can compare trends in the abilities of entering cohorts.

Objective tests have several advantages, but the difficult and time-consuming task of creating good local examinations is a deterrent to many potential users. The most serious disadvantage of developing objective tests is the difficulty of writing items that examine higher-order thinking skills (Diamond, 1998). With respect to analyses of multiple choice items, Appelbaum (1988) reports that "this form of test item rarely, if ever, operates beyond the level of simple recall and recognition" (p. 125). As Appelbaum points out, even experienced item writers have difficulty producing items that test above this level. This, in turn, reinforces the fear of some faculty that objective examinations will encourage instructors to "teach to the test" and, in the process, lower expectations for students. In addition, some tests are focused at such a general level of information that they do not yield the kind of detailed results that are useful for improvement of teaching and learning. For example, faculty at SUNY College at Fredonia experienced some difficulty in translating results from their general education exams into specific recommendations for change (Hurtgen, 1997). The trend toward using performance measures for assessment is an attempt to overcome some of the limitations of objective tests.

The attitude of students toward large-scale assessment testing is another consideration. For example, objective tests provide little opportunity for students to demonstrate the skills they have acquired or to receive useful feedback on their work. Participation rates and motivation levels may be low if a test is unrelated to what students care about. After using volunteers or sampling for several years, faculty at the University of Memphis finally required all seniors to take part in testing. Refreshments, a prepared introduction, and gentle greeters were added to help improve the atmosphere. In addition, students who left early or gave inadequate effort were asked to retake the test. After several years of sharing results and building support, the senior test became part of the campus culture (Poje, 1996).

Developing Good Tests

When developing objective tests, information about reliability and validity must be provided. Test blueprints or tables of specifications are particularly important for assessment tests, which typically cover a wide range of subjects. Test blueprints show the subjects covered by the test and the number or percentage of items addressing each subject. Because they also indicate the level of knowledge being assessed, blueprints encourage test developers to address complex thinking skills. A blueprint can be used to answer important questions about how well the content of a particular test matches the content of the curriculum—a key issue with respect to the test's validity (Erwin, 1991). Some indication of the relationship between the performance of students on the test and other measures of academic performance such as success after graduation is also important.

Item analysis should be used to examine the difficulty of individual items, as well as their ability to discriminate between test takers who are performing well and those who are not. However, most criterion-referenced tests set 80 to 85 percent as the overall level of proficiency with less concern about the difficulty and discrimination of individual items (Jacobs and Chase, 1992). Pilot testing provides the opportunity to review and edit items. Items that are not working should be revised or eliminated.

The length of the test is an important consideration with respect to the test's reliability. Time allocated for administration must be constant from one administration to the next. This is sometimes difficult to achieve when test conditions vary. For example, the time available in orientation for entry-level testing may differ from the time available for upper-division testing in classrooms.

A standardized test is one where conditions of administration and scoring are constant. A good test will have a set of procedures for administration that can be implemented by all users. A standard set of introductory comments and directions should be developed and used with all test takers. Specific scoring procedures that allow for consistency in the way results are evaluated should also be available.

Locally developed objective tests are appealing to many faculty because they have had experience using them in their own classrooms. In most cases, these tests are implemented without the formal documentation that is important for assessment. Whereas classroom tests are almost always the result of an individual teacher's effort, tests that are locally developed for programmatic assessment often reflect a group effort. These tests may cover content from an entire program or across multiple sections of a given course. Because these tests are often developed and used by a group of faculty, documentation about content, administration, and scoring procedures need to be available and understood by all users.

Faculty at the University of Arkansas at Pine Bluff (UAPB) followed a carefully developed design process in creating comprehensive examinations for each major. The process included delineation of learning objectives, prototype testing, and test refinement. Criterion-referenced tests were designed to assess students' mastery of concepts and principles, and their ability to make sound judgments and interpret material. Tests are administered twice each semester, as well as in the summer upon request. Faculty introduced these tests to help ensure UAPB graduates, many of whom are economically, socially, and culturally disadvantaged, receive educations comparable to students elsewhere (Ellison and Heard, 1996).

Writing Good Items

A typical test item consists of a question (sometimes called the stem) and a set of possible responses. The most important strategy for writing good test items is to use clear, easily understood language for all parts of the item, avoiding unnecessary words. Include as much of the item in the stem as possible to avoid repetition. It is helpful to use positive language rather than negative. In particular, avoid using double negatives. All aspects of the question need to be checked for accuracy. Test developers should avoid giving clues when posing questions. All possible responses should be similar in length and complexity. Items should be checked against the test blueprint to see if there is correspondence between the content and level of thought addressed by the items and that which was planned (Jacobs and Chase, 1992; Freeman and Lewis, 1998). The construction of locally developed assessment examinations can be facilitated by using readily available resources to help in writing items, including existing finals, exams created for courses taught in multiple sections, curriculum materials developed locally, and materials available through book companies. Asking faculty outside the department or college to review locally developed tests is also very helpful.

Commercially Available Instruments

If faculty are interested in purchasing an examination, they must compare the subject matter covered by the instrument with the content of the local curriculum. Testing companies should be able to provide detailed information about the test's content. Examination copies of the instrument, technical information about reliability and validity, and descriptions of the groups used to establish norms should be available. It is often helpful to check with other users. Gary Pike's regular column in *Assessment Update*, entitled "Assessment Measures," frequently deals with technical information about commercially available examinations.

Several instruments are available to assess general education. Overall, these instruments examine analytical skills as well as recall, include writing samples as well as multiple-choice items, and, in some versions, provide group rather than individual scores. Some include matrix designs with skill areas examined across subject areas so that items contribute to more than one subscore. However, faculty often have concerns about the ability of these instruments to align with local curriculum and to guide programmatic improvement.

The American College Testing (ACT) College Outcomes Measures Program (COMP) was designed specifically to address general education outcomes necessary for effective functioning in society. Using a matrix design, COMP examines three process areas (communicating, solving problems, and clarifying values) as they apply to the content areas of functioning within social institutions, using science and technology, and using the arts. The long form of this test is being phased out; however, a version that can be completed in two and one-half hours is available. The latter is an objective test containing questions based on various stimuli such as magazine articles and television documentaries. Separate subtests of COMP are also available to assess writing, speaking, reasoning, and communication. Although some authors have concluded that the COMP examination measures aptitude or ability and is "relatively insensitive to educational effects" (Krotseng and Pike, 1995, p. 64), COMP is used on many campuses. Austin Peay State University has found some relationship between COMP scores and performance in courses and has used item analysis of COMP results to identify specific areas for improvement of instruction particularly in communications and mathematics (Rudolph, 1996).

ACT has developed another instrument designed for administration at the end of the sophomore year. This instrument, Collegiate Assessment of Academic Proficiency (CAAP), is aimed at both improvement in instructional programs and individual development through assessment of foundation skills. The examination is a battery of instruments available in self-contained modules that address the content areas of reading, writing, mathematics, science reasoning, and critical thinking. Each module requires forty minutes for testing plus additional time for administration. Students can be tested on one or several modules, and scores can be aggregated to provide group results.

The Educational Testing Service and the College Entrance Examination Board have developed the Academic Profile. This examination provides a total score as well as subscores in the content areas of humanities, natural science, and social science. Subscores are also reported for the skill areas of reading, writing, mathematics, and critical thinking. The latter scores are norm referenced, and criterion-referenced scores are also provided in writing, mathematics, and reading/critical thinking. (With respect to criterion-referenced scores, critical thinking is considered a higher-level reading process.) This test is available in a long form that takes three hours to administer, and a short form that can be administered in fifty minutes. The latter is a group test with items spiraled across four forms.

An additional comprehensive general education test is the College Basic Academic Subjects Examination (BASE). This is a criterion-referenced test that is available in both long and short forms, as well as an "institutional-matrix" (group test) form. The long form takes three and one-half hours to administer, the short form takes two hours, and the matrix form takes fifty minutes. The long form of College BASE addresses four subject areas (English, mathematics, science, and social studies) and provides three reasoning scores. All of the subject scores are further divided into cluster and skill scores. For example, the two cluster scores in science include laboratory and field work and fundamental concepts. The short form is made up of two modules that test English and mathematics. The institutional matrix form of College BASE is a group test and does not provide scores for individual students.

Based on a thorough review of assessment practices on nine campuses, T. Dary Erwin notes a move away from norm-referenced measures such as the ACT-COMP toward criterion-referenced measures such as the ETS Academic Profile and College BASE. For example, East Tennessee State University switched from ACT-COMP to College BASE because the latter provided a better match to its curriculum. Test results are used to demonstrate the strengths of the general education program for performance funding and for regional accreditation. In an attempt to align assessment instruments with curricula, Erwin points to considerable interest among these campuses in developing local assessments to supplement commercial measures. In addition to using the Academic Profile for performance funding purposes, Northwest Missouri State University uses an end-of-core writing assessment that involves writing a rough draft as well as a finished paper (Erwin, 1998).

Commercial instruments are also available for testing in the major. Many institutions use the Educational Testing Service Major Field Tests, which are available in more than a dozen disciplines, including economics, history, English, biology, and political science. In addition, faculty in several disciplines, including nursing, teacher education, and accounting, track the performance of their students on national or state licensing examinations.

Preparing Students

Because objective tests provide an opportunity to examine large numbers of students simultaneously, faculty must think carefully about the way students will be affected by testing. In many cases, interest is in the performance of the group rather than in individual performance, so students may be asked to participate in assessment testing that does not affect their grades. Some institutions or programs require participation as a condition for graduation. In these cases, notations may be entered on students' records when they have met testing requirements.

Reservations about the match between test items and the curriculum create sufficient concern about results from commercially available instruments, either for general education or the major, that faculty are reluctant to use the scores to influence students' grades or graduation status. However, if individual scores are generated, they may be shared with students to help increase their motivation to perform well on examinations. If students know faculty will see results, or if they anticipate receiving results, they may be motivated to do well. In fact, some institutions report test results on students' transcripts. Sharing individual-level results is not possible when group tests are used and is one of the disadvantages of this type of test.

With locally developed assessment examinations, faculty are often more comfortable with respect to test content and its relationship to the curriculum, and are more likely to include results in the grading process. In some cases, students' scores are factored into their course grades. (In fact, faculty may choose a test they already use for grading as an assessment measure). In other cases, students are given points toward an overall course grade for participation in testing, rather than for how well they do.

Because there are many possible approaches, students must be informed of the effect, if any, that their performance or participation will have on their grades. Students need to know the overall purpose of the testing and how the information will be used. If the test is an important part of the assessment program, students should be told. If a test blueprint or outline is available, students should be allowed to examine it if they choose to do so. Another good practice is to make available examples of items or practice exams. Students may even be invited to contribute items to the test or to review the test as it is being constructed.

A rather high percentage of respondents to a recent *Campus Trends* survey expressed reservations about the use of large-scale standardized testing. About two-thirds agreed that assessment will significantly improve undergraduate education, but more than half indicated that the use of nationally standardized tests risks distorting the educational process (El-Khawas, 1995, p. 44). Yet many campus assessment programs include objective tests. Tests that contain well-written items, adequately cover the appropriate subject matter, test the appropriate level of thinking, and are given under standardized conditions can reveal much about the learning of students.

Using Classroom Assignments for Assessment

If, in fact, the goal of assessment is to improve educational institutions, then at some point assessment needs to be linked with what goes on in classrooms. In a significant shift away from large-scale testing, many assessment programs now include information that is generated at the course level. For example, faculty in a general education program may be asked to demonstrate that particular learning goals are being addressed in their classrooms. Rather than creating new, additional instruments, faculty may use existing classroom materials.

All kinds of assignments, such as tests, essays, posters, laboratory notes, oral reports, book reviews, term papers, and works of art are currently used to evaluate individual students in courses and to determine their course grades. What faculty learn from these activities can provide information that is also useful for assessing the effectiveness of programs, departments, or institutions. As Walvoord and Anderson note, grading is a process that "has nearly universal faculty participation, enjoys superb student participation, is never accused of violating academic freedom" (1995, p. 8; 1998, p. xvii). It is closely linked to objectives for learning and to the planning of classroom teachers. Because of these characteristics, several educators believe faculty can and should use the grading process as a basis for assessing programs (Wright, 1997).

Walvoord and Anderson, although quite aware of the criticisms of using course grades for programmatic assessment purposes (discussed in Chapter Three), argue for use of "the *process* by which a teacher assesses student learning through classroom tests and assignments, the *context* in which good teachers establish that process, and the *dialogue* that surrounds grades and defines their meaning to various audiences" (1998, p. 1). Course grades are not something that magically appear at the end of the semester. They are the result of activities that occur throughout the semester—activities that tell much about learning.

Using the Grading Process

For grades to work in the assessment process they need to be based on tests and assignments that are linked to the learning goals of the course and on established criteria and standards for learning. They must allow feedback of results that help students improve their learning and that can be used to improve classroom teaching—criteria that exist for all good assessment techniques.

The key to using the grading process for assessment is developing faculty expertise. As Walvoord and Anderson note, "Effective assessment must arise from what happens in classrooms. If effective classroom assessment is not going on now, it is hard to believe that effective departmental or general education assessment will occur in the future" (1998, p. 4). What must faculty do to make the process of grading work? As with all assessment methods, effective grading starts with individual faculty intentions about learning. Faculty must then develop criteria and standards for grading assignments. Most important, they must be willing to share this information for assessment purposes in ways that are more public than in the past.

Faculty will need to submit various information to an assessment committee for centralized analysis. What kind of information is needed? Walvoord and Anderson suggest that faculty submit their course objectives, one or more assignments or tests that measure their objectives, the scoring scales they use to evaluate students on these tests and assignments, samples of student work they have graded or scored, scores of students on these tests and assignments over time, and information about how the results were fed back into the teaching and learning process (1995, p. 11).

The committee or individuals in charge of the analysis can combine the information received from individual instructors to see how an overall academic program is working. In reviewing this information, the assessment committee will be able to examine the subject matter that is being addressed, the techniques used to assess individual students, criteria and standards with respect to various types of learning, the relationship between content and assignments in various courses, and trends in student scores over time (Walvoord and Anderson, 1998, p. 152). Faculty at Raymond Walters College, a branch campus of the University of Cincinnati, have found that sharing results among faculty in the department is sufficient to generate discussion and improvement. In their project to assess critical thinking across campus, the collegewide assessment committee and dean needed to know that good assessment was taking place and that problems were being identified, but did not necessarily need to see results from individual classes (Walvoord, Bardes, and Denton, 1998).

Primary Trait Analysis

A key to the success of using the grading process for assessment is the method teachers use to develop their criteria for grading.

Walvoord and Anderson (1998, p. 69) recommend primary trait analysis. The first step in using primary trait analysis is to identify the factors or traits that will be considered in scoring an assignment. Generally, the traits chosen for evaluation are expressed as nouns. A teacher grading a research project may look at traits such as "statement of hypothesis," "analysis of information," and "conclusions." For each trait, a three- to five-point scoring scale is developed for use in scoring performances of students. Each number is accompanied by an explicit statement that describes performance at that level. For example, "statement of hypothesis" may be given a grade of 3 if the hypothesis is clearly stated, of 2 if it is present but unclear, or of 1 if it is incomplete or missing. See Exhibit 6.1 for an example of primary trait analysis scoring.

In practice, each possible grade will ordinarily be described by several aspects of performance. A score of 5 on a "conclusions" section of a research paper may require an overview of issues, a restatement of major positions, the student's own judgment about the position that is superior, and an indication of further avenues for study. Lower grades will be assigned to students whose "conclusions" section is incomplete on one or more aspects of the performance

Exhibit 6.1. Primary Trait Analysis for a Research Paper

Traits	Scoring Scale	
Statement of hypothesis	3	Clearly stated
	2	Present, but unclear
	1	Incomplete or missing
Analysis of information	3	Thorough and appropriate
	2	Present, but not complete
	1	Not attempted
Conclusion	3	Complete and appropriate
	2	Present, but not completely appropriate
	1	Not articulated or not appropriate

necessary to receive a grade of 5. Reviewing samples of former students' papers is a useful strategy when identifying traits and developing scoring scales. Scoring scales developed for primary trait analysis should be tried out in practice and revised if necessary. Several departments at North Dakota State University are using primary trait analysis to assess the performance of their master's and doctoral students. For example, traits identified with respect to final oral examinations include analyzing and synthesizing approaches to the field; determining conclusions that are theoretically, empirically, and practically sound; and demonstrating commitment to the value of science within the field. Faculty in the Zoology Department expect the introduction and literature reviews of theses or dissertations to include clear statements of the problem to be investigated, the hypothesis to be tested, the significance of the problem, and the contributions the research will make. Most departments use a three-level rating scale that includes the following categories: exceeds expectations, meets expectations, and needs improvement. Emphasis is on using assessment activities to help departments identify strengths and weaknesses in their programs (Murphy and Gerst, 1997).

Potential for Programmatic Assessment

The success of this approach rests on the willingness of faculty to share explicit information with others about what they are doing in their classrooms, including their objectives for learning, their assessment instruments, and the grades assigned as a result of the assessments. Some faculty may fear sharing this information. Although almost all faculty are willing to share their syllabi and most, if not all, of their assignments, some are reluctant to share the actual grades they have assigned to projects and papers. They are not comfortable having these grades examined by others. Some faculty will resist investing the additional time needed to compile the information. This is not true for all faculty. Many much prefer to draw on assignments and examinations they already have in place. These faculty strongly resist the need to create additional layers of assessment materials and intuitively understand that what they are already doing has value for programmatic assessment.

Besides the reluctance of some faculty to share information, an additional limitation is the difficulty involved in getting results from individual faculty to add up to a meaningful whole—one that can be used to address relevant issues. For example, in the absence of a capstone course, it may be difficult to see how students are integrating what they are learning. Clearly, making sense of disparate materials from individual classes requires judgment on the part of the oversight committee. Materials need to be carefully examined before conclusions are drawn. Walvoord and Anderson (1995) note this aggregation problem and recommend the development of primary trait scales using common language. In addition to documenting that appropriate assessment is occurring in individual classrooms, faculty discussion about how individual sections and courses come together to make up a program must be encouraged. If not, some of the benefits of programmatic assessment will go unrealized.

The approach described by Walvoord and Anderson seems to hold particular promise for course-based assessment programs. When an assessment process is focused on the contribution of individual courses to an overall academic program, using classroom assignments as the source of information about these courses makes a great deal of sense, especially for those taught by a single instructor. However, a curriculum committee may want faculty teaching various sections of a multiple-section course to provide some aggregate information. Assessment often reveals great differences in coverage among different sections of the same course and this might be less apparent when looking at unique materials from each instructor. In these cases, faculty may need to develop some common assignments or exam questions, or information generated from classroom activities may need to be supplemented with information from other assessment measures. Faculty may also have to develop new materials to address aspects of instruction that they were not previously examining, such as critical thinking, global awareness, or learning to learn skills.

Walvoord and Anderson's approach rests on their strong belief that learning is context specific—that skills such as critical thinking and problem solving are best measured within the context of specific disciplines and courses (1998). Their recent book, *Effective Grading: A Tool for Learning and Assessment*, makes a strong case for using and improving the process of grading and drawing on the information this process provides. They have argued that the willingness of faculty to cooperate in this endeavor provides "the best chance of retaining control of the content and criteria for learning in their disciplines and classrooms" (1995, p. 11).

Using Classroom Assessment Techniques

Since 1988, Tom Angelo, K. Patricia Cross, and their colleagues have developed and shared classroom assessment techniques as a means to bring assessment issues into closer alignment with faculty interests. Prominent in assessment literature, classroom assessment techniques also appear in the literature of good teaching. In his book *Becoming a Critically Reflective Teacher*, Stephen D. Brookfield (1995) shares several classroom strategies that teachers can use to examine how they think and work as seen through the eyes of their students. Linda B. Nilson also includes classroom assessment techniques in her recent book, *Teaching at Its Best* (1998). The classroom assessment movement has been very influential in fostering the view that both teaching and learning can be improved if faculty listen to the voices of their students. In the spirit of what David Schön (1983) describes as reflective practitioners, teachers who use classroom assessment techniques can seek out connections to their students' thoughts and feelings and reflect in action. They can use the information they gain to help adjust and reframe how they teach. Here, we review classroom assessment—its purposes, methods, and potential impact.

Definition and Purposes

Many teachers have developed informal methods to assess whether students understand class materials. Watching the expressions on students' faces, providing opportunities for students to ask questions, and asking them to respond to faculty questions are popular methods of getting their feedback. Classroom assessment techniques provide more systematic means to acquire information from students about how well they are learning. According to Angelo, the main purpose of classroom assessment is "to improve learning *in progress* by providing teachers with the kind of feedback they need to inform their day-to-day instructional decisions, and by providing students with information that can help them learn more effectively" (1994, p. 5).

Classroom assessment is made up of small-scale assessment techniques that provide information to teachers and students about what is going on in the classroom. Generally, classroom assessment techniques (CATs) can be administered in a few minutes at the beginning of, end of, or during the class period. CATs, which are usually ungraded and anonymous exercises, help teachers get a sense of how much and how well students are learning and provide information about the processes students use to learn. Because CATs are used by teachers to help adjust instruction and improve learning rather than to assign grades, they are considered formative methods of assessment. As Angelo notes, "CATs are meant to be used *between* teaching and testing, to find out how well students are doing in time to help them improve" (1994, p. 10). Unlike large-scale assessments where classroom teachers often must cooperate in an assessment activity that was designed by others, classroom assessment techniques are selected, designed, and used by individual teachers in specific classes for the benefit of the class. Teachers make all the choices, including how to handle the results.

Angelo and Cross (1993) have worked with classroom teachers across the country to develop a set of fifty techniques that can be used, adapted, and expanded by all classroom teachers. Their book,

Classroom Assessment Techniques: A Handbook for College Teachers, contains complete descriptions of these techniques, provides examples of how the techniques have been applied in various classrooms, and shares the pros and cons of each CAT.

Examples of CATs

Classroom assessment techniques fall into three broad categories. The techniques in the first group are used to assess course-related knowledge and skills. Teachers use these techniques to find out how much prior knowledge students have about a topic, determine how well students are following instruction, discover areas of confusion, and reinforce the material that is being taught. These techniques assess various levels of cognition, including recall, analysis, synthesis, and application of knowledge.

According to Angelo and Cross, the *minute paper* is the most popular classroom assessment technique. Teachers simply ask students to use a half sheet of paper to indicate the most important thing they learned during that class period and their most important unanswered question. This straightforward CAT asks students to recall and evaluate what they have learned and to engage in some self-assessment. Teachers can respond to this information by reviewing information or clarifying points in their lectures that were confusing. Teachers can spend some time addressing unanswered questions that were not part of the class material or can provide references. Although usually used at the end of the period to get students' reactions to the day's material, it can be used at any time during class to ask for reactions to lab assignments, readings, group work, or other aspects of instruction. The questions asked can also vary. Students can be asked about the most surprising thing they learned or the most interesting thing they read. Any question that prompts a short written response from students can be considered a minute paper.

Another helpful technique for learning about course-related knowledge and skills is the *background knowledge probe*. In many cases, teachers ask students to list any related courses they have taken previously. Rather than focusing on course taking patterns, this probe focuses on students' prior learning. Teachers ask students to rate their degree of knowledge on a four- or five-point scale. For example, an economics teacher might prepare a short questionnaire asking students if they are familiar with different theories about the economy. Rather than having students check yes or no, they may be asked to choose between a set of responses ranging from never having heard of the topic to having a clear idea of what it means. The background knowledge probe, which can be given at any time during the term, enables teachers to find both a starting point for presenting material and the appropriate pace for covering various subjects. Sharing results with students lets them know how their knowledge compares to that of others in the class and gives them strong signals about what is expected.

The second group of classroom assessment techniques is used to find out about attitudes, values, and self-awareness of students. These techniques help students gain personal insight and understanding about their own approaches to learning through assessment of their self-confidence, goals for learning, and ways of learning. Collecting this information is a significant departure for those faculty who see their role as providing instruction about their disciplines. Faculty who use these techniques show concern for students as learners and convey that concern directly to students.

Process analysis is a CAT that asks students to keep logs of the steps they use to carry out their assignments and to draw conclusions about their own approaches. This technique focuses on how students do their work rather than on their content knowledge. It can be used for in-class or out-of-class assignments. Examples include a biology teacher who asks students to document the procedures they use to carry out an experiment or an English teacher who asks students to indicate how they go about creating an essay, such as developing outlines or drafts of their work.

Teachers who use *punctuated lectures* actually stop the class and ask students to reflect on their activities during the previous few minutes. Some students may say they were relating class material to their own lives or drawing connections with information they learned in related classes. However, some may say they were daydreaming. To foster self-awareness, students are also asked to write down any insights about how what they were doing helped or hindered their learning. Teachers then collect, summarize, and share the written responses.

Brookfield (1995) suggests using the *critical incident questionnaire* to capture "vivid happenings" that students consider significant. It asks students, "At what moment in the class this week did you feel most engaged with what was happening" (pp. 114–115) or most distanced, and what action was most helpful and affirming?

The third set of classroom assessment techniques is used to assess students' reactions to specific aspects of instruction, including class activities, assignments, and materials, as well as teaching. Classroom assessment techniques differ from end-of-semester faculty evaluations in that they are given by the teacher for the teacher. The results need not be shared with the department chair or anyone else unless the teacher chooses to do so. At the end of the semester, Brookfield asks his students to write "letters to successors" identifying the essential things students need to know to survive the experience (p. 107).

Since 1993 Leslie Gardner (personal communication, Sept. 1, 1997) has asked students to suggest and help make improvements to her Quantitative Methods course, which is a component of the undergraduate business curriculum at the University of Indianapolis. A regression analysis performed on student ratings of twelve aspects of instructor behavior in this course over seven semesters demonstrates that the students' suggestions have helped Gardner improve: the ratings have increased significantly ($p < .05$).

Sharing Results

To provide benefits to students, teachers who use classroom assessment techniques must summarize responses and share results with the class. This need not be difficult. For example, the minute paper can be summarized by quickly categorizing answers in broad groups. In large classes, teachers can select samples of responses to examine, rather than trying to summarize every response. Teachers can also break their classes into groups of students and ask each group to share its best responses with the entire class.

Teachers must also indicate to students how they intend to respond to results. Perhaps they will spend some time reviewing difficult material or assign additional readings. Teachers' responses should also indicate to students what they, as students, need to do to be more successful. In his workshops and writings, Angelo (1996) is quite clear that classroom assessment is a three-step process, including planning, implementing, and responding. Teachers who collect information using CATs but do not summarize the information and share results with the class may be opening up some lines of communication, but they are not tapping the full collaborative potential of classroom assessment.

Benefits

In his 1995 review, Angelo notes the widespread appeal of classroom assessment for obtaining information about learning in individual classes. At that time, Angelo and Cross had spoken to more than thirty-five thousand faculty about classroom assessment, had trained nearly four hundred workshop and campus leaders, and thirty-five thousand copies of their original (1988) and revised (1993) handbooks had been published.

Classroom assessment has great potential to improve classroom teaching. Teachers have more information about the background knowledge of students in the class, the ways that students approach their assignments, and the learning that is taking place. Teachers can use the information gained from students to identify specific problems, such as preconceptions, misconceptions, sequencing issues, and unclear concepts, and to determine what needs to be reviewed (Nummedal, 1994). Classroom assessment also has potential to improve learning. Using CATs helps students become more aware of teachers' expectations, more actively engaged in learning, and more self-conscious about their own learning. As Cross and Steadman (1996) point out, grades alone do not provide useful information to students about their progress as learners, nor do grades help them build self-assessment skills. CATs have the potential to do both. Studies of the impact of classroom assessment indicate positive effects on student learning and satisfaction (Steadman, 1995).

Part of the appeal of classroom assessment techniques is their close link to what is known about teaching and learning. By selecting appropriate CATs and engaging students in classroom assessment, faculty can help them set high standards for themselves, pay attention to their own ways of working, organize what they are learning in personally meaningful ways, seek real-world applications of what they are learning, work productively with other students, and invest high-quality effort in their work (Angelo, 1995, p. 12).

Lisa Jansen, an instructor in computing at Northeast Wisconsin Technical College, has developed two CATs that turn what used to be boring review sessions before tests into exciting games that the students enjoy (personal communication, Sept. 25, 1997). Both assessment games give students opportunities to review course concepts in three settings: individually, in a small collaborative group, and in a competitive whole-class environment. Each game can consume an entire fifty-minute class period, but students say that what they learn is worth the time and Jansen has found that the games have produced higher test scores.

The use of ungraded and anonymous exercises provides teachers and students with a collaborative way to exchange information. Because the focus is on the performance of the group rather than on individual performance, using CATs provides a means of communication that is more comfortable than a grading situation. Giving students the opportunity to provide their reactions encourages them to become more involved in class. In fact, faculty who use classroom assessment strategies can offer students an opportunity to be "coresearchers" engaged in exploring significant aspects of teaching and learning. This approach embodies the notion of participatory human inquiry—inquiry as a means of doing research *with* people, rather than *about* them (Reason, 1994).

Based on a study in which several instructors each taught two classes, one incorporating the use of CATs and one not, Michelle L. Kalina and Anita Catlin (1994) report positive effects on retention, more A grades, and greater student satisfaction in the classes using CATs. Susan G. Nummedal (1994) provides several examples of classroom assessment projects that had beneficial results such as increased involvement of students in the classroom.

As with all assessment techniques, there are some potential negatives. Some faculty fear using CATs will take too much time or that students will not take CATs seriously. Other teachers are concerned that they may discover negative things they would rather not know. Indeed, some feedback may be negative. Each teacher must choose whether to take that risk. Teachers need to start by determining if they have a question that needs to be answered and if there is an appropriate CAT to address it. If planning is appropriate, answers should be valuable, even if some are negative.

Seeking Help

Some campuses have introduced classroom assessment techniques by inviting an experienced practitioner to visit campus; others have sent representatives to national conferences to attend sessions or workshops led by nationally known practitioners. Frequently, those who initially learn about classroom assessment share what they know with others on campus. Often faculty from a number of disciplines come together to learn techniques and approaches and to share classroom experiences. Some campuses have been particularly successful using working groups to introduce classroom assessment to faculty. In this approach, faculty meet for several sessions to become familiar with classroom assessment. Then they try out what they have learned in their classes and return to the group to report on their experiences. Other campuses have faculty groups that continue to meet long after they have become experienced practition-ers. In fact, the Minnesota Community Colleges have published a document capturing results from classroom assessment projects undertaken by several faculty on their campuses (Minnesota Community College Faculty, 1994).

Angelo laments that many classroom assessment groups "have been difficult to maintain over time, often sputtering out after two or three years" (1995, p. 12). He recommends several conditions that are helpful in maintaining long-term interest such as engaging in "a very small number of significant and sustainable projects" and helping faculty draw on research about teaching and learning to "develop skills and knowledge they can adapt and apply to their specific disciplines, courses, and students" (p. 13).

Using Classroom Assessment Outside the Classroom

Some instructors use computers to enhance classroom assessment. Angelo and Cross (1993) suggest using electronic mail feedback. Teachers who use this CAT pose questions on e-mail to which students respond anonymously. At the United States Military Academy, all cadets and instructors participate in a local area network that supports a variety of traditional testing methods, as well as a number of CATs. Approximate analogies, one-sentence summaries, and minute papers are used to obtain quick assessments of how well students are understanding class materials. Results are summarized automatically and the system provides immediate feedback to students. For CATs such as the minute paper, where responses are open-ended, the system provides samples of how other learners responded. By focusing on their own learning, the system encourages students to prepare more actively for examinations. The developers of the electronic assessment system feel its benefit to students may even surpass classroom assessment's already-proven value to instructors on their campus (Gandolfo and Carver, 1995).

Classroom assessment techniques can be used in other settings as well. For example, out-of-class learning activities, such as leadership training or community experiences, can be evaluated using these techniques, as can workshops, conferences, and seminars. A recent American Association for Higher Education Assessment Conference provided evaluation instruments for each session, asking attendees to indicate "What was the most important idea this session sparked for you?" Attendees were also asked what should be retained or changed if sessions were repeated. All feedback forms were returned immediately to the presenters so they could summarize them as they wished—very much in the spirit of classroom assessment.

The Potential for Programmatic Assessment

In their writings, Angelo and Cross (1993) portray classroom assessment as a reaction to some of the less-appealing aspects of mainstream assessment. Classroom assessment is clearly focused on the individual classroom—the ultimate site for improvements in teaching and learning (Angelo, 1994). Practitioners of classroom assessment can change the quality of teaching and learning in their own classrooms through their own actions. An important question remains, however. What potential does classroom assessment have to provide helpful information about how programs are working overall?

Because classroom assessment projects are often done at the initiative of individual teachers, it is a challenge to get the results to add up to a coherent picture of what is going on in a program. Angelo notes that classroom assessment projects "have been very difficult to link to departmental, program, and institutional assessment efforts" (1995, p. 12). He suggests reaching consensus on the most important instructional goals and learning outcomes, then focusing individual classroom assessment projects "on a finite number of critical common goals" (p. 13). Thus, even if faculty are using different classroom assessment techniques at their own convenience to answer a variety of questions, the results can be meaningfully shared across teachers and courses. Often a regularly scheduled faculty meeting can be used for discussion about what has been learned. Alternatively, a short questionnaire can be developed for faculty, asking them to reflect on what they learned about critical common goals through the techniques they used during the semester.

In addition to agreeing on a set of learning goals, faculty could also agree to use a small set of classroom assessment techniques. For example, faculty may all agree to use a background knowledge probe at the beginning of the semester and, again, at various key points during the term. Using a common set of CATs makes it easier to obtain an overview of results. Care must be taken, however, not to impose so much direction that the strongest appeal of classroom assessment techniques—the ability of individual teachers to frame the questions, select the techniques, and analyze the results for their own use and the benefit of students—is lost. At Martin University, the campus assessment committee introduced a single classroom assessment strategy across campus, asking faculty to administer a brief questionnaire, Improving the Teaching and Learning Process, four times during the semester. Faculty shared their experiences using the form with the committee and indicated the changes they had made in their classrooms as a result of using it. Changes included clearer assignment specifications, additional visual materials, and greater use of guest speakers (Imasuen, 1998).

Faculty can use recent work by K. Patricia Cross and Mimi Harris Steadman (1996) to become familiar with classroom research, a collaborative process for investigating teaching and learning issues. According to the authors, their handbook *Classroom Research: Implementing the Scholarship of Teaching* is about learning rather than teaching. Classroom assessment asks questions about what and how students are learning, but classroom research is concerned with questions about why students learn. Classroom researchers are interested not only in what works in the classroom but why. According to Angelo (1994), classroom research is one level up from classroom assessment. As such, classroom research focuses on student learning in a particular course rather than an individual class meeting. If focused on broad questions, classroom research has great potential to address issues related to programmatic assessment.

7

Listening to Students' Voices

LISTEN (*v.*): pay close attention so as to hear

The focus of academic assessment is on helping to improve the preparation of graduates. One of the ways faculty and professional staff can accomplish this is by being receptive to the voices of students. Through questionnaires, interviews, focus groups, and other listening and observing approaches, educators can learn from students. Likewise, these techniques can be used to obtain insights from alumni, employers, parents, and other groups.

Most assessment programs have several objectives in terms of the type of information being collected. In addition to measures of student learning and development, faculty are often interested in the satisfaction of students with their educational experiences. Techniques such as surveys and focus groups are particularly helpful in answering questions about student satisfaction because they allow examination of the attitudes and opinions of students. These techniques can be used to gather information about many aspects of students' actual experiences, and they are useful in finding out about the successes of students after they have left campus. In addition, although they do not provide direct evidence of learning, they allow students to reflect on their learning.

In this chapter, we describe the use of surveys, focus groups, and other qualitative methods for assessment purposes. As our examples demonstrate, part of the value of these techniques lies in the wide range of topics they can address and their flexibility in reaching a variety of target groups. Often these methods provide information that cannot be collected easily in any other way.

Using Surveys for Assessment Purposes

In this section, we provide an overview of the use of surveys for assessment purposes and include some specific suggestions for implementing survey projects.

Definition

A survey is a method of collecting information from people about their characteristics, behaviors, attitudes, or perceptions. Surveys most often take the form of questionnaires or structured interviews. Questionnaires can be administered by mail or completed on site. In fact, many assessment questionnaires are administered in college classrooms or in offices of units that provide student services. The latter may use computers for administration rather than paper forms. Questionnaires are usually self-administered—that is, completed by individuals who are working alone. In contrast, interviews require at least two people: one to ask questions and one to answer. Interviews are typically conducted by phone or in person. Both questionnaires and structured interviews require researchers to decide on specific questions, provide appropriate instructions, and carefully construct a data collection instrument (Fink, 1995; Fink and Kosecoff, 1998; Suskie, 1992).

Topics for Assessment Surveys

There is almost no limit to the types of information that can be collected through surveys. In fact, surveys sometimes suffer from an unwillingness to narrow the topics covered. To decide what topics to include in an assessment survey, faculty need to refer to their goals and objectives for learning and to the subject matter they have agreed upon as relevant for assessment.

Experiences

Many surveys ask students to report on their actual experiences, including the amount of time they spend studying, their class attendance patterns, and their out-of-class activities, such as participation in various planned events and membership in organizations. C. Robert Pace strongly encourages educators to use this kind of information. As he notes, "All the evidence that we have indicates that college students are conscientious and generally accurate reporters about their activities, that they express their opinions and satisfactions forthrightly" (1985, p. 13). Students can also indicate their future plans, including those for involvement in college activities and for continuing education and careers after college.

Values, Attitudes, and Expectations

Surveys offer one of the best approaches for examining the values and attitudes of students, often so important in general education programs. Students can be asked about the importance they place on various college goals, such as gaining a broad education and increasing their capacity for self-reflection, as well as life goals, such as making a meaningful contribution to society or continuing to learn. Many surveys are designed to gain an understanding of factors that are important in program completion. Thus a freshman year experience survey may include questions asking about students' goals for college, adjustment to college life, and needs for various kinds of support services. Charles Parish and John Emert, mathematics professors at Ball State University, believe negative attitudes toward math are having negative effects on course completion and performance and have developed an attitudinal survey to test this hypothesis (personal communication, Sept. 18, 1997).

Satisfaction with Experiences and Services

Students are often in the best position to evaluate whether what educators are doing is working. Many assessment surveys ask students to indicate their level of satisfaction with overall campus experiences, as well as with specific aspects of their majors. Questions typically ask students to reflect on academic factors such as class size, instructional strategies, and feedback from instructors. Seniors in social work at the University of Tennessee, Knoxville, were asked to complete surveys addressing the helpfulness of the portfolio process in which they had just participated. Students rated portfolios very highly in terms of helping them understand curriculum themes (Spicuzza, 1996).

Satisfaction with specific services, such as advising in the major, career counseling, and financial aid, is also determined. At Sinclair Community College, every department in the Student Services Division uses a "point of service survey" to acquire immediate information about levels of student satisfaction with the services they provide (A. M. Mays, personal communication, Sept. 19, 1997). Eleven factors associated with good service are rated in terms of importance and satisfaction, and differences between the two ratings on each factor are inspected to see how closely departments are meeting expectations.

Reflections on Preparation

Many surveys include questions asking students to reflect on their preparation by completing various rating scales or responding to open-ended questions. Although self-reported, these reflections can help determine relative areas of strength and weakness. Survey questions can concentrate on specific learning objectives of the major. At Southern Connecticut State University, nursing faculty annually survey the previous year's graduates of their programs and their employers to ask how well each graduate is performing in the work setting based on the seven learning objectives faculty have used to organize the curriculum. Specific items addressed on the surveys developed by the Department of Nursing include the following:

1. Using a nursing model to guide nursing practice

2. Appreciating values that reflect the worth, dignity, and uniqueness of individuals and groups

3. Using effective communication in clinical and professional situations

4. Using leadership and management principles to facilitate change

5. Analyzing the impact of environmental influences on health care and nursing practice

6. Valuing the culture of nursing

7. Evaluating research findings for application to nursing practice

Both graduates and employers use a four-point scale to rate preparation in these seven areas (C. Thompson, personal communication, Nov. 11, 1997).

Anne Hummer (1998) of the University of Detroit Mercy has developed an instrument that measures student perceptions of their communication skills. The fifty-item instrument includes questions asking students to assess their gains in knowledge with respect to communication skills, to reflect on their use of peer and faculty input about their skills, and to evaluate program practice opportunities. Students are asked to think carefully about each item on the instrument and to accurately assess their achievement levels.

Surveys are frequently administered as part of the evaluation of general studies programs. They may be administered to a representative group of all students in the program or they may be administered to students within specific courses. Generally they are used to examine whether students believe the goals and objectives of the program are being met. For example, students may be asked whether the program developed their abilities to solve problems and to communicate effectively. Faculty at Hawaii Pacific University have derived thirteen student outcomes from the liberal arts themes and the underlying institutional mission statement. They ask graduating students to compare their abilities upon entry to those upon graduation on each of these outcomes (D. P. Lohmann, personal communication, Sept. 18, 1997). The students are also asked to estimate the proportion of their personal growth and development that is attributable to the university.

Surveys administered in the classroom played an important role in the recently completed general studies course evaluation at Ball State University. In this evaluation, faculty teaching general studies courses were asked to demonstrate that their courses were meeting program goals. These goals include development of students' abilities to clarify their personal values, to be sensitive to the values of others, and to assess their own unique interests and talents. Several faculty assessed these goals by administering survey instruments at the end of the semester. Usually questions were stated in language specific to the course. For example, global geography students were asked about their sensitivity to the cultural values of individuals from those countries studied during the semester. As this example illustrates, students can be asked to reflect on their development of attitudes and values as well as knowledge and skills.

Background Questions

In cases where students are not identified by mailing labels or code numbers, surveys usually include demographic and background questions asking for such things as age, gender, class level, and major. To help interpret answers on course-based surveys, students can be asked about related courses they completed previously, their interest in the subject, their study habits with respect to the course, their class attendance, and their anticipated grades. Responses to these questions are helpful when examining students' opinions about the value of the course in achieving learning goals.

Selecting and Using Various Target Groups

Surveys can reach a wide variety of specific audiences, including current and future students, nonreturning students, graduates, faculty, employers, and parents. Once general agreement about issues has been reached, target groups can be selected and specific questions can be developed.

If an assessment plan calls for separate surveys of several target groups, it is often useful to include a common core of questions. For example, both faculty and students can be asked about the importance of various areas of study. Entering, current, and exiting students can all be asked about the importance of various life goals. They can also be asked about their preparation in various academic areas. Because assessment is usually concerned with issues of growth and change, administering the same survey to several target groups or including a common core of questions on surveys that otherwise differ are good strategies for obtaining assessment information.

In addition to questions that can be asked across target groups, faculty frequently have questions specific to particular groups. For example, students who are entering a program might be asked about their reasons for selecting the program, their expectations about the program, and their plans for involvement in various activities. In contrast, a survey of exiting students might contain questions about their satisfaction with academic programs, their experiences in their majors, and their immediate and future plans. Faculty surveys can explore several assessment issues, including goals and objectives for a program, strengths and weaknesses of a program, and perceptions of student performance. Austin Peay State University included a faculty survey about philosophy and attitudes toward teaching in their assessment of general education. Results indicated unevenness across the curriculum in addressing general education skills such as numerical ability and critical thinking. In response, a number of faculty development initiatives were put in place (Rudolph, 1996).

Surveys are widely used to obtain information from alumni. Many of these surveys are employment oriented, including questions asking graduates if they have obtained jobs in their field, if they are satisfied with their employment, and if they are continuing their education. In addition, many alumni surveys contain questions asking graduates to reflect on their preparation in various academic areas. Employers, too, can be surveyed to find out, in general, about their expectations with respect to skills of college graduates they hire or about the preparation of graduates from specific institutions. Chapter Eight contains specific suggestions for involving alumni and employers in assessment efforts.

Response Categories

Along with the wide variety of questions that can be asked on surveys, several response categories can be used to capture respondents' answers.

Agreement Response Scales

Because assessment surveys are often concerned with student attitudes and opinions about their programs, response categories based on a Likert scale are commonly used. These response categories might include "strongly agree," "agree," "undecided," "disagree," and "strongly disagree." Variations in wording are common, and many times the "undecided" option is eliminated to produce four response categories rather than five.

These response categories can be used for all types of reflective questions where faculty are interested in whether students agree or disagree with various statements. For example, many surveys contain questions asking exiting students to indicate their satisfaction with various aspects of their major departments. Students may be asked to select the response that best completes statements such as "I am satisfied with opportunities to interact with departmental faculty" or "I am satisfied with opportunities to participate in internships, practicums, or co-op experiences." Usually the initial statement "I am satisfied with" is included as a stem and followed by a series of items. Students can also be asked to agree or disagree with a series of free-standing statements such as "My advisor was very helpful" or "I felt comfortable using computers to access information." Statements can be worded either positively or negatively.

Importance and Preparation Response Scales

Importance and preparation ratings scales ask students to choose their responses from a set of ordered categories. Students may be asked to indicate the importance of various learning goals, objectives, and activities. A typical response scale for this type of question would be worded "very important," "somewhat important," and "not important." A preparation scale might include the categories "very well," "satisfactorily," and "poorly." Often these scales are used together as shown in Exhibit 7.1.

Participation Response Scales

Assessment surveys often contain questions about student participation in various activities and can include a response scale with the categories "very often," "often," "sometimes," "rarely," and "never." Another approach is to provide a series of categories containing intervals of numbers as a response scale. Alternatively, students can be asked to fill in a blank indicating the actual number of times they participated in the particular activity. The selection among these approaches depends on students' abilities to provide accurate information and the precision of response needed. The choice is important because it affects the type of analysis that can be provided (discussed in Chapter Eleven).

Semantic Differentials

Another approach to scaling is to ask students to choose a position between two extremes. Such scales, called semantic differentials, consist of a series of dashes or marks that are anchored with words or brief phrases that are opposites of one another. Respondents circle or check where they place themselves between the two extremes, such as "well prepared" and "poorly prepared." See Exhibit 7.2 for an example of a semantic differential scale.

Unordered Choices

The response categories just described allow researchers to obtain information about strength of opinion, degree of involvement, and frequency of participation. Essentially, these response categories provide the respondent with a series of ordered choices. Many survey questions do not lend themselves to ordered-choice responses. For

Exhibit 7.1. Ratings of Skills and Abilities

Please indicate how well *your* experiences prepared you in the following skill and ability areas. *(Consider all activities that you participated in, including those outside the classroom.)* Check the second column to indicate your view of the importance of each skill or ability.

How well did your experiences prepare you in these areas, and how important is each area to you?

	Very Well	Satisfactorily	Poorly		Very Important	Somewhat Important	Not important
Writing	☐	☐	☐		☐	☐	☐
Speaking	☐	☐	☐		☐	☐	☐
Listening	☐	☐	☐		☐	☐	☐
Problem solving	☐	☐	☐		☐	☐	☐
Analyzing and evaluating ideas	☐	☐	☐		☐	☐	☐
Conducting research	☐	☐	☐		☐	☐	☐
Using library resources	☐	☐	☐		☐	☐	☐
Using mathematics	☐	☐	☐		☐	☐	☐
Creative thinking	☐	☐	☐		☐	☐	☐
Critical thinking	☐	☐	☐		☐	☐	☐
Using computers in your field	☐	☐	☐		☐	☐	☐
Providing leadership	☐	☐	☐		☐	☐	☐
Persuading others	☐	☐	☐		☐	☐	☐
Managing time	☐	☐	☐		☐	☐	☐
Conflict resolution	☐	☐	☐		☐	☐	☐
Interacting with diverse groups of people	☐	☐	☐		☐	☐	☐
Making informed decisions	☐	☐	☐		☐	☐	☐
Self-evaluation	☐	☐	☐		☐	☐	☐
Working cooperatively	☐	☐	☐		☐	☐	☐
Clarifying personal values	☐	☐	☐		☐	☐	☐
Experiencing and responding to the arts	☐	☐	☐		☐	☐	☐
Lifelong learning	☐	☐	☐		☐	☐	☐
Maintaining physical health and well-being	☐	☐	☐		☐	☐	☐

Exhibit 7.2. Semantic Differential Scale

1	2	3	4	5	6	7
Poorly						Well
Prepared						Prepared

example, if students are asked why they entered a particular program, faculty need to provide them with a set of responses from which to choose, such as academic reputation, location, and size. For these kinds of questions, faculty need to think carefully about the choices they provide for possible answers, and to include all those that have a high likelihood of being chosen by respondents. Often practitioners can get good ideas by looking at surveys that have been developed elsewhere and modifying response options for their own use.

Open-Ended Questions

Surveys often include open-ended question asking respondents to write their own answers rather than to choose among responses that have been provided. This allows for answers that were not anticipated. Sometimes the open-ended question is no more than an invitation for the respondent to provide "additional comments." More often, open-ended questions are specific. For example, a survey of students at the end of their freshman year might contain a question asking them to describe the aspects of the campus that were most helpful to them or to describe their most important learning experiences. Many alumni surveys contain open-ended questions asking respondents to indicate the strengths and weaknesses of their academic programs and to provide suggestions for improvements. Responses to these types of questions can be especially useful if respondents' answers are sorted into categories or topics using content analysis. Examples of actual quotes can be provided to illustrate the topics included in the analysis.

Occasionally a question with predetermined response categories contains an open-ended choice such as "other (please specify)." For example, if researchers are not sure they have thought of all the important reasons why students may have chosen to study in a program, providing a category for "other" responses helps ensure that everyone's reasons will be included.

Writing Good Questions

Faculty who are asked to design surveys for assessment purposes often find they have little previous experience on which to draw. Following some general guidelines can help in avoiding common pitfalls. Survey items should be worded as clearly and simply as possible, focused on obtaining information respondents will be able to provide. For example, alumni should not be asked about courses using current names and titles that differ from those in use when they took the program. Ambiguous terms, such as part-time status, need to be defined.

To reduce bias, surveys should avoid leading respondents into providing particular answers. Asking students how much they agree or disagree with a series of statements is preferable to simply asking them how much they agree. Also, avoid the use of leading words. For example, asking students if they are satisfied with the "inadequate" selection of books in a particular course would be a leading question. Each question should be able to stand alone. Inquiring whether students received helpful career information from faculty or career counselors is asking two separate questions. If the answer is "no" it is impossible to tell what action should be taken. The tendency to ask two questions rather than one is a very common error made on survey instruments. Response categories provided for questions about continuous variables such as age or grade point average should cover all possibilities and not overlap.

In general, the layout of questions should be logical, with related questions appearing together. Providing topic headings for various subsets of questions such as "employment information" and "further education" can make a survey easier to complete. Start with familiar or more general questions that are easy to answer. Personal questions should be asked only if necessary and are best placed towards the end of the questionnaire. Instructions should be clear, using phrases such as "select only one response" or "choose all that apply."

Special care should be taken for items that are to be answered by only some of the respondents. Skip patterns on surveys should be clearly marked. For example, a survey of exiting students may contain items that are to be answered by transfer students only. All others need to be directed to the next appropriate question through instructions on the survey. Bold type, arrows, or brackets are used for this purpose. Pretesting the survey with a small number of respondents helps to create a better survey.

Cover Letter

The cover letter needs to capture the interest of potential respondents. It helps, therefore, to provide a good explanation of the reasons for the survey and to let potential respondents know their answers are important. The cover letter should also explain how the information will be used. If respondents will be identified, the cover letter should indicate that responses will be treated confidentially. If possible, the cover letter should be signed by the most responsible person in the unit. College or university presidents often sign cover letters for alumni questionnaires that are going to all graduates of the institution. College deans, department chairs, or program coordinators frequently sign cover letters as well. In addition to the cover letter, potential respondents should be provided with a return-mail envelope for which postage has been prepaid.

Anonymous Versus Confidential Questionnaires

One of the important decisions that must be made about mailed questionnaires (and even some interviews) is whether respondents will be anonymous or identified. If respondents are anonymous, then the questionnaire will usually need to contain several items asking for background and demographic information, such as gender and age. In contrast, if respondents are current students or alumni who are identified, the institution's student records can be used to provide some of the necessary information. This can be helpful in controlling the length of a survey instrument. Identification of respondents also facilitates follow-up mailings. However, there are some topics and situations where it is better not to identify respondents. Surveys that focus on personal behaviors such as seeking help with academic and social problems may be answered more accurately by students who are responding anonymously. In addition, some questionnaires filled out in the classroom, particularly those that reflect on the value of the course, may be filled out more accurately by anonymous respondents. In cases where students are identified, it is important to remind them that information will be treated confidentially. This means that only group data will be reported, not individual responses.

Encouraging Responses

Good choices about topics, wording, instructions, and layout can increase the survey's appeal and, therefore, the response rate. The length of the survey is also important. Anything that takes more than twenty minutes to complete is long for a mail or telephone survey, although personal interviews may take as long or longer. The time schedule of the survey also matters. Avoid sending mailed questionnaires around the holidays or during finals week. Response rates for mailed questionnaires vary greatly, with some studies reporting no more than 20 to 25 percent return rates and others reporting greater than 60 percent. Many times, reminder postcards or follow-up mailings are used to boost the overall response rate. In fact, in some cases, a postcard is sent before the actual mailing to alert study subjects that a survey will be coming. Incentives such as prizes or coupons can be offered to respondents. Regardless of response rate, it is important to demonstrate how well those who completed the survey represent the overall group of potential respondents.

Jeff Seybert and Karen Conklin report on a survey methodology that routinely attracts 70–80 percent response rates (personal communication, Sept. 12, 1997). Each year Seybert and Conklin conduct a follow-up survey of students who completed one of Johnson County Community College's forty career programs during the previous academic year and the employers of those completers who are working in a job related to their course of study. First they ask career program administrators to verify the accuracy of lists of completers of their programs. Completers are mailed a survey with a cover letter in mid-November and a follow-up mailing occurs a month later. Nonrespondents are telephoned in January and a third questionnaire is mailed if a phone call produces a new address. In February a list of nonrespondents is given to each program administrator, who then tries to encourage a few more completers to respond. A question on the survey asks for employer's name and address. Employer surveys are mailed in January with one follow-up mailing two weeks later.

Cautions

A substantial investment of time is required to design a good survey, as well as to administer the instrument and analyze results. Each of these steps is often more difficult than imagined. Sometimes results are difficult to interpret and can be affected by placement and wording of items. Except for open-ended questions, surveys offer few opportunities to probe areas of interest or to pursue areas of investigation that were not predetermined. In addition, survey information is self-reported. Evidence about learning is indirect, and even factual information such as GPA or income may not be accurately provided. For these reasons, some observers have indicated that information from surveys "is highly inferential, anecdotal information that should never be confused with hard data on actual program quality" (Johnson, McCormick, Prus, and Rogers, 1993, p. 161). Surveys, nevertheless, remain an extremely popular assessment technique. In fact, practitioners often choose alumni surveys as one of the most valuable assessment techniques.

Seeking Help

Designing good surveys takes a considerable amount of knowledge and expertise. Thus we strongly recommend that faculty and administrators who are developing surveys have them reviewed by survey experts before they are distributed. Although it is very important that faculty create the general topics and questions, experts can be helpful in finalizing the wording of questions and formatting the survey.

Institutional resources should be drawn upon to identify the pool of individuals to receive surveys. Alumni offices can usually provide current addresses for past graduates. Help may be available from various sources for administering the survey, entering responses electronically, and summarizing results. Many computer centers offer these kinds of services. Staff in mailing services should be able to provide recommendations about the most efficient way to send questionnaires.

Campuswide Projects

Many institutions conduct comprehensive surveys of current students or alumni that provide information to divisions and departments about their own majors. If respondents are identified through mailing labels or other means, campus records can be used to determine their majors and other demographic information. Separate reports can then be created for each unit. In cases where students are not identified, they can be asked to self-report their major, and this information can be used to disaggregate results. Those who are planning assessment activities at the division or department level should inquire about the availability of unit information from campuswide studies before designing their own questionnaires.

The Office of Information Management and Institutional Research at Indiana University–Purdue University Indianapolis (IUPUI) sends a Research Brief summarizing university-wide survey results to each academic dean along with a customized report for the school containing results at the unit level. Office staff also conduct workshops or personally present findings to those units expressing an interest (V.M.H. Borden, personal communication, Sept. 18, 1997). Ohio University's Office of Institutional Research reports results of its institutional impact studies disaggregated by academic college and department. These data are used for academic program reviews of departments that are conducted every seven years by the university's assessment council (Williford, 1997).

Ball State University's Office of Academic Assessment provides several college- and department-level reports that follow particular themes. For example, one report focuses on results having to do with career issues; another focuses on students' computer competence. These reports contain department-level tables with college and university comparative figures. Each college can then compare its results to university averages (B. K. Pickerill, personal communication, Sept. 25, 1997).

Several campuses including both IUPUI and Ball State practice another helpful strategy in allowing colleges and departments to prepare supplements for institution-wide surveys. This approach allows colleges and departments to prepare questions that are of particular concern to them. The supplements are then mailed with the main survey to the relevant target group. This coordination helps avoid the situation where respondents are asked the same or very similar questions by more than one office.

Choosing a Survey Method

Although mailed questionnaires and structured interviews are similar in the types of information they are able to obtain, there are several factors to consider in choosing between them. For a large number of potential respondents, mailed questionnaires can be distributed quickly across a wide geographic area. In addition, it may be easier to obtain up-to-date addresses than to obtain current telephone numbers. If the number of potential respondents is large, it is almost always easier to do a mass mailing than to schedule telephone or in-person interviews. Mailed questionnaires can generally cover more content in a given time than other approaches. Respondents, too, may find a mailed questionnaire more convenient because they can fill out the instrument when they want. Thus mailed questionnaires are often the better choice if convenience is a primary consideration.

Interviews are the preferable method if respondents may have difficulty in reading or following items on a self-administered questionnaire. Interviews are also preferable if faculty want the opportunity to probe certain areas in depth, especially if the survey instrument allows for follow-up of specific questions. Many departments interview their graduating seniors to get in-depth reactions about their experiences.

Telephone interviews are preferable when practitioners think respondents will have little interest in returning a mailed questionnaire. For example, mailed questionnaires of nonreturning students almost always produce very low return rates. However, nonreturning students are often willing to answer questions on the telephone about why they left and what they are currently doing. Sometimes a parent or sibling may be able to provide information to the interviewer about whether or not the nonreturning student has transferred to another school.

Cost is difficult to compare. Telephone surveys are very expensive if done by consultants, but inexpensive if done by staff or students who volunteer to help. The first consideration in deciding among the various survey methods needs to be the assessment questions and the approach that will lead to the most accurate and useful results. And, as with other aspects of assessment, the decisions about topics, target groups, and survey methods should be reached through consensus among faculty, staff, and students involved with assessment.

Using Focus Groups for Assessment Purposes

Focus groups provide an excellent opportunity to listen to the voices of students, explore issues in depth, and obtain insights that might not occur without the discussion they provide. As a result, the use of focus groups has become increasingly popular as an assessment method.

Definition

Focus groups are carefully planned group discussions conducted by trained moderators. They are designed to generate in-depth consideration of a narrowly defined topic. A small number of questions is developed in advance of the meeting and serves as the basis for discussion. Typically, the goal is to examine perceptions, feelings, attitudes, and ideas rather than to reach consensus or solve problems. Focus group participants are given adequate time to respond to questions and to discuss topics at length. Group interaction is encouraged. Participants include a moderator, an assistant moderator, and a small number of carefully selected interview subjects who are usually similar with respect to some key characteristics that relate to the topic of interest.

Sharon Vaughn and her coauthors (1996) recommend developing a general purpose statement at the initiation of a focus group project that identifies topics of interest as well as how the information will be used. Specific intended outcomes for the project, such as determining key ideas, describing participants' language, and finding direction for further analysis, should be included.

Topics and Target Groups

Focus groups allow researchers to consider a number of different topics with a variety of target groups. Students can be asked about their activities and plans, their satisfaction with various aspects of their academic programs, and their perceptions of what and how much they have learned. Recent or longer-term graduates, members of alumni boards, employers of graduates, and local business leaders are often willing to share their opinions. Alumni can be asked about their satisfaction with their college experiences, as well as about their success after graduation. Current or potential employers can be asked about the kinds of skills they expect of graduates and their satisfaction with the skills of those they hire. As with surveys, the target groups that are selected should be the relevant ones to address assessment questions.

In order to examine the success of their interns and graduates, faculty in the Human and Organizational Development program at Vanderbilt University conducted a series of focus groups with internship supervisors and employers of graduates. Participants discussed students' preparation for their jobs and how students in the Vanderbilt program compared with other graduates whom employers and supervisors had hired or used as interns (Barker and Folger, 1996).

Although focus groups generally provide indirect rather than direct information about learning, they often allow real insight into the strengths and weaknesses of educational programs. In an unusual approach to using focus groups, faculty in the Department of Sociology/Anthropology at North Dakota State University have determined that focus groups can provide just the kind of direct measures of student learning they need to assess program effectiveness (P. D. Murphy and G. A. Goreham, personal communication, Sept. 9, 1997). The department has developed specific statements of outcomes in these areas—concepts, theory, and methods—and selects random samples of graduating students in sociology, anthropology, criminal justice, and the graduate program to take part in focus groups of four to nine individuals. Each focus group involves three faculty: one who serves as moderator and two who evaluate students' responses on a prepared matrix.

Each focus group is given a scenario appropriate to its discipline. Then the facilitator asks questions in each of the department's three outcome areas—concepts, theory, methods. The students discuss each question without comment from the faculty who are present. The faculty recorders give each student in the group a mark on each question, as follows: O (didn't know the answer), 1 (wrong answer), 2 (weak but correct answer), or 3 (strong, correct answer). Responses are tallied, not to give individual students scores but to determine strengths and weaknesses of the group. These assessment findings are shared with all faculty, who look for directions for improving course content and instruction.

Some Practical Considerations

Use of focus groups requires careful planning. Faculty must decide on the specific topics and questions to be addressed, the appropriate types of individuals to be included, and the actual number of sessions to be conducted. An impartial moderator and assistant moderator need to be selected. (In some cases faculty will moderate sessions with students from their own classes, but in order to allow for a wide range of opinions someone other than the teacher may be selected to lead the focus group.) Potential participants need to be identified and invited. Consideration must be given to possible incentives. These need not be the same for each type of group. Community leaders may be invited to lunch; students may be given pizza. Sites and meeting rooms need to be selected. The actual site should be a neutral one. Students may feel inhibited discussing aspects of their academic programs if they are sitting in the department conference room. Rooms must allow for appropriate seating. Everyone should be clearly visible, so circular seating is preferred. Arrangements must be made for recording and analyzing the information. In addition to note taking, audiotapes are often used and occasionally videotapes as well.

The Moderator's Role

Richard Krueger's 1994 book, *Focus Groups: A Practical Guide for Applied Research,* has many helpful suggestions about moderating focus groups. The moderator must be able to conduct the group effectively, remaining impartial with respect to the discussion. Extensive training is usually not necessary, but the moderator must have some prior knowledge of focus group functioning. Although they need not be experts on the topic being considered, moderators need enough familiarity with the subject matter to be able to lead the discussion.

Moderators set the tone for focus groups. They need to create a comfortable environment where all participants feel free to express their thoughts and opinions. They must make sure all of the participants have opportunities to contribute and that the groups' discussion stays focused on the topics being examined. The moderator needs to exert some subtle control of the group, encouraging shy participants to express their opinions and shifting attention away from those who seek to dominate the conversation.

Moderators should start off the session with planned opening remarks that provide an overview of what will occur and what is appropriate behavior. For example, moderators usually caution participants to speak one at a time. They should let participants know at the start that they need not reach consensus in their thinking, and that, in fact, a variety of viewpoints is encouraged. Opening remarks should let the group members know why they have been brought together and how their responses will be summarized and shared. In some instances, participants may be cautioned to keep the discussion confidential. The introduction can also be used to clarify any important terms likely to be used in the discussion.

Rather than participating in the discussion, the job of assistant moderators is to take notes. The notes need not be verbatim but should capture the essence of the discussion as well as various points of view. Attention should be given to important themes rather than to details. Quotes that seem representative can be included. Care should be taken to capture comments in sequence because opinions often change between the beginning and end of the session.

Neither the moderator nor assistant moderator should show any verbal or nonverbal reaction to the group's comments. Both individuals must be perceived as neutral by the participants. In fact, both should be impartial about the outcome of the discussion. If not, the summary and notes of the proceedings may not truly reflect what has occurred. Occasionally, notes from focus groups bear too little relationship to what has been said.

Even if arrangements are made to tape focus groups, assistant moderators need to take notes. These notes provide an immediate record of what has occurred and a helpful backup if taping fails. Note takers should end sessions with brief overviews from the notes they have taken. Participants can then be invited to make additions or corrections as needed.

Choosing Participants

Although discussion groups and roundtables may be much more lively when they include representatives of a broad cross section of interests, with focus groups the aim is to bring together a set of participants who are well matched on characteristics of interest so that results can be associated with these characteristics. For example, if the issue to be discussed is whether a requirement for a course on women and gender studies should be added to a sociology major, the department may decide to conduct separate focus groups for seniors, alumni, and faculty, as well as males and females. The idea is to avoid a situation where the thinking of one group will dominate that of another. A recent focus group for freshmen was less than a success because one talkative sophomore was inadvertently invited. (What a difference a year of school can make!)

A number of strategies are available for identifying specific participants. Campus records can be used to generate a list of students' names from which a random selection of individuals can be drawn. These students can be invited through telephone calls or mailings. Faculty can invite students in class. Occasionally, student clubs are used as the source of participants, but this may lead to results that are not representative of the class as a whole. Flyers or ads can be used to locate volunteers. Occasionally, a snowball technique is used in which initially selected participants are asked to suggest additional individuals who have characteristics similar to their own. It is not necessary for all participants to be strangers. However, too much familiarity can sometimes inhibit candid discussion.

One of the more difficult aspects of focus groups is finding willing participants, especially if the target group is students. Sometimes the topic will be compelling enough to pique their interest. Many students are happy to get together to talk about various aspects of their major. Occasionally, teachers give small incentives such as extra points towards students' grades. Some practitioners have good luck finding students to participate if they provide sodas and pizza. Marketing researchers routinely pay $15 to $30 to subjects who participate in focus groups. Occasionally, a small stipend is paid to students or alumni who participate in focus groups related to assessment issues. Regardless of the strategy used to obtain potential participants, they will need to be reminded of the session a day or so before it occurs.

Developing Questions

A critical aspect of preparing to conduct a series of focus groups is selecting a precise set of questions. (Occasionally, moderators will guide sessions based on topic lists rather than sets of specific questions, but this requires more skill.)

Ordinarily, the first question will be one that all participants can answer, giving each participant the chance to speak. For example, students can be asked their major or class level. These questions are useful to note takers as they put future comments in context. As an icebreaker, sometimes the opening question is about hobbies or interests. This round-robin question is followed by four or five questions about the topic of interest, usually starting with general questions and following with those that are more specific.

A recent focus group conducted on behalf of faculty in a geography department was designed to see how well their course was meeting general studies goals. Students were asked about their understanding of what the general education program was trying to accomplish and how the geography course fit into it. Students were also asked about several specific goals and how well the course addressed them. The session ended with a question about ways faculty could alter the course to address program goals more effectively. Students were candid in their remarks and provided useful information about the course.

In addition to open-ended questions, moderators sometimes introduce exercises such as asking each participant to respond to a specific statement about the department or to provide a word that best describes the department. Frequently, the last question is used to identify participants' final conclusions, preferences, or recommendations. Richard Krueger (1994) recommends avoiding questions that result in yes or no answers. Asking participants to "think back" about their experiences is also preferred to asking them to project forward.

Moderators may modify questions slightly or be unable to cover every question because of time constraints, but they should follow the predetermined questions insofar as possible. To help generate useful information, moderators are expected to ask follow-up questions and probe for responses, but should not suggest answers. Often the moderator will ask participants to expand or clarify their answers. Moderators can include a quick round-robin check to see how each participant feels about a key discussion point.

Generally, four or five central questions are sufficient for what is ordinarily no longer than a one-and-a-half-hour session. If the project involves several types of groups, such as current students, alumni, and employers, the questions should be coordinated but need not be exactly the same for each group. Occasionally, the questions for later sessions will be modified on the basis of findings from initial sessions.

Summarizing Results

Notes taken by assistant moderators should be summarized to provide permanent records of meetings. These notes can be organized by question, with important points summarized under each. Alternatively, they can be organized by findings. (This usually involves coding and sorting responses into a number of broad categories.) Several important points can be raised with quotes and narrative that support each of the findings. Highlights can reflect how often comments were made and how strongly they were expressed. Body language, tone of voice, and group dynamics should be noted, if important. The summary should be put together fairly quickly after the session has been conducted. If an audiotape is used, it will usually be transcribed. These transcripts can be made available as a whole, or they too can be summarized in narrative form. Videotapes can also be provided as a permanent record. In some cases, researchers carefully analyze videotapes looking for particular responses or behaviors.

Issues of Reliability

To be confident in their conclusions, researchers need to replicate focus groups. More than one focus group should be conducted for each type of participant. For best results, Krueger (1994) recommends six to nine people per group and three to four replications for each type of group. For example, if alumni and current students are of interest, practitioners could conduct three groups for each. Of course this is not always feasible and, in fact, researchers can often find out what they need with a relatively small-scale project.

Ordinarily, any set of participants chosen for focus groups is brought together only once. Groups that meet on a regular basis to wrestle with related assessment issues are discussion groups or round tables, not focus groups. The essence of focus groups is the interaction that occurs among a group of individuals who have been brought together to discuss a narrowly defined topic. Focus groups are not made up of individuals who work together over time.

Some find the value of individual opinions to be the most compelling aspect of focus groups, but one drawback is the restricted ability to generalize from results. Although participants may be representative of their group, they are usually not selected at random and may not reflect accurately the opinions of the larger group about the topic of interest.

Strengths and Weaknesses

Practitioners need to remember that there are some research questions for which focus groups are not appropriate (Vaughn, Schumm, and Sinagub, 1996). For example, focus groups are not helpful in determining frequencies of various behaviors or counts of students possessing particular attitudes. Focus groups do not yield results suitable for statistical testing and may not work with sensitive issues. Moderators need to be adept at eliciting accurate rather than socially desirable responses.

With respect to their strengths, perhaps foremost, focus groups allow for in-depth discussion of a topic. In addition to information about the kinds of attitudes and opinions held by participants, they also allow an exploration of why the opinions are held. Focus groups allow for interaction among group participants, providing them with the opportunity to consider their own attitudes, opinions, and preferences in a group setting. This group interaction may cause participants to discover new insights. Opinions often change as a result of group discussion.

Because of their flexible format, focus groups allow for consideration of ideas and insights that may be entirely new to those who are conducting the group. For example, the purpose of a focus group may be to find out why students are having difficulty with a particular aspect of a program. Students may mention reasons that were quite unexpected. Perhaps they are having difficulty with a prerequisite course and faculty are not aware of this.

Compared to other methods, focus groups can be relatively low in cost. Expenses may include paying the moderator and assistant moderator, renting a room and recording device, supplying refreshments, providing for analysis of the information, and offering an incentive for participants. In an educational setting, many of these expenses can be minimal. If faculty or staff run a focus group in an on-campus room with volunteers from the student body, costs will be quite low.

Another strength of focus groups is that results can be gathered rather quickly. The process of carrying out a focus group study can often move along much more quickly than methods such as testing and surveying students. Frequently, real insight into a problem can be gained almost immediately.

Potential Uses

Focus groups can be used to help facilitate or interpret results from other assessment methods. Focus group findings can provide useful insights for designing surveys. For example, students in a particular program could be asked to participate in a focus group to discuss whether or not to require internships for seniors. Participants may generate ideas for a short survey to determine the interest of other majors in the proposed requirement.

Focus groups are also helpful in interpreting information that has already been collected. For instance, a survey about satisfaction with aspects of a major department may reveal that students are not satisfied with the advising they are receiving about possible career paths. A focus group could determine the types of problems students are encountering and the kinds of career information they would find helpful. Thus focus groups are useful in clarifying survey results and in identifying appropriate next steps.

Seeking Help

Focus groups offer a very appealing way to obtain information from students and others. Sometimes there is a tendency to underestimate the expertise it takes to conduct successful focus groups. Thus we recommend seeking expert assistance. Usually there are individuals on campus who have some experience with conducting focus groups. Many student affairs professionals, including counselors, have developed this expertise and will be willing to help. Professional staff engaged in marketing or public information activities may also be available. If faculty want to learn how to conduct focus groups themselves they can attend workshops. Richard Krueger and his associates conduct workshops on focus groups at regular intervals. In the absence of training, it is helpful to sit in on focus groups led by others. Much can be learned through observation.

Other Qualitative Approaches

Focus groups represent only one of several possible qualitative assessment methods. Typically, these methods allow for interaction between the researcher and respondents, adding depth to the information that is obtained. Qualitative methods are based on the assumption that there are multiple views of reality requiring educators to examine diverse opinions and perspectives. Generally, the goal of qualitative research is not to generalize but rather to describe findings within a particular context (Vaughn, Schumm, and Sinagub, 1996). Qualitative projects usually are designed to study a small number of cases and situations in depth and detail.

Michael Quinn Patton (1990) describes three kinds of qualitative data collection approaches. These include in-depth open-ended interviews, direct observations, and analysis of written documents. All of these approaches have been used for assessment projects. One of the most well-known applications of qualitative assessment is the Harvard Assessment Seminars. In these, more than one hundred faculty and administrators from two dozen colleges and universities met regularly in small working teams to design and organize assessment projects. Several of the projects involved in-depth interviews with students, many of whom were interviewed several times. Interviews were conducted by faculty members or fellow students and lasted one to three hours, yielding "some detailed and remarkably personal data about students' experience at college" (Light, 1992, p. 4). In contrast to structured interviews with preset questions and response categories, in-depth interviews can proceed in various directions.

Joe V. Chandler and Bettie Horne (1995) at Lander University report very good results from conducting exit interviews of seniors graduating from the Division of Physical Education and Exercise Studies. Interviews were conducted by individuals from outside the department and included a wide range of questions about both the major and general education program. Interviewers recorded important points made by students.

At the University of Hawaii at Manoa, seniors were randomly selected to participate in interviews about their experiences with writing-intensive courses. Several open-ended questions focused on the benefits of these courses, their relationship to students' majors, and ways to improve the program. Answers to interviews conducted by graduate student research assistants were transcribed and coded. The final report containing actual words of students was well received at the university (Hilgers and Bayer, 1993).

At Miami University students have participated in time-usage studies where they were beeped on a random basis and asked to write a detailed description in a log of what they were doing (Schilling and Schilling, 1993a). Portfolios, journals, diaries, and free writing are additional qualitative approaches that provide important opportunities to examine the processes as well as the products of learning (Herman, Aschbacher, and Winters, 1992). For example, journals allow students to "explore their interactions with new knowledge and ways of knowing through expressive, personal, and ungraded writing" (Courts and McInerney, 1993, p. 115).

Based on their work with faculty who represent a diverse group of disciplines and campuses, Mary Kay Kramp and W. Lee Humphreys (1995, p. 10) argue for the use of narrative as a "powerful way for learners to self-assess," allowing students to write about what learning means to them. The authors describe their use of a multistage narrative process. Students in a variety of courses were asked to tell initial stories about their experiences with the course's subject matter, to write short vignettes during the course about their learning experiences, and to review these materials near the end of the term to construct individual stories as learners of the subject. Although faculty did not grade the stories, they reflected with the class on certain experiences shared by several students and used the stories to shape class activities. In the view of Kramp and Humphreys, narrative forces educators to listen to the voices of students about their learning experiences.

These methods tap the potential of assessment to examine not only what students are learning but "why they care about it, what they want to learn, how they think they learn best," and how their views match our own thinking (Courts and McInerney, 1993, p. 25). Chapter Twelve contains further discussion about using qualitative methods for assessment purposes and the opportunity they provide "to study human experience from the ground up, from the point of interacting individuals" (Lincoln and Denzin, 1994, p. 584).

8

Relating Assessment to the World of Work

RELATE (*v.*): to connect

Although many faculty believe their primary role is to educate students about their disciplines, many also feel responsibility to prepare students for the workplace. The Teaching Goals Inventory developed and administered by Angelo and Cross (1993) provides information about how teachers view their roles. In their 1990 study of more than 2,800 classroom teachers, about 21 percent of respondents from community colleges and 11 percent from four-year colleges chose "preparing students for jobs/careers" as their primary role as a teacher. In comparison, 25 to 30 percent of both groups chose "teaching students facts and principles of the subject matter" as their primary role. Similar percentages chose "helping students develop higher-order thinking skills" (pp. 399–406). Of course these objectives are not mutually exclusive; many faculty see themselves fulfilling more than one role.

Whether or not educators have been successful in helping students prepare for the workplace remains a subject of much debate. Philip D. Gardner's recent review of research evidence identifies a consistent theme: "College students show strength in their content or academic skill base but lack competencies to handle successfully the principal complex issues of work: interpersonal communication, teamwork, applied problem solving, time management, setting priorities, and taking initiative" (1998, p. 61). Creativity and risk taking, flexibility, and openness to new ideas are additional skills graduates need to succeed in the workplace (Gardner, 1998).

The federal government has become sufficiently concerned about the workplace skills of college graduates to undertake studies aimed at defining and ultimately assessing these skills. In 1994 the National Center on Postsecondary Teaching, Learning, and Assessment at Pennsylvania State University received funding from the National Center for Education Statistics to conduct surveys of faculty, employers, and state policymakers for the purpose of identifying essential skills in writing, speech and listening, and critical thinking for college graduates (Jones and others, 1994). Goals inventories were developed and administered to more than six hundred people using Delphi probes and focus groups. The study revealed substantial areas of agreement on skill definitions and perceived importance among the three groups involved.

Many campuses have introduced initiatives to help improve the transition of seniors from college to the workplace. These initiatives reflect a view that institutions should be more accountable for the career success of graduates, particularly with respect to professional skills that are not task specific. They also reflect the fact that "most students pursue degrees as preparation for careers" (Holton, 1998, p. 96). In fall 1997, 75 percent of respondents to the widely used freshman survey conducted by the Cooperative Institutional Research Program indicated that "to be able to get a better job" was a very important reason for deciding to go to college. In comparison, about 61 percent indicated "to gain a general education and appreciation of ideas" was very important (Sax, Astin, Korn, and Mahoney, 1997, p. 27).

In this chapter we review assessment approaches that can be used to examine whether campuses are adequately preparing students for the workplace. Most of the applicable techniques have been presented in previous chapters, but here we examine how these techniques can be used to learn from three groups: alumni, employers of our own graduates or those of similar programs, and individuals who supervise internships, practica, or student teaching experiences. We review several ways to obtain their insights, reactions, and suggestions, and we also discuss some strategies for assessing group work and service learning.

Involving Alumni in Assessment

One of the most useful approaches for addressing questions about the preparation of graduates for the workplace is to ask graduates themselves. Many institutions regularly conduct surveys of their alumni; others ask alumni to participate in focus groups or interviews. Inviting alumni to serve on advisory boards that provide assessment information is an additional approach. In each case, alumni can provide important insights into the levels of preparedness they experienced when they entered the job market and about the strengths and weaknesses of educational programs in contributing to their readiness.

Conducting Alumni Surveys

One of the most widely used assessment methods is mailing questionnaires to alumni. When institutions conduct these surveys varies. Some programs survey their graduates within six months of program completion. Others wait one or two years. It is not unusual to conduct both short-term and long-term surveys of alumni, perhaps beginning one year after graduation and repeating the process at five years out.

Employment-Related Themes

Most alumni surveys contain several questions asking graduates about their employment. These questions inquire about the current employment status of alumni, the occupation and industry in which they are working, the length of time it took to find employment, the relationship of their job to their major, level of satisfaction with their employment, and perhaps current salary.

The purpose of employment questions is to generate information about job placement and career paths. Do graduates obtain jobs in the field within a reasonable time? Do they advance in their careers? Job placement information can tell a great deal about immediate opportunities for graduates. Prospective students and their parents often ask these questions before enrolling in programs. It is important to remember that results from employment-related surveys vary greatly depending on the economy. Employment information obtained from alumni must be interpreted in the context of information about the job market in general.

Some alumni surveys ask about specific job responsibilities. For example, a recent Ball State University survey included questions for alumni about the writing tasks they routinely perform at work. A checklist was provided that included various examples of writing assignments such as memos, sales letters, and research reports. Alumni were also asked about the quantitative tasks they perform and the types of computer programs they routinely use. These checklists provided helpful information about the specific responsibilities of alumni in various disciplines (B. K. Pickerill, personal communication, Sept. 25, 1997). In addition to questions about employment, many alumni surveys contain questions about further education. Surveys may include questions about current or completed educational activities as well as about plans for additional education.

Programmatic Issues

Most alumni surveys include several questions asking graduates to reflect on their experiences in their programs, including their opportunities to interact with faculty, availability of required courses, information about internships, feedback from instructors, and faculty advising. The specific content of the questions should focus on areas that are related to departmental mission. For example, faculty may feel responsible to provide advice to students about planning their careers, but not to help graduates obtain jobs.

Alumni may be asked to rate their level of preparation with respect to various skills such as creativity and critical thinking, as well as to indicate the importance of these areas to them. Comparing the importance alumni attach to skills with an indication of their preparation in these areas can provide valuable information about programmatic strengths and weaknesses. Particular attention needs to be paid to skills that alumni rate high in importance but low in preparation.

In addition to mailed surveys, some departments conduct telephone surveys of alumni. These are most often conducted among recent graduates and may focus on broad questions about academic preparation and readiness for work. A telephone survey of recent nursing graduates included questions asking if their program had changed them personally, if they felt confident at the completion of their program, and whether they had any plans for continued learning.

Because departments are unique in their goals and objectives for learning and in the experiences they provide for students, it is not unusual for several departments within an institution to conduct their own alumni surveys. Some institutions, including Indiana University–Purdue University Indianapolis, have tried to coordinate these efforts through designing institution-wide alumni surveys and inviting departments to prepare their own supplemental questions. This approach allows the institution to collect information that is comparable across departments and yet still meets special needs of departments.

Other Approaches

Many departments ask their graduates to participate in focus groups. In these cases, alumni are asked to concentrate their discussion on a few questions of significance to the department. Questions may be quite broad, asking alumni about the department's strengths and weaknesses. Alternatively, alumni may be asked about specific aspects of their experiences, such as internships or practica, or they may be asked about preparation in a specific area such as computer training for their jobs.

To encourage current seniors to do their best work in preparing a portfolio, graduates of the baccalaureate program in social work at the University of Tennessee, Knoxville, are invited to the Senior Integrative Seminar to discuss their portfolio experiences (F. J. Spicuzza, personal communication, Sept. 2, 1997). The graduates say that employers and graduate school admissions committees are impressed by the portfolio work and that they themselves gained an important sense of self-accomplishment, enhanced self-esteem, and a realization of the need for continued learning.

Several academic programs invite their graduates to serve on alumni boards, which can be involved in the assessment process in a number of ways. In some departments, faculty present results of their assessment studies to their board members in order to obtain reactions and suggestions. Assessment results may be presented orally or through written summaries. The National Alumni Board of Ohio University is briefed on various aspects of the institution's assessment program each year. This allows alumni to evaluate efforts at programmatic improvement. Influential alumni often encourage additional improvements based on the information they receive (Williford and Moden, 1993; Moden and Williford, 1996). Some departments provide curriculum information to alumni boards to obtain their recommendations about program structure and requirements. Having completed the program and acquired some on-the-job experience, alumni board members can provide valuable insights about how the program is working. For example, faculty in a telecommunications department recently introduced a foreign language requirement partly because of recommendations from their alumni board.

Alumni board members are often willing to participate in other ways. Several alumni from one college attended a round-table discussion where participants critiqued a proposed survey designed for short-term and long-term alumni. At Virginia Polytechnic Institute and State University, alumni board members of the Department of Civil Engineering were asked to meet over dinner with a group of junior, senior, and graduate students to discuss various aspects of the department, such as availability of faculty, the mentor program, advising, use of computers, and the cooperative education program. To facilitate an open discussion about these topics, alumni board members met with students without any faculty present. Because faculty encouraged this open discussion between students and alumni, they were able to identify a number of issues and introduce several improvements in their program (Walker and Muffo, 1996). Returning to alumni for additional feedback after program changes have been introduced is another effective strategy.

Involving Employers in Assessment

In addition to alumni, employers can provide valuable insights. Employers are in the best position to tell about the needs of the workplace, both in terms of the number of employees they require and the types of skills employees must possess. Employers can provide information about specific expertise needed, including computer skills, communication skills, and personal abilities. Many of the approaches used to obtain information from alumni are also helpful for obtaining information from employers. To ensure employer participation, faculty must explain the project's purpose and the value of employer contributions.

Conducting Employer Surveys

Many programs obtain helpful information about the importance of various skills through the use of employer questionnaires. These generally contain lists of specific job skills, which employers are asked to rate. The list must be well designed. If skill categories are very broad it is difficult to obtain information that can be used for curriculum improvement. For example, as Gardner reminds us, there are at least three forms of writing that may be relevant to the work situation, including report writing, research writing, and technical writing (1998, p. 66). A questionnaire for employers can include all three of these categories. The National Center for Education Statistics study of important skills for college graduates included information from employers as well as from faculty and policymakers (Jones, 1996a). In their responses, many employers indicated that new employees had weak communication and other fundamental skills.

The development of scales to rate performance levels required of employees is also important. Gardner describes a scale used by the Collegiate Employment Research Institute at Michigan State University that contains six points adapted from Bloom's taxonomy of cognitive skills. The scale was used to rate the level of thought (awareness, application, analysis, and the like) required with respect to various skills and subskills commonly required in the workplace. Employers were also asked to distinguish between requirements and preparation of technical employees and nontechnical employees (Gardner, 1998, pp. 66–67). This latter distinction is important because findings can differ for the two groups both in terms of job preparation and expected performance. The study described by Gardner found that reading and selected writing skills of technical graduates needed improvement when compared to the level of performance expected on the job.

Another important distinction is between skills required at the new-employee stage and those required of experienced employees. Holton notes, "The breaking-in stage should be considered a distinct and unique career stage with special rules and special relationships" (1998, p. 99). At this stage employers are concerned with such factors as willingness to learn new things, fitting into the culture, earning respect and credibility, and discovering unwritten expectations. Whether students are prepared for these experiences can be examined with several of the assessment approaches described in this and other chapters.

Identifying Employers

Several strategies can be used to identify employers for assessment surveys. In some cases, alumni who receive surveys are asked to provide their employers' names and addresses so they can be contacted. In these cases, it is particularly important to let alumni know the purpose of the employer survey. There are a number of possibilities. For example, employers might be asked general questions about the types of knowledge and skills that lead to success in the field. Alternatively, employers could be asked about the preparedness of typical graduates from the institution's program. In some cases, employers are asked questions about specific individuals. If alumni are providing names of their employers, they must be told whether the survey will include specific questions about their own job performance.

Faculty at the State Technical Institute at Memphis use the latter approach to obtain information about alumni from the Department of Chemical Engineering Technology. Two surveys are sent to graduates, who are asked to forward the second copy to their supervisor. Both surveys ask for a description of work being done, as well as about qualifications of employees and their potential for advancement. Alumni and employers are also asked to rate the importance of ten specific program objectives. Because both groups have recognized its importance in their survey responses, the curriculum has been modified to include more exposure to computers (Van Dyke and Williams, 1996).

An alternative to obtaining current addresses from alumni is to identify employers from existing records of those who have hired graduates in the past. Some departments maintain records based on information supplied by graduates at the time they accept jobs. The institution's career services office may also have information about employers. An approach that sometimes works is to obtain mailing lists from professional organizations. For example, addresses for both architects and urban planners can be obtained this way.

Some institutions have designed separate surveys for recruiters of their graduates. Recruiters can usually be identified through career services offices or other administrative units that schedule their visits to campus. These surveys may focus on the recruiters' knowledge of programs and services on the campus and their impressions from interviewing candidates for jobs. The College of Business and Administration at the University of Colorado has designed a survey that is applicable to both employers and recruiters. It provides a category of "unsure" with respect to ratings of graduates' actual performances on the job that can be used by recruiters who are unfamiliar with on-the-job accomplishments of individuals. However, both recruiters and employers are asked to rate the importance of various skills, as well as the relative preparation of Colorado's graduates (Singell and Palmer, 1998).

Using Parallel Surveys for Employers and Alumni

Questions asked of employers can be designed to parallel those asked of alumni so that responses of the two groups can be compared. Employers of architecture alumni were asked how well the preparation of Ball State University's graduates met their expectations in several areas, including aesthetic, conservation, and energy issues and how well the preparation of BSU graduates compared to that of recent graduates from other schools. The survey determined the weight employers give in their hiring decisions to various aspects of degree programs such as internships, socialization skills, design ability, and computer skills. The survey of employers paralleled the one for alumni in that graduates were asked to rate their preparation in the same areas considered by employers. Although employer ratings tended to be higher than alumni ratings, a need for more preparation in office management and in using computers for analysis was evident in the responses of both groups.

At Virginia Military Institute, surveys of graduates and employers are conducted annually by academic departments (Z. Zhang and

R. S. RiCharde, personal communication, Sept. 18, 1997). Over time these surveys have shown repeatedly that the most needed workplace skills are oral and written communication, problem solving, critical thinking, and computing. These findings have been incorporated into a seven-factor structure for VMI's assessment model. Several departments have strengthened their written and oral presentation requirements and added courses in computer applications. The Department of Civil Engineering has replaced FORTRAN programming with a course on relational databases in response to suggestions made by graduates and employers.

At Western Carolina University, alumni and employer surveys contain items that are also completed by seniors. These items allow the university to obtain and compare graduates' self-assessments with employer assessments of general education skills and perspectives (Hinson and Stillion, 1996).

Focused Surveys

Employer surveys can be focused on particular needs as opposed to a range of topics. For example, faculty may be concerned about experiential education, communication skills, or computer literacy. An employer survey can be developed to focus on any one of these areas of interest. A survey about current practices with respect to computer technologies could help faculty with respect to curriculum planning in that area.

Background Questions

Surveys of employers generally contain a number of basic questions to help classify responses. For example, employers may be asked to indicate the number of professional employees in their firm, the number of entry-level employees they hire in a given year, and the firm's areas of industrial specialization. These kinds of questions are helpful in analyzing responses.

Focus Groups

Focus groups can be an effective way of obtaining information from employers and is particularly cost effective if it includes employers who are located close by. Community colleges are often in a position to draw on local employers to determine the educational needs of the local community. Asheville-Buncombe Technical Community College (A-B Tech) has had great success using focus groups of employers to help identify changing entry-level employment needs. Employers are able to tell the college what they value in employees and to provide a rationale for emphasizing certain skills and abilities in the curriculum. The college has developed a comprehensive process that begins with focus groups of chief executive officers of the major industries in the community. Information from focus groups is supplemented with survey information from graduates and their employers. Advisory committees in each curriculum area also play a role. Findings and recommendations from focus groups are presented to faculty, staff, and students. Suggestions for new programs are evaluated by the faculty and advisory committee of the curriculum most likely to be affected. Final decisions are made only after a comprehensive survey of all employers in that sector of the local economy is completed. Thus A-B Tech uses several approaches to draw on employers for assistance in identifying curriculum objectives (Morris, 1995).

Other Approaches

Similar to alumni, employers are often willing to help collect assessment information from students. Some departments invite professionals in the field to interview their students about their satisfaction with their experiences or to help evaluate their graduates. These professionals may serve on panels or juries as external reviewers. Inviting professionals to observe students or critique their work is particularly helpful with respect to performance assessment measures. For instance, the Court Reporting program at the State

Technical Institute at Memphis asks professionals in the field to assess the quality of two-party transcripts, jury charges, and literary production tests generated with a minimum of two hundred words per minute and 95 percent accuracy (J. Van Dyke, personal communication, Sept. 30, 1997). As Barbara Wright notes, using external judges to evaluate publicly displayed work can help provide a sense of realism about what the future holds for students who are getting ready to graduate, as well as "concrete models for less advanced students" of what will be expected of them (1997, p. 580).

W. Tracy Dillon (1997) has formed a corporate advisory board to help assess students in the professional writing program at Portland State University. In addition to offering advice about curriculum development issues, the board participates in an annual contest involving the assessment of student portfolios. The board chooses first-, second-, and third-place winners using a holistic writing assessment procedure. Each student's portfolio includes a cover letter explaining the communication context for the items in the portfolio. These letters provide the judges with background information needed to evaluate writing performances. When inviting potential board members, Dillon emphasizes the contribution they can make to the debate over the role of higher education in preparing competent citizens. Dillon strongly believes that assessment ought to stimulate dialogue between the university and others in the community.

A unique approach to drawing on professionals for assessment purposes is used by Ball State University's Entrepreneurship Program. Donald F. Kuratko (1996), the director of the program, has devised a challenging assessment procedure to evaluate potential graduates. All seniors in the program must complete a New Venture Creation course. In this course, each student is required to complete a business plan. At the end of the semester, students present their business proposals to a board of professional consultants, investment bankers, entrepreneurs, and venture capitalists. If the plan is judged as an acceptable venture, the student receives an A grade in the course. If the plan is judged unacceptable, the student receives an F. The rationale for this approach is to let students experience the challenge and fear that confront entrepreneurs. In addition to grading individual students based on their plans, the board of professionals provides useful information about how the overall program is working. The board critiques the class as a whole with respect to communication and planning abilities and provides general feedback about the curriculum. Miami University of Ohio uses a similar approach, but projects count for only half of students' grades. The two universities have recently introduced a national case competition for students studying to be entrepreneurs.

Evaluating Experiential Education

Experiential education is a general term used to describe academically related work experience. Internships, practica, cooperative experiences, and student teaching all provide ways for students to become acquainted with the world of work. By presenting an opportunity to obtain practical work experience before graduation, these experiences provide a bridge between learning in the classroom and learning on the job. The assessment of experiential education can provide information about whether graduates are likely to be well prepared when they begin their professional lives.

The term *internship* is usually used to describe work experiences that allow participants to explore a profession while they apply their academic skills. Students often earn credit and may receive pay for their involvement. Many internships occur before the senior year in college. Some academic programs, such as journalism, require all of their majors to participate in internships; others provide options about participating. Practica are programs that stress development of academic and work-related skills. Typically, students earn course credit for participating in practica, but generally they are not paid for their experiences. Cooperative education involves alternating work and learning experiences related to a specific course of study. These experiences usually begin after the freshman year. Generally, students earn pay as well as course credit.

All types of experiential education can be assessed by three groups: students participating in the experience, faculty monitoring the experience, and on-site supervisors. Each brings a unique perspective and opportunity to examine how experiential education is functioning. To develop an evaluation tool for assessing the clinical performance of students in a three-course practicum, Elizabeth Howard of the Graduate School of Nursing at Northeastern University asked alumni of the graduate school and clinical preceptors to list observable clinical behaviors that reflect achievement of each course objective (personal communication, Sept. 8, 1997). Then she asked a second group of alumni and preceptors to rate each of the behaviors as suitable evidence of achievement. Behaviors with high levels of congruence with a course objective were selected for inclusion in an evaluation tool for the practicum.

Assessing Internships

The assessment of internships can be an involved process. In many cases, departments maintain computer or paper files that list suitable opportunities for internships. However, students often locate their own internships. In these cases, departments generally provide some kind of screening process to verify that the internship will provide meaningful work related to the student's major. Most internship programs insist that students be supervised by appropriately trained professionals who can participate in evaluating students' work. Most also insist on a minimum number of hours of participation, such as twenty hours a week for ten weeks. In order to be sure these minimum requirements will be met, interns generally meet with internship coordinators prior to beginning their work experiences.

Self-Assessment

Many academic programs ask for self-assessment on the part of interns. Some programs ask interns to complete written statements at the beginning of their internships that describe job responsibilities as well as goals they have set for themselves with respect to their internship experiences. Some faculty ask interns to maintain descriptive journals during the course of their experiences. Interns may be asked to provide weekly reports summarizing their activities. One approach is to ask interns to complete time logs that show their activities on a daily basis. An alternative approach is to have interns describe their actual activities. In this case, their weekly reports might indicate projects completed, new projects started, and ongoing projects. Students in Ball State University's internship program for journalism majors have an option between these two types of weekly reports (S. Swingley, personal communication, Sept. 26, 1997).

In addition to weekly reports, most interns are asked to complete final reports that summarize their experiences. These final papers can be used to provide overall descriptions of their activities and critiques of their internship experiences as a whole. Interns can also be asked to state whether they have met the goals they set for themselves at the beginning of their experiences and to illustrate how these goals have been met. Interns can respond to a series of specific questions in their reports by indicating the activities they engaged in most frequently, the courses that best prepared them for their experiences, and whether their experiences had any impact on their career interests.

Some programs ask students to prepare final papers that relate their internship experiences to specific themes that are important to the major. For example, political science interns can be asked to prepare research papers on political issues or professional concerns raised by their experiences. Honors students at the Colorado School of Mines who are interested in earning a minor in public affairs complete an internship that requires them to keep a journal as well as write a final report (B. M. Olds and R. L. Miller, personal communication, Sept. 3, 1997). The journal provides a reflective record of the student's experiences and the paper assesses the internship in light of program goals and objectives. In particular, students are asked to observe the official and unofficial office organization, interactions within and outside the company, and the ethos of the workplace.

Interns may be asked to fill out evaluation forms that ask them to rate their satisfaction with various aspects of their experiences such as these:

- The level of support provided by their internship coordinators

- The level of support provided by their supervisors at work

- The reporting requirements involved in their internships

- The amount of work required

- The relationship of work to their academic programs

- Their growth in various areas of learning

- Their own performances as interns

The form may include open-ended questions as well. For example, interns may be asked to provide suggestions for improving the program.

Supervisors' Evaluations

An important aspect of assessment with respect to internships is the information that is provided by the on-site supervisor. Some programs ask supervisors to work with students to develop goals for the experience. Written statements of these goals are then signed by both students and supervisors. Most programs will provide a form for supervisors to use in evaluating the work of individual students. Evaluation forms may contain open-ended questions asking about the strengths and weaknesses of the intern's performance, specific areas where the intern could improve his or her performance, and recommendations for improvements in the academic program based on the intern's performance. The supervisor can be asked if he or she would consider hiring the intern if an open position was available at the workplace.

Most evaluation forms for supervisors will include some rating scales. The supervisor may be asked to indicate satisfaction with various aspects of the intern's performance, such as the intern's ability to write, work independently, provide accurate information, work with clients, be prompt, solve problems, respond to criticism, and meet deadlines.

Coordinators' Evaluations

The role of faculty who coordinate internships varies by department. In almost all cases, coordinators will approve proposed internship experiences. Coordinators also collect assessment materials that are completed by interns and supervisors. In some departments, internship coordinators are expected to make one or more visits to the workplace to observe students on the job. The role of coordinators in assigning grades also varies. In many cases the on-site supervisor recommends the grade, but the grade may also be based on the evaluation of both the supervisor and coordinator. Some internships are graded on a pass-fail basis, others carry letter grades.

All Alverno College students take at least one internship and participate in a concurrent seminar with students from a variety of disciplines (D. C. Balistreri and L.F.L. Scheible, personal communication, Sept. 15, 1997). In addition to reflections on internship experiences, the seminar focuses on reading an organization's culture, applying various learning theories, and identifying components of professionalism appropriate to the student's discipline. Alverno's Experiential Learning Committee has articulated rigorous academic learning outcomes and assessment criteria for internships, and the seminar instructors and site mentor observe and judge a student's performance based on explicit criteria related to the outcomes. The student's self-assessment and the diagnostic feedback from instructors and internship supervisor (mentor) help the student integrate theory and practice.

Because internships play such a key role in preparing students for the workplace, it is important that the information gathered through evaluation activities be shared with others in the department. Internships need to be seen as part of students' entire programs rather than as separate activities. In some departments, internship coordinators present summary information to faculty about the performance of students with internships. The suggestions contained in Chapter Six about sharing assessment information generated from classroom activities and assignments apply to internships as well as to other courses. Assessment information about internships should be an important part of the unit's overall assessment program and included in discussions about how well the unit is achieving its learning goals.

Other Information

In addition to the materials generated through the internship experience itself, a number of other ways exist to assess how internships and work-related experiences are functioning. Many senior surveys include questions about the availability and usefulness of internships. Focus groups can also address these issues. One of the topics discussed at the meeting of Virginia Tech alumni and students described earlier was the cooperative education program. This program, which requires students to alternate semesters of class attendance with semesters of full-time employment, was considered very desirable by participants (Walker and Muffo, 1996).

Assessing Real-Life Projects

Some departments ask students to participate in client-oriented project work. In these situations students are assigned tasks that are based on clients' needs, allowing students to practice oral and written communication skills and, if working with a group, teamwork skills as well. Because students generate products or reports that are shared with clients, clients are generally involved in project evaluation. Clients can be asked to complete rating sheets that address various aspects of performance, such as accuracy, timeliness, and usefulness. Open-ended questions can ask clients to indicate how well their needs have been met. Generally, faculty supervisors will also participate in project evaluations.

Lawrence D. Fredendall has developed a primary trait scale for use by members of business firms who rate business management team projects completed by Clemson University students. The scale asks clients to assess several aspects of the way the team and its members have functioned, including the following:

- Customer satisfaction skills such as punctuality, courtesy, and enthusiasm

- Project management skills including plan awareness, problem definition, plan feasibility, and plan presentation

- Data analysis skills including collection methods, tool selection, and analysis of results

- Development of recommendations including clarity and impact

- Personal skills such as self-confidence and reliability

Each area is accompanied by descriptions of quality at three levels and is rated on a ten point scale. For example, problem definition includes the following three descriptions:

1. The team's definition of the problem was absent or vague.
2. The problem was clearly defined. Data were provided measuring the scope of the problem.
3. The problem's importance and relationship to the firm's goals were clearly stated.

The entire scale is reproduced in the Walvoord and Anderson book *Effective Grading* (1998, pp. 212–217).

Lord Fairfax Community College uses a capstone course in Computer Information Systems that brings students from six related degree concentrations together to solve applied information technology problems with guidance from six faculty members and business representatives (E. H. Crowther and J. E. Callahan, personal communication, Sept. 15, 1997). Students demonstrate their learning through group work, final projects, presentations and interactions with external practitioners. The external experts evaluate most of the final presentations and through their involvement help faculty improve coursework continuously.

Students at the Colorado School of Mines participate in a four-semester course in which they work on a series of increasingly complex real-world projects for customers outside the university. The course emphasizes the development of professionalism, such as meeting deadlines, arriving for meetings on time, and meeting clients' expectations. The course was recently modified to introduce Total Quality Management principles. One of several new modules that were introduced deals with conducting an effective meeting. Among other means, the value of this module is assessed through group discussion at the end of each meeting. Students are required to discuss and agree on the quality of their teamwork and the progress they have made in completing the project. Using a self-assessment instrument, students consider questions about the tasks they accomplished at the meeting, the cooperation they exhibited, and the clarity of their goals. Participating in self-assessments has contributed to better use of meeting times and more effective team interactions (Olds and Miller, 1997).

Assessing Group Work and Team-Building Skills

In addition to client-related projects, many academic programs include a variety of opportunities for students to work in groups, developing team-building skills that are highly desirable in the workplace. These skills are valued in both general education programs and the major. In order to be confident that teams are functioning effectively and students are learning what they should be, assessment of group work and team-building skills is important. In many cases, faculty develop assessment instruments to be used by group members.

Faculty at Rockhurst College use several instruments to provide peer feedback at the executive MBA level. In one rating form, developed by William R. Ferris (Marcic and Seltzer, 1998), members of the group are evaluated on various aspects of teamwork, including willingness to volunteer, verbal communication skills, listening skills and attentiveness, level of preparation, consensus-building ability, open-mindedness, and ability to offer and accept constructive criticism. Each of these aspects of team building is accompanied by a set of five descriptors carrying points from zero to one hundred in increments of twenty-five. For example, with respect to preparation, students who are tardy, disorganized, and do not read assignments are assigned zero points. Students who attend class, read most assignments, and usually are organized are assigned fifty points. Those who obtain additional outside materials, share relevant outside experiences, and are well organized and committed to their roles in the group receive one hundred points. Each member of the group fills out a form assigning points to all group members (Miller, 1997).

According to Charles Walker, problems in group process rather than differences in the talent or achievement of group members may contribute to poor group performance. To help build effective, autonomous groups, Walker developed a classroom assessment technique to help instructors detect problems early in the semester. The Group Process Assessment Technique is designed to help students learn "organizational skills that will help them work effectively with others in small groups" (1995, p. 4). Based on a specific model of team building, this classroom assessment technique (CAT) asks students about team goals, strategies, and resources. For example, students are asked whether each member of the group has been assigned unique responsibilities to help the group do its work. Questions are specifically focused on the process of group work rather than on individual performances. Group members are asked to fill out the CAT individually and then to meet as a group to discuss responses. The teacher then receives a summary from each group about results, as well as the group's plans to address team building.

Students often need some preparation before they can rate themselves or their peers effectively. In fact, they may feel reluctant to play this role. Faculty must make it clear to group members how peer evaluations will be used. Gainen and Locatelli (1995) recommend that peer evaluations be advisory and used only to supplement the instructor's own judgment. Instructors can evaluate group work in a variety of ways. Faculty or professionals can observe various aspects of the way the team is functioning. For example, group presentations can be evaluated for evidence of teamwork. In some cases, groupwork can be taped and viewed at a later time to examine interactions among group members.

Robert M. Diamond (1998) suggests assigning students a final one- or two-page paper asking them to describe the insights they have gained about working with groups. He also suggests giving each member a specific responsibility within a group project or presentation, thus allowing the instructor to evaluate the contributions of individual members as well as the overall project.

As with all assessment, instruments must reflect what faculty and students care about. As Gardner (1998) notes, successful teamwork requires agreement among members about expectations and performance, about how decisions will be made and conflicts resolved, and about the role of each member. Assessment instruments should reflect these important elements of teamwork along with traditional elements such as preparation and timeliness.

The Foundation Coalition of the National Science Foundation, partner schools engaged in engineering or preengineering education, identifies several criteria for effective team membership that are addressed on survey instruments for students and employers.

Among others, performance criteria include the following (National Science Foundation, n.d., p. 7):

- Initiating and maintaining task-oriented dialogue

- Working for constructive conflict resolution

- Striving for group consensus

- Supporting other members in their roles

- Participating in the development of ideas

Effective team members are also expected to display appropriate listening skills, including paying attention, avoiding interruptions, and using appropriate nonverbal skills. Speaking criteria include asking appropriate questions and speaking in a clear and concise manner.

Assessing Service Learning

Many institutions provide opportunities for students to engage in service learning experiences. These experiences range from intensive long-term projects such as service in a culture abroad to one-time events such as cleaning up a neighborhood community. Although definitions of service learning differ, Barbara Jacoby defines it as "a form of experiential education in which students engage in activities that address human and community needs together with structured opportunities intentionally designed to promote student learning and development. Reflection and reciprocity are key concepts of service-learning" (Jacoby, 1996, p. 5). According to Thomas Ehrlich, service learning is "the various pedagogies that link community service and academic study so that each strengthens the other" (1996, p. xi). Ordinarily, service learning is based on experiences that take place outside of classrooms and campuses. Service learning occurs in local neighborhoods, states, and the global community. With its intentional focus on goals for student learning, these activities can help students in their transition to the workplace. As defined by Jacoby and others, service learning involves reflection on the part of students, as well as feedback from those being served, peers, and program leaders. An important aspect of service learning is the mutual respect between individuals in the learning exchange (Jacoby, 1996, p. 8).

Several descriptions of good practice for service learning exist, and all highlight the importance of evaluation as a means to give direction for program improvement. Mintz and Hesser (1996) describe the self-reflection and evaluation efforts involved in the University of Maryland's service learning program. In this program, commuter students spend one year working with homeless, runaway, and abused youth. In regular reflection sessions, students discuss what they have learned from the youngsters they work with and how they have applied these insights to their service. Students meet regularly with agency volunteer coordinators to obtain feedback on their work and to determine additional needs of the agency. Ongoing evaluations from student participants, agency staff, and community participants are also used to strengthen the program.

One-time and short-term learning events can be evaluated through a postevent gathering of participants during which they share reactions and ideas. McCarthy (1996) recommends an additional follow-up session sometime after the event. In his view, it sometimes takes a period of time before the significance of a service learning event sinks in. Meeting again after a reasonable time gives an additional chance to discuss whether expectations were met and to reflect on the experience.

Many of the classroom assessment techniques suggested by Angelo and Cross (1993) could be adapted for use with service learning, such as the minute paper or process analysis. Asking students to keep reflective journals is another good strategy. Pointing out the serious consequences of failing to meet service learning commitments, Morton (1996) stresses the need to make sure these commitments are honored. He recommends self-reporting on the part of students and written reports or time sheets signed by students and site supervisors.

Faculty at Portland State University have developed a workbook of strategies and methods for assessing the impact of service learning on students, faculty, the community, and the institution. The authors identify key variables, indicators, and measurement strategies that help determine the effect of service learning on each of these groups. Strategies include the use of interviews, focus groups, observations, journals, and contact logs. Emphasis is on reflection as well as documentation (Driscoll and others, 1998).

Assessing Professional Orientation

Observers have challenged institutions of higher education to examine their roles and responsibilities in preparing graduates for professional success. These institutions have been encouraged to recognize that subject matter knowledge and skills are only part of what students need to know. Students need transferable skills such as the ability to negotiate and compromise. Qualities such as adaptability, openness, and empathy are needed as well (Holton, 1998). Curry and Wergin (1997) specifically criticize licensing and certification examinations for their emphasis on knowledge and skills rather than judgment and insight.

Some disciplines are redefining the meaning of adequate professional practice to include "judgment and wise action within complex, unique, and uncertain situations" (Curry and Wergin, 1997, p. 352). In addition to skills in reflective practice, emphasis is on effective critical thinking, communication, and awareness of values and perspectives within the profession.

Faculty in the Smeal College of Business Administration at The Pennsylvania State University have instituted assessment for every one of its major programs, all built on a common foundation of skills (such as writing and speaking), knowledge (such as a functional understanding of business logistics or systems analysis), and perspectives (such as global or ethnic issues) (M. J. Dooris, personal communication, Sept. 10, 1997). Faculty in each department defined the skills-knowledge-perspectives content for their majors and developed or chose their measurement tools, such as student and employer surveys and syllabus reviews. Assessment findings convinced faculty to reconstruct the core curriculum of the college, integrating heretofore tightly compartmentalized separate courses in accounting, marketing, and management, for example. Assessment has been placed on a multiyear continuing cycle and linked with annual strategic planning for the college.

As is the case with their peers in some other disciplines, accounting graduates are now expected to develop professional competence and skills of lifelong learning. The Accounting Education Change Commission (AECC) has identified three key outcomes related to professional orientation: an attitude of lifelong learning, professional integrity, and professional capacities and attitudes. In addition, the AECC identifies "learning to learn" as an underlying capacity that integrates knowledge, skills, and values (Gainen and Locatelli, 1995, p. 92). As described by Francis, Mulder, and Stark (1995), intentional learners exhibit five traits: questioning what is to be known; organizing what is learned; connecting new knowledge with old; reflecting on what, how, and why they are learning; and adapting what is learned to a changing world.

We mention the expectations of the AECC here because their statements provide an excellent example on the part of a particular profession to define the meaning of workplace readiness. The recent work of Joanne Gainen and Paul Locatelli (1995) contains a thorough description and analysis of the specific meaning of workplace competence for future accounting graduates. Graduates will be expected to value self-improvement; to welcome uncertainty; to make ethical decisions; and to possess attitudes such as persistence, empathy, and leadership. How can these qualities be assessed? In addition to using existing inventories such as the Critical Thinking Dispositions Inventory and the Defining Issues Test (described in Chapter Nine), Gainen and Locatelli suggest assessment measures such as faculty evaluations of case presentations, overall ratings of class discussions, and ratings by employers of graduates' skills in addressing ethical issues.

Campuses offer rich and varied experiences that help prepare students for the world of work. Assessing these experiences and using the findings can help make them even more valuable.

9

Assessing General Education

GENERAL (*adj.*): applying to all

One of the most challenging aspects of assessment is its application to general education programs and to the goals for learning and development on which these programs are based. In this chapter, we address some of the issues and concerns that come into play when examining how general education programs are functioning. We present an overview of recent thinking about the role of general education in college curricula, discuss some of the many choices involved in assessing general education programs, and focus, in particular, on the assessment of critical thinking.

The Nature of General Education

The meaning of general education and its role in college curricula are not without controversy and debate. Historically, the focus of general education has been on providing broad exposure to the skills and attitudes that help graduates function in society, rather than on developing specialized knowledge about particular disciplines. However, the notion that general education requirements can be satisfied simply by taking a sampling of courses from a variety of disciplines has been challenged (Association of American Colleges, 1994; Ratcliff, 1997b). Perhaps as a result, 87 percent of respondents to the 1996 *Campus Trends* survey reported introducing new general education requirements since 1985–86 and 76 percent reported increased coherence of general education (El-Khawas and Knopp, 1996).

In the old view of general education, students could satisfy their "distribution" requirements by taking one of several introductory courses in various academic departments. These courses were viewed as foundations for more important specialized knowledge. Faculty teaching these courses often believed they were providing a "service" to students majoring in other areas. Based on a project involving faculty and administrators from seventeen colleges and universities, the Association of American Colleges (AAC) issued a report in 1994 called "Strong Foundations: Twelve Principles for Effective General Education Programs." The AAC report captures much of the current thinking about the role of general education in college curricula. As the report points out, a new concept has emerged recognizing that "general education must be much more than breadth and simple exposure to different fields of study" (p. iii). General education programs should provide students with the opportunity to learn specific thinking and communication skills in courses offered throughout the curriculum. Students should study other cultures as well as the diversity in their own culture, be able to integrate thinking and ideas across disciplines, and develop personal qualities characteristic of all college graduates. Perhaps of most importance, students should "experience a coherent course of study, one that is more than the sum of its parts" (p. iv).

In the current view, courses must be selected for general education programs because they address certain goals and objectives for learning, rather than represent certain disciplines. Although the vast majority of general education programs use "distribution" systems, approaches to achieving coherence within these systems differ greatly. Some campuses require all students to take several core courses; others offer interdisciplinary courses, and many now require senior capstone seminars. Coursework clusters are also offered on some campuses (Ratcliff, 1997a; Erwin and Fuller, 1998). Regardless of structure, a commitment to assessment remains important. The final principle for effective general education programs addressed in the AAC report states that "Strong General Education Programs Assess and Monitor Progress Toward an Evolving Vision Through Ongoing Self-Reflection" (p. 52). Assessment plays a vital role in helping to determine whether general education programs are achieving their purposes and, of equal importance, helping these programs evolve and improve.

Assessment Choices and Issues

In the current view, general education programs are dynamic systems that evolve as they mature, rather than fixed, unchanging sets of discrete courses. How do faculty go about assessing these programs? The process of assessing general education programs is the same as that of assessing the major. Once the overall mission and purposes of the program are defined, specific goals and objectives for learning must be articulated, an approach for organization must be selected, assessment methods must be chosen and administered, and results must be examined and used. As with assessment of the major, faculty and students must be involved in all aspects of the process. What is particularly challenging about assessment of general education is that, in almost all cases, programmatic assessment calls for consensus and agreement among faculty who are housed in different academic departments and who represent various disciplines. Almost all successful programs to assess general education are led by strong interdisciplinary committees that include faculty from across campus. Ordinarily, these committees select the approach to assessment, evaluate information, and issue recommendations.

Agreeing on Program Purposes and Learning Objectives

The most important question for faculty to answer with respect to any general education program is, "What is the point . . . ?" (Association of American Colleges, 1994, p. 3). The answer to this question becomes the foundation for the program and provides the rationale for what and how faculty teach in the program. Many institutions embrace the current view that general education programs prepare students for effective citizenship in a democratic society. However, institutions vary greatly in how this purpose is articulated on their own campuses. Agreement about purposes is a crucial first step and must occur before any attempts to develop programs for assessment. At the University of Texas at San Antonio, faculty have designed the core curriculum to "enable students to assess the perspectives and accomplishments of the past and to move to the future with an informed and flexible outlook. It promotes intellectual adaptability, ethical awareness, and transfer among diverse modes of thought" (University of Texas at San Antonio, 1998, p. 114) An essential aim is to activate the verbal, numerical, and visual skills necessary to analyze and synthesize information, construct arguments, and identify and solve problems. Faculty foster understanding of the intellectual and cultural pluralism of modern society and encourage interdisciplinary study (R. Tullous, personal communication, Aug. 25, 1998).

Once there is agreement about the purposes of general education, faculty can articulate specific goals for student learning and development and provide opportunities in the curriculum for these objectives to be addressed. Although there are differences across campuses, common goals include preparing students who can understand and deal with diverse ideas, populations, and cultures and who possess a set of competences including critical thinking, creative thinking, oral and written communication, quantitative reasoning, and problem solving. Important aspects of personal development include abilities to negotiate with others, to tolerate ambiguity, and to be sensitive to the values of others. Students should also develop a sense of responsibility for actions, enthusiasm for learning on a continuous basis, and a sense of professionalism (Association of American Colleges, 1994; Ratcliff, 1997b). Because definitions of various competences (such as critical thinking) often differ across disciplines, reaching consensus about general education goals and objectives is a particularly challenging task. Before proceeding, faculty must clearly define the meaning of their learning objectives and express them in ways that are assessable.

Selecting an Assessment Approach for General Education

Once goals and objectives for learning have been articulated, faculty must decide the approach they will use for collecting and using information. A key decision is whether to focus on individual or groups of courses for data collection, or to create special opportunities to assess students outside of the course structure. We describe several approaches here. The approaches are not mutually exclusive; in practice, campuses draw from all of them and adapt them to serve their own needs.

Individual Course-Based Approach

In this approach, assessment information is collected about the learning that is occurring in individual courses. Faculty are asked to explicitly demonstrate that students in their courses are acquiring the knowledge, skills, and values associated with one or more general education goals. They may be asked to evaluate specific goals, or they may choose the learning goals they address. Then, faculty use a variety of assessment activities to evaluate whether students in their classes are making appropriate progress with respect to these goals. Although course instructors may draw on existing classroom tests and activities, they may also develop new assessment instruments such as writing exercises, exam questions, or surveys. They may conduct focus groups to concentrate on specific aspects of the course. New instruments may need to be developed for assessment of multiple section courses if common measures are not in use.

Assessment that focuses on individual courses is particularly appealing if there is concern about the value of these courses in the overall general education program. Given the history of general education, faculty may want to ensure that each course is making a legitimate contribution to overall goals, rather than merely functioning as an introductory course in the major. Because most instruction takes place within structured courses, a course-based approach has great potential for making connections between assessment results and needed curriculum improvements. Many times, differences in content coverage across multiple section courses become quite clear as instructors plan for and carry out assessment activities.

In order for this assessment approach to provide meaningful information about the program as a whole, results from individual courses need to be aggregated in some way. For example, faculty responsible for reviewing the material generated in individual courses can use checklists or rating sheets to make sure that all of the goals of the general education program are addressed in at least some courses, and that, across all courses, students have adequate exposure to each of the program's goals. This may involve secondary readings of classroom materials or evaluating reports submitted by classroom teachers. In either case, the value of the overall general education program is demonstrated by first looking at the role of individual courses, and then summarizing results across courses. At the U.S. Air Force Academy two faculty teams independently rated the extent to which each individual core course addressed three areas: integrated knowledge, framing and reasoning, and intellectual curiosity. Then results were compared for the teams and across courses to get an overall look at the core (Porter, 1998).

Although it has the advantage of maximizing faculty involvement, course-based approaches to programmatic assessment can be very labor intensive. If existing instruments do not address general education goals explicitly, separate instruments may need to be developed for each course, requiring faculty to work independently or in small groups to design tests, surveys, and other assessment instruments. Surveys may need to be developed to address the affective goals often included in general education programs.

A criticism of course-based assessment is that, although it can be used to look at the general education program as a whole, it may not provide a perspective on the overall learning of individual students. Thus the important ability of students to integrate knowledge across disciplines may be overlooked. However, if there is a capstone course that addresses general education objectives, results from this course can be used to demonstrate the ability of students to integrate what they have learned.

Multicourse (Theme-Based) Approach

Rather than focusing on individual courses, faculty from a number of disciplines may be asked to provide evidence that certain learning objectives are being met in their courses. Santa Clara University has used this approach (which is a step up in aggregation level from individual course-based assessment). The Assessment Task Force created six subgroups, each designed to assess a single core goal. Three or four faculty from each of the departments most directly involved in supporting a particular requirement were included. In the first year of the project, focus was on areas such as critical writing, ethics, mathematics, and religious studies. After clarifying their outcomes statements, the subgroups selected various assessment instruments including essays, class discussion, and existing assignments. Newly designed questionnaires and focus groups were also used, as was an abbreviated version of the Defining Issues Test of moral reasoning. Although this approach relied primarily on course-embedded activities, its focus was on how a set of particular competences were addressed across several courses (Gainen and Facione, 1996). In a similar approach, Winthrop University created interdisciplinary faculty teams, including a Quantitative Team and an Aesthetics Team, to create assessment tools that can be used in campus classrooms. Exercises and instruments that address attitudes and skills have been developed (Tebo-Messina and Sarow, 1996).

Noncourse-Based Approaches

Typically, these approaches are campuswide and focus on individual or groups of students rather than courses. General education assessment instruments are administered to all or a sample of students outside of the course structure. Often selected on the basis of their class level, students may be invited (or required) to fill-out mailed surveys or to attend sessions to complete assessment instruments. Examples include a campuswide sophomore survey or a junior-level test of writing competence. Instruments may assess specific skills such as writing, computer competence, or critical thinking. Alternatively, instruments may cover all or a substantial portion of the learning objectives addressed in the program. Instruments may be purchased or designed locally. For example, Capital University has developed a thirty-item Core Assessment Measure covering the areas of global awareness, lifetime health, science and technology, and quantitative reasoning. This instrument is administered to all sophomores as part of a mandatory testing policy (Schalinske, Patterson, and Smith, 1996).

The ability of students to integrate knowledge can be demonstrated through portfolios, research papers, or other projects that demonstrate achievement with respect to several learning goals. At the University of Hawaii–West Oahu all seniors are required to complete projects that represent a culminating experience and that demonstrate writing ability, critical thinking, and research skills (Oshiro, 1996). Rather than establishing requirements that exist outside the course structure, capstone or other required courses (in general education or the major) can be used to collect this information, allowing a look at individual students and at courses as well.

Selecting Assessment Methods

Because general education programs usually include a broad range of learning goals and objectives, including critical thinking skills, communication skills, and values and attitudes, faculty must be particularly careful to ensure that the instruments they select will address all of these objectives. Creating a matrix to match goals and methods (described in Chapter Four) can be useful for this purpose. Most likely, the techniques selected will include one or more direct assessment methods such as portfolios, performance measures, classroom assignments, or locally developed or commercial tests. Faculty are often unfamiliar with approaches to assess values and attitudes. Indirect methods such as surveys, focus groups, and other qualitative techniques may be particularly helpful for addressing affective goals. Information can be collected from alumni and employers as well as from current students. Assessment of general education programs is also likely to include a review of course syllabi, and perhaps an inventory of classroom assignments as well.

To reduce the need for individually developed instruments, some institutions have developed surveys that can be administered in several different courses using a cafeteria-style design. These surveys address attitudes and values as well as knowledge and skills. For example, a generic survey instrument may include questions that ask students how well a particular course helped them become aware of their own interests and talents, develop sensitivity to the values of others, and develop various thinking and communication skills. Faculty who use the survey in their own classes can select the particular items that reflect the goals and objectives they address. In addition to asking for self-reflections on their learning and development, these surveys can ask students about specific types of activities included in courses, such as writing and speaking assignments. Faculty at Southeast Missouri State University report good results using surveys that ask students to rate their progress in various areas and that are analyzed based on the importance assigned to goals by the instructor (Holt and Janzow, 1995).

Reporting and Using Results

Results from campuswide general education assessment activities can be reported in various formats, including project reports or theme reports that concentrate on particular areas of study. Responsibility for report preparation will ordinarily fall to a campuswide assessment committee. However, institutional research or assessment office staff may prepare reports, sharing results from surveys or instruments they administer. Reports prepared by staff will usually include comparisons and analysis but leave the development of programmatic recommendations to a campuswide committee.

If a course-based approach is going to be implemented, it is particularly important that faculty understand how the assessment program will be conducted. Faculty need to know the types of data and analysis they are responsible for generating and sharing, the format they need to use for reporting their results, and the process that will be used for evaluation. Most important, faculty must know the possible consequences of the information they provide. Generally, an interdisciplinary assessment committee will play a key role in evaluating information provided by faculty. The committee may be primarily a vehicle for faculty discussion and overall problem identification (Walvoord, Bardes, and Denton, 1998). However, in some cases these committees have the authority to recommend that courses be removed from the general education program if assessment information reveals they are not contributing to program goals. With so much at stake, faculty need to have clear directions about their role in the evaluation process. Ball State University recently completed its first five-year cycle of general education assessment. Based on a careful review of reports from course instructors, the general education subcommittee of the University Senate recommended several modifications to the program. Some courses were redesigned and others were removed from the program because they were not addressing program goals (B. Thomas Lowe, personal communication, Sept. 21, 1998).

Faculty at The Pennsylvania State University have conducted several studies focusing on general education, the most productive of which have involved surveys of baccalaureate alumni two and five years after graduation and alumni focus groups (M. J. Dooris, personal communication, Sept. 10, 1997). The messages from alumni were very clear: in their lives after graduation they found the skills of writing, speaking, working collaboratively, and information literacy to be of utmost importance. Due in part to this information from alumni, the Faculty Senate's General Education Committee developed a set of five learning elements, three or more of which have to be integrated in any course approved for the list of general education distribution requirements.

Assessing Critical Thinking

"Evidence of adults exercising critical thought is one of the chief things we look for when assessing the democratic health of a society" (Brookfield, 1987, p. 66). If we examine the mission statements of higher education institutions, we find a large number that include at least a sentence or phrase about the importance of critical thinking. Many campuses place great value on the ability of their graduates to be critical thinkers. Yet critical thinking is a concept that is difficult to define and therefore difficult to assess. What exactly is critical thinking? Does it differ from problem solving? How does it relate to other kinds of thinking? Although rarely identified as a separate discipline on college and university campuses, the development of critical thinking skills plays a key role in both general education and the major. Because of its importance, we turn now to a consideration of the definition and assessment of critical thinking.

Definitions of Critical Thinking

Every year conferences are held, workshops are conducted, and lectures are given, all dealing with critical thinking: what it is, how to teach it, and how to assess it. Because many definitions are possible, it is extremely important that faculty who are going to assess the ability of their students to think critically reach a consensus about its meaning in the context of their own curriculum. We do not advocate any particular definition, but we offer several here to provide various points of view.

In their 1989 book *Evaluating Critical Thinking*, Stephen P. Norris and Robert H. Ennis define critical thinking as "reasonable and reflective thinking that is focused upon deciding what to believe or do" (p. 1). In their view, critical thinking is based on sound reasoning that contains deliberate reflection about the reasonableness of one's own thought as well as that of others. Critical thinkers rely on many sources such as background knowledge and experience, observation, and information from others to infer decisions. Critical thinkers focus on a particular purpose—what to believe or what to do. In the view of Norris and Ennis, critical thinking can be used to evaluate actions as well as statements. Dispositions, such as open-mindedness, also play an important role in the process of critical thinking. In Brookfield's view, critical thinking entails a readiness to ask questions, to speculate on alternatives, and to be skeptical (1987).

Some writers define critical thinking by placing it within the broader context of thinking as a whole. Barry K. Beyer (1987) distinguishes between microthinking skills, such as those contained in Bloom's taxonomy, and more complex operations, which he refers to as *strategies*. In his view, problem solving is a strategy involving a sequence of steps, such as recognizing a problem, devising a solution, executing a plan, and evaluating the results. Decision making is another strategy involving identifying, analyzing, ranking, and choosing among alternatives. Microthinking skills are building blocks for strategies and are used repeatedly in implementing these strategies. Beyer distinguishes critical thinking from both microthinking skills and strategies. Critical thinking contains analysis and evaluation, but is used specifically to judge the authenticity, validity, or worth of a claim, source, or belief. Critical thinking is not a strategy itself because it does not consist of a series of sequential operations. It is a collection of specific operations that may be used alone or in combination with other operations. Beyer identifies several critical thinking operations, including abilities to identify ambiguous claims or arguments, identify unstated assumptions, and detect bias. Critical thinkers can recognize logical inconsistencies or fallacies in a line of reasoning and can determine the strength of an argument or claim (p. 27). Whereas Norris and Ennis describe the critical thinking process as part of problem solving, Beyer sees critical thinking as a distinct set of operations that can be used at various stages of problem solving, decision making, or other strategies.

In 1990, the American Philosophical Association issued a report describing expert consensus on the concept of critical thinking (Facione, 1990). Using a Delphi technique, forty-six experts from several academic fields characterized critical thinking as "the process of purposeful, self-regulatory judgment. . . . the cognitive engine that drives problem-solving and decision-making" (Facione and Facione, 1994a, p. 1). This view includes interpretation, analysis, inference, evaluation, and explanation as the five key skills used to make judgments about what to believe or do. In fact, these skills are used interactively. For example, critical thinkers can explain their interpretations and analyze their own inferences. They can monitor, correct, and improve the process of coming to a judgment. Thus self-regulation is an important critical thinking skill. In addition, those who are inclined to value and use critical thinking skills possess certain attributes such as open-mindedness, inquisitiveness, and cognitive maturity.

The consensus view just described was used as the basis for a national study of the definition and value of critical thinking held by educators, employers, and policymakers (Facione and Facione, 1994a). In fact, the National Center for Education Statistics (NCES) commissioned several studies through the National Center on Postsecondary Teaching, Learning, and Assessment to identify the specific skills required of graduates who will be effective in the workplace and in society. The results of this study indicate substantial agreement among the three groups about the importance of critical thinking skills identified through the Delphi process (Jones, 1996b).

Elizabeth A. Jones, principal investigator of the NCES study, and others have developed inventories for critical reading, writing, speaking and listening, and problem solving as well as critical thinking.

As Jones notes, their intention is not to provide definitions of these skills but to stimulate discussion so that faculty may decide themselves which expectations are most appropriate on their own campuses (1996b, p. 2).

This brief review makes clear that critical thinking, as well as other kinds of thinking, can be defined in many ways. For example, materials describing the Minnesota Community College Teaching for Thinking Project (1996) identify four kinds of thinking: factual thinking that seeks out facts and finds ways to remember them with accuracy and clarity; insightful thinking that sees the possibilities in things and draws on the imagination; rational thinking that allows individuals to think logically and to analyze information; and evaluative thinking that leads them to take positions about things and to examine feelings and values. Faculty associated with this project have developed self-assessment rubrics to help students examine their own thinking as well as scoring rubrics for use in evaluating papers.

Instruments to Assess Critical Thinking

A number of commercially available instruments can be used to assess critical thinking. Several are described here. All can be used within particular disciplines as well as in general education programs. The value of any of these instruments depends on how well their specific content corresponds with the concept of critical thinking that is shared by faculty teaching in the program.

Watson-Glaser Critical Thinking Appraisal

Although first developed in the 1930s and revised several times, this test is still widely used to assess critical thinking skills. The Watson-Glaser instrument includes five subtests that are used to determine how well students can reason analytically and logically. The subtests examine inference, recognition of assumptions, deduction, interpretation, and evaluation of arguments. Response scales differ by subtest. With respect to evaluation of arguments, students indicate whether the argument presented is strong or not strong. With respect to recognition of assumptions, students indicate whether or not particular assumptions are made. Each section is introduced with a description of the specific aspect of critical thinking that is being examined and a sample question. The test can be completed in fifty minutes, although the instructions do not call for a limited administration time. In fact, the instrument is designed to be "a test of power rather than speed" (Watson and Glaser, 1980). This test can be scored locally, and test booklets can be reused, keeping the cost very reasonable. It is available through the Psychological Corporation.

California Critical Thinking Skills Test (CCTST)

This instrument was developed in 1990 to reflect the consensus definition about critical thinking mentioned earlier (Facione and Facione, 1994a). As such, it addresses the major core skills of critical thinking: analysis, inference, and evaluation. The CCTST is a standardized multiple-choice test with thirty-four items designed to be completed in forty-five minutes. As described in the manual, items range from analyzing the meaning of sentences to integrating critical thinking skills. In most cases, test questions are introduced with a short narrative describing a situation, but in some cases, a longer passage is provided as the basis for responding to two or more questions. Response scales differ by item, often asking students to judge the truthfulness of conclusions based on various statements or to indicate whether good thinking has been demonstrated. The CCTST results in an overall score as well as subscores in five areas: analysis, evaluation, inference, deductive reasoning, and inductive reasoning. This test is available in two forms with scoring keys available for local use.

Tasks in Critical Thinking

The Educational Testing Service (ETS) has developed a performance-based assessment instrument called Tasks in Critical Thinking. This instrument asks students to demonstrate various skills and subskills by carrying out multiple extended tasks such as completing short-answer questions and preparing a long essay or report. The major skills addressed include inquiry, analysis, and communication. Tasks that address inquiry ask students to plan a search, use various methods of observation and discovery, comprehend and extract information, and sort and evaluate that information. Analysis includes subskills such as formulating hypotheses, applying models to solve problems, and evaluating assumptions, evidence, and reasoning. Communication involves organizing a presentation, writing effectively, and communicating quantitative and visual information. Each Task takes ninety minutes to complete. ETS can train faculty to score responses or can arrange for scoring off campus. According to ETS materials, a group of at least one hundred students is required for reliable score reporting because this allows about ten students per Task. Reported scores reflect group proficiency in using various skills.

Choosing Among Instruments

Norris and Ennis (1989) provide several guidelines for selecting among instruments that assess critical thinking. Because items on critical thinking tests are often subject to more than one interpretation, they strongly recommend that faculty take the test themselves and compare their own answers to those provided in the test guide. Although faculty may not agree completely, the scoring guide should provide answers that can be justified. Norris and Ennis also recommend that faculty ask whether the test covers enough of what they have defined as critical thinking to be useful. An additional issue is the difficulty of the test. If it is a challenge for faculty to finish the test in the allotted time, it may be very frustrating for students.

In a recent report for the National Postsecondary Education Cooperative, T. Dary Erwin reviews the psychometric properties of several critical thinking instruments as documented in test materials. Both the Watson-Glaser and CCTST have high reliability coefficients, whereas those for Tasks in Critical Thinking are moderate. Erwin points out the strong content validity of the CCTST as it is based on a consensus definition of critical thinking. He also notes that the American College Testing Program is currently piloting a critical thinking instrument that contains objective items and essays (U.S. Department of Education, 1998).

Other Instruments

In addition to their work with the CCTST, Peter A. and Noreen C. Facione have developed additional instruments related to the evaluation of critical thinking. In 1994, they issued a *Holistic Critical Thinking Scoring Rubric* that contains a four-point scale. This rubric can be used to score critical thinking demonstrated in essays, presentations, or other types of performances. It is designed to "mix skill measurement with dispositional measurement" (Facione, Facione, and Giancarlo, 1996, p. 73). Students who receive a score of four must demonstrate important critical thinking skills such as analysis and evaluation. They must also demonstrate fair-mindedness and a willingness to follow evidence where it leads. The Faciones (1994b) recommend a training session for faculty raters to score samples of work and establish consistent expectations. They recommend having two raters evaluate each item and using a third rater to reconcile disagreements. The Faciones encourage conversation among raters about differences in scoring and strongly discourage the mechanical averaging of disparate ratings.

As a companion to the CCTST, the Faciones (1992) have developed the California Critical Thinking Dispositions Inventory. This instrument assesses seven factors that are exhibited by those who possess dispositions to be critical thinkers. Among others, these factors include truthseeking, open-mindedness, systematic thinking, inquisitiveness, and maturity. An overall score and seven subscores are provided. Respondents are asked to use a six-point Likert scale to indicate the strength of their agreement or disagreement with the seventy-five items contained in the instrument. Among other questions, respondents are asked about the value they place on understanding what others think and on acquiring information.

As Peter Facione and his coauthors (1995) have pointed out, these dispositions are an important aspect of critical thinking. General education programs will achieve their educational goals for critical thinking only if they "succeed not just in teaching the skills, but in actually cultivating in their students the disposition toward critical thinking" (p. 22).

The Faciones have created a ten-item evaluation form, the Teaching for Thinking Student Course Evaluation Form, that can be used to indicate how much emphasis on the teaching of thinking is exhibited in a particular course. All of the instruments developed by the Faciones are available through the California Academic Press. A close look at these instruments can stimulate useful ideas for assessing critical thinking.

Locally Developed Approaches

Rather than using commercial instruments, many faculty develop their own approaches for assessing critical thinking. These approaches include research papers, presentations, case studies, simulations, and other methods. Some faculty videotape in-class presentations of students and review them later for evidence of critical thinking and other skills. Indiana University at Bloomington has developed an instrument that addresses critical thinking, the Indiana University Student Performance Measure. It requires students to read extensive materials on a given topic and to answer several open-ended questions based on the readings. Faculty and students value the academic work captured in the instrument (Gray, 1995a). Faculty at Towson State University have used portfolios to examine both higher-order thinking and writing skills using locally developed scoring guides (Gibson-Groshon and Miller, 1995).

When using local measures, the Faciones and Giancarlo (1996) recommend taking a close look at the processes students use in accomplishing their work, not just the products. By studying the processes students use to think and solve problems, faculty can assess whether students are employing solid reasoning to answer questions. For example, faculty can analyze tapes of class discussions or of students delivering services to clients. The Faciones and their coauthor suggest that faculty encourage students to keep reflective journals and voice their thinking by talking aloud as they work through problems. Faculty who develop rubrics "that integrate the habits of mind with the thinking skills" should share these rubrics with students and encourage students to use them to evaluate their own work (p. 77).

Assessing Other Aspects of General Education

In addition to critical thinking, most general education programs address written and oral communication skills, problem solving, and values and attitudes. How can these be assessed?

Writing

Along with critical thinking and problem solving, the ability to communicate effectively has been identified by the National Education Goals Panel (1992) as an important skill necessary to compete in the global economy and to practice effective citizenship. Approaches to the instruction of writing differ. For example, Portland State University embeds writing requirements into all its general education coursework, rather than in separately identified writing courses (Reardon and Ramaley, 1997). Regardless of structure, faculty must reach agreement about important learning objectives with respect to writing. The NCES study of faculty, employers, and policymakers revealed widespread agreement about many aspects of writing. Students must develop awareness of their audience—and they must be able to address more than just an academic audience. They should be able to comprehend and carry out various purposes for writing, organize and shape their ideas in coherent narratives, and prepare a variety of products such as memoranda, letters, and reports. According to the NCES study, employers place more importance on the use of visual aids such as tables and graphs than do faculty (Click, 1996). Faculty place more importance on the process of writing, including skills for drafting and revising (Jones, 1996a).

Faculty approach the assessment of writing in various ways, often reflecting the way writing is embedded in the curriculum. In addition to classroom assignments, some programs include tests of writing competence. Truman State University requires a Sophomore Writing Experience that gives students the opportunity to check on their growth as writers. After their papers are evaluated, students meet with faculty from across the curriculum to set personal goals for their writing (Magruder, McManis, and Young, 1997). Many institutions evaluate writing as part of a portfolio review. Case studies and research reports can also be evaluated for writing skills, as can various products such as proposals, memos, and essays. In addition to adopting a common definition, it is important that faculty agree on their criteria for evaluating writing and that students are aware of these criteria.

The nationally recognized Writing Program at Washington State University requires students to complete both a placement exam and a junior-level writing portfolio. The latter includes three papers from already-completed courses, as well as two timed essays that are similar to those in the placement exam. Trained faculty read the portfolios using a two-tier rating system. Papers receiving a "pass" are scored only once, but a second group of raters rereads all portfolios that receive a "needs work" or "pass with distinction" on the first reading. All students at WSU take two writing-intensive courses within their majors (Erwin, 1998; Haswell and Wyche-Smith, 1996).

Oral Communication Skills

The NCES work led by Elizabeth Jones (1994, 1996a, 1996b) helped articulate a set of advanced communication skills about which there is widespread agreement. Oral communication skills include both speaking and listening. Basic speaking skills include giving directions and expressing a point of view, and advanced speaking skills for college graduates include such things as adapting messages to the demands of the situation or context, using appropriate examples, and using language that maintains audience interest. Listening requires identifying important issues and understanding the messages of others (Rubin and Morreale, 1996). The NCES study notes the importance of reasoning in communication.

Although objectives formulated elsewhere can be very helpful, faculty need to consider for themselves which aspects of oral communication will be taught and assessed in their own programs. Rebecca B. Rubin and Sherwyn P. Morreale (1996) identify several instruments that are available to assess oral communication, including Rubin's Communication Competence Assessment Instrument. Locally, many faculty have developed strategies for assessing oral communication. For example, speaking skills can be assessed through individual or group presentations in class, debates, and mock interviews. Faculty usually develop their own scoring rubrics to assess presentations and performances. Listening skills can be evaluated by asking students to summarize the main points of a group presentation or to judge the appropriateness of presentations for particular audiences. Rating scales that address group work often include aspects of oral communication.

An additional aspect of communication skills that was included in the NCES study is that of critical reading. Many of the skills covered in the critical reading inventory are also covered in the critical thinking inventory. In her review of the NCES study, Joanne Carter-Wells (1996) cautions that many current critical thinking instruments have a high correlation with reading. She asks whether these instruments are tapping reading or thinking, and recommends a careful consideration of the way these skills overlap. Carter-Wells notes the fundamental importance of reading skills, particularly in such emerging activities as utilizing the World Wide Web and the Internet.

Information Literacy

Closely related to communication skills are those related to searching for and locating information related to a given topic. James Madison University (JMU) considers information-seeking skills to be an essential part of a general or liberal education. In 1989, the Carrier Library began to assess the library skills of sophomores using a pencil-and-paper test developed locally by librarians (L. Cameron and D. Sundre, personal communication, Sept. 15, 1997). At the time all freshmen were required to complete a self-paced, individualized library skills workbook in English composition classes during their first semester at JMU. The purpose of the assessment program was to determine whether JMU students were learning basic library skills by the end of the sophomore year, to gather data about student attitudes toward the library and technology, and to include seniors in selected majors: psychology, English, business, chemistry, and communication. Librarians who served as liaisons to academic departments developed instruments that measured skills related to strategies and sources important to each major. The program was also expanded to include freshmen, who were tested the day before they began coursework at JMU to obtain baseline data that could be used for comparison.

Since 1989 the librarians have discovered that JMU students are indeed learning basic essential library skills by the end of the sophomore year. They are confident in their use of library sources. They prefer electronic sources over print, and they are comfortable using technology. Students show a strong preference for teaching methods that provide active learning experiences. Sophomores score significantly better than freshmen.

Assessment results in some majors have shown deficiencies in library skills. For example, in 1992, about half of the English majors were not familiar with the MLA Bibliography, the most important index for finding literary criticism. In response to learning about this deficiency, the English Department made some changes in the curriculum that would require all majors to take a literature course that requires library research.

In 1993, JMU began to develop a new competence-based General Education program that includes the following information-seeking objectives as a formal part of the curriculum:

- Formulate and conduct an effective information search that includes a variety of reference sources, such as encyclopedias, library catalogs, indexes, bibliographies, statistics sources, government publications, and resources available on the Internet.

- Evaluate information sources in terms of accuracy, authority, bias, and relevance.

To provide support for these objectives, the Carrier Library developed a Web-based instruction program that includes instructional content, on-line exercises, and suggested course-related assignments. The on-line exercises require students to answer multiple-choice questions by searching electronic sources. These exercises are scored electronically, and students may send their score to their professor, showing evidence of successful completion of the instruction program.

Given a decade of experience with assessment of information-seeking skills, JMU faculty and librarians have concluded that assessment efforts will provide the most useful information and results if the following are true:

- Skills are measured by active demonstration of the skill, not by pencil-and-paper test.

- Both the instruction program and the assessment are based on clearly stated objectives that are part of the curriculum.

- Students have the opportunity to practice the skills and competence in the instructional program before they are assessed.

The new Web-based instruction program, accompanied by performance-based assessment, is fully integrated into the curriculum and satisfies all these criteria.

Problem Solving

Most general education programs, as well as those in many majors, expect college graduates to be competent problem solvers. B. Christopher Dougherty and Patti Fantaske (1996) point to considerable consensus about important skills in this area: "All effective problem solving includes the search for a clear and concise statement of the problem along with the efficient generation, selection, and implementation of alternatives" (p. 56). Although analytical step-by-step approaches may characterize the solution of well-structured problems, the solution of ill-structured problems also requires the use of intuition and experience. Both types of problems often require an iterative rather than a clear step-by-step approach to reach solutions. Personal abilities such as patience, persistence, and creativity also come into play. The ability of students to solve problems can be assessed in a number of ways, including problem-solving exercises, case study analysis, simulations, and group work projects. Based on a careful review, Erwin concludes there is no adequate commercial measure of problem solving, although content of the ETS Tasks in Critical Thinking aligns closely with the NCES definition (U.S. Department of Education, 1998).

Another strategy, the Reflective Judgment Interview (RJI), can be used to evaluate how students approach solving problems that do not have clear-cut answers. The RJI is based on the Reflective Judgment model that views cognitive development as occurring in a series of discrete stages rather than along a continuum. In the first stage of intellectual development, knowledge is viewed as concrete, based on direct observation. At intermediate stages, knowledge is viewed as uncertain, understood within a context. At the seventh and highest stage, knowledge is viewed as the outcome of a process of reasonable inquiry (King and Kitchener, 1994). The RJI asks students to address a series of ill-structured problems, dilemmas for which answers are relative rather than absolute. In semistructured interviews, students are asked to express their opinions about four dilemmas. Emphasis is on the justification students provide for their positions, and the assumptions underlying their reasoning (Wood, 1997). Faculty in several disciplines have had success using essay questions adapted from the RJI to examine the assumptions students use when facing ill-structured problems in their disciplines (Wood and Lynch, 1998). In 1996, Gary Pike devoted several of his *Assessment Update* columns to a review of the RJI as well as several other measures of critical thinking.

Ethical Reasoning

Many graduates face ethical dilemmas when they enter the workplace. Ethical behavior requires that individuals be able to recognize and articulate the situation, identify important stakeholders, analyze situations, and develop responsible solutions. Some faculty have developed strategies to examine ethical reasoning, including case study analysis, simulations, and other methods. Gainen and Locatelli (1995) suggest the use of rating forms that ask students to rank the importance of various criteria in evaluating ethical situations. The importance students place on criteria such as keeping a job and getting promoted, as opposed to personal integrity and professional responsibility, can provide an indication of their thinking about ethical dilemmas.

The Defining Issues Test (DIT) is a commercially available instrument that can be used to measure ethical reasoning. The purpose of this test is to examine how individuals think about social problems. Students are asked to read a set of stories that illustrate moral dilemmas and then indicate their recommendations for what the person described in the story should do. They are also asked to consider what issues are important in making the choice. Several scores are generated for this test, the most important of which provides a general index of the development of moral judgment. High values indicate students place importance on optimizing mutual human welfare and applying universal ethical principles. Students with high scores emphasize the value of due process and safeguarding basic rights rather than personal advantage or maintaining approval (Rest, 1993). The DIT is available through the Center for the Study of Ethical Development at the University of Minnesota.

Values and Attitudes

Most general education programs include intended outcomes that address values and attitudes. Among other possibilities, faculty may expect that students will be sensitive to the values of others, value lifelong learning, and be able to assess their own learning and development. Whether or not they possess these values and attitudes can be examined by directly observing the way students behave and by asking them to reflect on their own preferences and behaviors. However, as Gainen and Locatelli (1995) point out, it is better to draw conclusions on the basis of "what people do rather than on what they say" (p. 92). Participation in activities, behaviors exhibited in group work, and even body language in focus groups can be examined for evidence about values and attitudes. Case studies, problem sets, and other assignments can be used to assess values and attitudes. Surveys, focus groups, and interviews can include questions asking students to describe their own preferences and behaviors.

Many general education programs, as well as programs in the major, are concerned with developing an appreciation for lifelong learning. Faculty expect students who exhibit this value to be able to access information, participate in professionally oriented organizations, and report plans for further study after college, either through degree, professional development, or personal enrichment programs. Survey instruments can address values with respect to life-long learning, such as enjoying learning for its own sake and valuing a broad education. Alumni surveys can include questions asking for self-reports on behaviors related to lifelong learning such as completing additional study after college.

According to the Foundation Coalition, a consortium of seven partner schools funded by the National Science Foundation (n.d., p. 6) to improve engineering and preengineering programs, students with a commitment to lifelong learning will

- Express an openness and desire for intellectual experiences

- Express confidence in their ability to independently acquire new knowledge

- Project a life of learning activities

This commitment is demonstrated by seeking intellectual experiences for personal and professional growth.

General education programs often help students develop a capacity for self-assessment. Indeed, this is one of the marks of a successful assessment program. Students' capacities for self-reflection can be examined through statements contained in portfolios, through self-assessment of various projects, and, in some cases, by examining the quality of student peer review.

In their writings about critical thinking, Linda Elder and Richard Paul (1996) espouse the use of what they call "universal intellectual standards" to help students learn how to think. In their view, questions based on these standards should be part of students' inner voices. They recommend that students be taught to ask whether their own thinking, as well as the thinking of others, is clear, accurate, precise, and relevant, as well as logical and significant. These questions form a useful basis for evaluating the work of students and for students to use in self-assessment.

In addition to valuing lifelong learning and being able to engage in self-assessment, most general education programs expect students to develop sensitivity to the values of others. This value can be assessed through self-reporting on the part of students and by observations of student behaviors. M. Lee Upcraft and John H. Schuh (1996) include several instruments that address multicultural awareness and attitudes in their inventory of assessment instruments. These include the Campus Diversity Survey, available through the University of Minnesota, and the Campus Opinion Survey, available through the National Institute Against Prejudice and Violence located at the University of Maryland. The Annual Survey of American College Freshmen, available through the Cooperative Institutional Research Program at the University of California–Los Angeles, also addresses a broad range of values. Additional versions of this survey are available for use at the end of the first year and during the senior year.

Integration, Development, and Learning Styles

A number of assessment approaches allow faculty to examine if students can integrate what they have learned. Portfolios allow faculty to do this, as do research papers and case studies. Oral presentations and simulations can also be designed to assess interrelated skills. In addition to locally developed methods, a number of commercial examinations are in wide use (described in Chapter Six) that address several subject areas, including reasoning skills. Other standardized instruments include the Scale of Intellectual Development (SID) and Learning-Thinking Styles Inventory (LTSI). Both are used at the Virginia Military Institute to measure qualitative change in cognition as a result of the college experience (Z. Zhang and R. S. RiCharde, personal communication, Sept. 18, 1997). Annual assessment is conducted with freshmen, rising juniors, and graduating seniors. The SID, developed by T. Dary Erwin, is adapted from Perry's scheme of intellectual development. It defines intellectual development in terms of dualism, relativism, commitment, and empathy.

On the basis of longitudinal studies of VMI students' scores on the SID, it appears that students become less reliant on external guidance, more responsible for their decisions and behavior, and more aware of their impact on others and society as they progress through college. The LTSI, developed within the framework of information-processing and trait theories, measures four dimensions: perceptual modality, distractibility, metacognition, and analytical global tendency (RiCharde, 1992). Metacognition is measured in terms of logical reasoning, probability estimate (the student's estimate of the likely correctness of his or her reasoning), and problem solving. LTSI scores of freshmen and seniors suggest that seniors have developed higher levels of metacognition as measured by logical reasoning and probability estimate. Moreover, students with higher grades demonstrate more metacognitive development than peers with lower grade point averages, and engineering and science majors gain more in this area than liberal arts majors (Zhang and RiCharde, 1998).

As noted, the LTSI also measures preferred perceptual modalities (auditory, visual, kinesthetic, reading) and general approaches to processing information such as global or analytic. At VMI use of the LTSI has increased faculty appreciation of learning style differences and led to more use of visual aids, graphic representation, and hands-on activities to accommodate the needs of different learners. Tutors and learning specialists in the VMI Learning Center also use LTSI scores to design intervention strategies, workshops, and other activities to help students who seek assistance at the Learning Center to become more effective learners.

Assessing General Education Outcomes Within the Major

Many disciplines have moved away from the view that they should emphasize only content knowledge, concepts, and theories specific to the field. Transferable skills such as communication and problem solving are now addressed, and appropriate ways of thinking and methods of judgment are emphasized (Jones, 1996b). A focus on general education skills within courses in the major helps communicate to students how important these skills are in terms of professional competence (Gainen and Locatelli, 1995).

In 1989, Bonnie Hagerty and Joan Stark noted how several accreditation bodies required undergraduates to link technical knowledge with appropriate values and attitudes and to develop abilities such as critical thinking, interpersonal skills, and professional ethics. Now, most professional accrediting bodies specifically address intended outcomes that are descriptive of all college-educated persons. Barbara S. Fuhrmann (1994) describes the positions of several accreditors. The National Association of Schools of Art and Design indicates that "artists and designers should develop an understanding of other areas of human achievement and competence in the communication arts of speaking, reading, and writing." The Accrediting Council of Education in Journalism and Mass Communications calls for instruction in the professional unit "to ensure that students learn to gather, analyze, organize, synthesize, and communicate information." This group calls for a minimum number of course credits in the liberal arts and sciences taught by experts in the disciplines. The accrediting body in social work also requires that students be trained in a liberal arts perspective (pp. 1–5).

Assessment methods administered in the major often have dual purposes. At the same time they examine discipline-specific knowledge and concepts, they address generic skills such as problem solving and critical thinking. Faculty may assign a project in a capstone course that provides students a chance to integrate what they have learned in general education areas with what they have learned in the major. Faculty can also use noncourse-based approaches asking students to complete portfolios that demonstrate competence in transferable skills or to sit for a writing examination that demonstrates critical thinking within the context of the major.

10

Assessing Campus Environments and Student Experiences

EXPERIENCE (*n.*): anything
observed or lived through

College campuses are not static environments. Although curricula and programs are in place, these aspects of college campuses are constantly changing in both small and dramatic ways. In addition, learning and development depend very much on how environments are experienced by students. Although assessment prompts a much closer look, educators readily accept the value of in-class experiences on student growth. In the past several years, many observers have recognized that experiences outside the classroom also have a strong impact on student learning and development. In fact, out-of-class experiences contribute to all kinds of college outcomes, including cognitive complexity, personal qualities like self-confidence and self-awareness, communication skills, and practical competence skills associated with effective job performance (Kuh, 1997, p. 71).

George Kuh argues that in-class and out-of-class experiences should work together to produce "seamless learning" (p. 67). Activities such as studying, using learning resources, interacting with faculty and peers, participating in campus programs, drawing on campus services, and using campus facilities should support in-class activities and help students gain as much as possible from their college experiences. As Kuh notes, these institutional aspects should be arranged to maximize the efforts students devote to their education. The latter is particularly important, because "quality of effort is the single best predictor of learning outcomes" (p. 68).

In this chapter, we look at several ways educators can obtain information about college environments—the educational "influences to which students are exposed" (Gainen and Locatelli, 1995, p. 109). We discuss strategies for examining curricula, a very important component of campus environments. We also discuss transcript analysis, students' reports of their activities, retention analysis, the use of performance indicators, and program evaluation. We begin with a brief review of Alexander Astin's model, which emphasizes the relationship between inputs, environment, and outputs.

Reviewing Alexander Astin's I-E-O Model

Alexander Astin has been very influential in helping educators periodically rethink higher education. In his 1991 work *Assessment for Excellence*, he describes his inputs-environment-outputs (I-E-O) model. In Astin's words, this model provides a "powerful framework for the design of assessment activities and for dealing with even the most complex and sophisticated issues in assessment and evaluation" (p. 16). The key point of the model is that outputs must be evaluated in terms of inputs and environment. Outputs include specific goals and objectives for learning and development, as well as global measures such as retention and graduation rates. Outputs alone do not tell very much about the educational impact of institutions and programs. For one thing, outputs must always be evaluated in terms of inputs. In Astin's model, inputs refer to personal qualities students bring to college with them, including their initial level of developed talent. Differences in personal qualities among students across campuses, as well as differences on a given campus, help explain outcome results. In Astin's view, important input characteristics include demographic attributes such as gender, race, and age, as well as educational background characteristics. Measures of the latter include performance in high school, performance on standardized tests, and course taking patterns in high school. Students' aspirations, expectations, and self-ratings are also useful as input measures.

According to Astin's model, good information about inputs and outputs is not enough; educators also need information about college environments. Environmental information tells about students' actual experiences during their educational programs. Information about the environment helps answer *why* questions. Why do students learn and develop in some situations but not in others? What kinds of experiences contribute to their growth? Several types of environmental experiences matter, including characteristics of individual classes such as size and teaching methods, course-taking patterns, use of time, and characteristics of peer groups (p. 92).

Leaving ample room for investigators to choose their own specifics, Astin has provided an extremely useful overall framework for examining the impact of college. Educators must look at the characteristics students bring with them when they enter college, the experiences they have while in college, and the changes that result from their experiences.

Examining Curricula

Curricula capture the academic policies of institutions. They capture educational aims and philosophies. Curricula are academic plans "purposefully constructed to facilitate student learning" (Stark and others, 1990, p. 2). They exist at many levels, including the course, program, and institution. Several authors have noted differences between the designed curriculum, the taught curriculum, and the learned curriculum. A coherent curriculum is one where aims, design, implementation, and evaluation work together, one where "most students will encounter logical sequences of coursework leading to useful and long-lasting skills and insights about the world" (Ratcliff, 1997a, p. 143). Previous chapters have focused on assessment of learning and development; here we look at issues of curriculum design.

Purpose

The key question of programmatic assessment is whether or not students have acquired the knowledge, skills, and values characteristic of graduates in their field. When looking at curricula, the key question is whether appropriate opportunities for this learning and development are in place. To realize the potential of assessment, its results must be linked to an understanding of curricula. In fact, as Peter Ewell (1997c) has stated, "Evidence strongly suggests that incentives for paying more systematic attention to documenting and monitoring curriculum functioning are here to stay" (p. 625). Michael F. Reardon and Judith A. Ramaley (1997) strongly advocate a "careful program of inquiry" into questions related to the curriculum (p. 522). Faculty take various approaches to achieving curriculum awareness. They may periodically concentrate on full-scale curriculum review, regularly examine questions related to their curricula, develop curriculum-related performance indicators, or combine these approaches. Whichever strategies they choose, they should consider curriculum development as a set of dynamic, interrelated decisions (Stark and Lattuca, 1997).

A careful look at curricula help faculty to determine whether planned academic programs actually are in place—to compare actions with intentions. Curriculum awareness is a process of looking at programs rather than at students and making sure appropriate conditions for learning exist. Faculty then ask questions about what is working and what needs to be changed. As James Ratcliff (1997b) notes, curricula constantly change, but most often in small ways. "The faculty does it every term in thousands of courses" (p. 5). As he points out, it is much harder to produce overall coherent change.

Asking Curriculum-Related Questions

Through a process of curriculum inquiry, faculty view their programs in a holistic way—at a level beyond individual courses. As described by Ewell (1997c), attention to the curriculum usually focuses on questions about sequence and structure, as well as about content and coverage.

As faculty examine their curricula, they determine whether goals and objectives for learning are adequately addressed in required and elective courses and whether requirements for courses within particular disciplines are appropriate. Faculty also examine whether learning goals are appropriately reinforced, ensure that courses are appropriately sequenced, and determine whether prerequisites for courses are appropriate given course content. Unnecessary overlap between courses can be examined and addressed. Faculty can also look at student credit hours assigned to various courses to see if they make sense.

A review of curricula can address the types of courses that are being offered, such as lectures, seminars, and discussion sections. For example, faculty might examine whether a lab setting would be appropriate in a science course, or whether students in a journalism program would benefit from participating in an internship. Instructional activities and types of assignments for students can also be studied. Expectations about out-of-class activities can be reviewed as well.

Mathematics faculty at The Pennsylvania State University reviewed student data from the two-course calculus sequence for science and engineering majors and were disappointed to find that only 45 percent of students who began the sequence completed the second course with a grade of A, B, or C (M. J. Dooris, personal communication, Sept. 10, 1997). They were teaching the course in a large-lecture, small-recitation section format and decided to experiment with some small sections of the course. Students in the small sections were much more successful and demand for the small sections grew. Over three years all freshman calculus courses were converted to the small section format and the percentage of As, Bs, and Cs for the sequence climbed from 45 to 66 percent.

The starting point for understanding a curriculum is often the same place as the starting point for assessment. Faculty begin by agreeing on the overall focus of their academic program and on their goals and objectives for learning. If clear statements of learning objectives do not exist already, faculty must carefully consider their expectations for their graduates. If statements do exist, faculty should review them to ensure they are reasonably up to date. Although a curriculum review may cause revision of objectives, faculty need a coherent starting place. Existing goals and objectives for learning in the program provide the best place to begin examining curricula.

Comparing Goals and Objectives to Course Content

Once goals and objectives for learning are identified, faculty can compare the actual content of each course to the intended outcomes of the program. Starting with a list of learning objectives, faculty can complete checklists indicating the objectives that are addressed in their own courses. This undertaking can be completed by faculty working independently or with others. However, those faculty teaching multiple sections of a given course should get together to compare their checklists or to develop a common checklist. An alternative is to ask a representative committee to examine the role of individual courses based on syllabi and descriptions submitted by course instructors.

As straightforward as this suggestion appears, it can be quite challenging. Faculty may differ among themselves in the language they use to describe similar learning objectives. It is a good idea to have some general discussion of programmatic goals and objectives and to reach consensus about what they mean before checklists are completed.

Faculty must respond to checklists and other information gathering on the basis of the way their courses are currently delivered and should be realistic when indicating the goals they cover in their courses. Sometimes there is a tendency to check nearly every goal. Letting faculty know they will be responsible for providing assessment information with respect to the goals they check can help them focus on the most important learning goals addressed in their courses.

The main point of reviewing curricula is to see how the subject matter of various courses comes together to accomplish programmatic goals. This responsibility will often fall to members of a standing curriculum committee. In some cases, a special task force or study group may take it on. The discussion and exchange among these faculty is one of the most important aspects of curriculum inquiry. Thus it is important that several faculty be involved, not just the department chair.

At this point, the checklists submitted by faculty need to be combined. A matrix that has course labels as column headings and learning objectives as row headings can be used for this. Based on the individual checklists completed by faculty, the matrix is completed by placing a check mark in each cell for courses that address the objective listed on a given row. Once completed, this matrix gives a visual picture of how courses fit together. In fact, some authors refer to this as a curriculum map (Gainen and Locatelli, 1995, p. 116). Exhibit 10.1 provides an example.

Rather than merely checking items, faculty can provide additional information about the importance placed on various learning objectives in their own courses. For example, they could indicate whether material related to learning objectives is introduced, reinforced, or built upon in their courses. Alternatively, they could indicate percentages of course time and effort spent on addressing particular objectives.

In her recent review of curriculum trends among programs for arts and science majors, Carol Schneider (1997) notes a move away

Exhibit 10.1. Curriculum Review Sheet

	Course			
Learning Objectives	100	101	200	201
Effective communication	✔	✔	✔	
Critical thinking		✔	✔	✔
Sensitivity to values of others			✔	
Global awareness			✔	✔

from programs where students "take courses in no particular order toward no clearly stated goal" to an approach that emphasizes "analytical and reflective practices." Thus, faculty reviewing curriculum in the major could examine whether students "learn first to use the field, then to gain critical perspective on it, and finally to connect the field's approaches with those of other communities" (p. 253).

Once the matrix comparing courses to learning objectives is completed, faculty should come together to discuss what it shows. Are courses aligned with objectives? Are there too many check marks, or too few? The matrix can be used to answer several curriculum-related questions. The approach we described can be used to articulate new programs as well as to examine existing programs. For example, multidisciplinary programs such as environmental studies or women and gender studies could be developed by examining existing and proposed courses that would meet learning goals.

Examining Syllabi and Catalogues

Many reviews of curriculum include the collection and examination of course syllabi. These materials can be very helpful in creating a picture of what happens in individual courses and how these courses fit together. However, not all syllabi are created equal. Some faculty are very thorough in documenting objectives of their courses in their syllabi; others are not. In fact, faculty examining syllabi for general studies courses might be quite dismayed at what is not shown. A syllabus may fail to mention that the course is in the general studies program, or may fail to mention the overall learning goals of the program. Instead it may emphasize discipline-specific topics. In many cases, however, syllabi do include helpful information about course goals and, through time lines and other information, may convey a clear picture of the content faculty intend to cover. Syllabi may also provide rich information about course assignments, such as writing tasks or computer competence exercises (Ewell, 1997c).

A review of syllabi at Austin Peay State University revealed that few faculty had enumerated the general education goals addressed in their courses. As a result, a model outline was developed, distributed to faculty for future use, and placed in the faculty handbook (Rudolph, 1996). At Oakton Community College, Trudy Bers, Diane Davis, and William Taylor (1996) undertook a content analysis of all class syllabi for social science courses taught in fall 1995. Using a coding sheet to evaluate syllabi from 114 classes, they found several areas where the syllabi were unclear. For example, types of tests and expectations about class participation were often missing. The project resulted in dissemination of good ideas to include in syllabi, a new section in faculty orientation describing how to design and write class syllabi, and lively department discussion.

Unlike syllabi, which can be changed and updated fairly regularly, opportunities to change college catalogues are less frequent. Thus, an institution's catalogue and the program and course descriptions it contains are often less useful in understanding the current content of the curriculum. However, catalogues can provide very useful information about program structure and choice. They should indicate the number of required and elective courses, the number of prerequisites, and the number of courses from which to choose electives (Ewell, 1997c). Out-of-class requirements, such as portfolios or writing competence examinations, should also appear in catalogues.

The Dynamic Nature of Curriculum

Some writers have drawn a useful distinction between various kinds of curriculum (Ewell, 1997c; Gaff, 1997). The written curriculum is the one described in official documents, particularly college catalogues and master course syllabi. This curriculum may differ from the curriculum actually being taught, as well as from that which is tested or learned. This can happen for a number of reasons. Individual faculty may choose to spend more time on some topics and less time on others, in spite of what their syllabi indicate. Sometimes topics get neglected or skipped completely. New topics may be added. Faculty teaching multiple-section courses may start with good intentions to cover common syllabi, but might wind up teaching quite dissimilar courses. Occasionally, new faculty are asked to teach courses with little direction about specific course content. Thus they may prepare syllabi that differ greatly from those of other instructors. Sometimes new textbooks appear with intriguing topics that have not been covered in the past, or current events may cause changes in the focus of courses. To help understand the curriculum, faculty need to share information about the curriculum they are actually delivering, as well as about the curriculum that exists in written documents (Ewell, 1997c). As with all assessment, educators get the best results if they concentrate on program activity rather than intent (Farmer and Napieralski, 1997).

Instructors' Activities and Expectations

Instruction brings life to curriculum goals and objectives. Thus a curriculum review may include an inventory of the methods instructors are using to deliver the curriculum. Faculty can indicate how they address different objectives. Some objectives may be addressed primarily through lectures; others may be addressed through group discussion, case study, or writing tasks. Perhaps faculty invite guest speakers to address particular topics, or make field trips to various sites. The materials used by faculty can also be inventoried, such as films, videos, and reading materials.

As faculty think about what they do in courses, it is important for them to think also about their expectations for students. Each faculty member can be asked to articulate the prerequisite knowledge assumed of students as instructional activities are planned. It is also helpful to examine the types of assignments students will be expected to complete. How will students be assessed in various courses? Will students take tests, write reports, prepare portfolios, or give presentations? Addressing these questions can provide particularly useful information with respect to learning objectives. For example, in many programs students are expected to excel in oral communication. Yet an examination of assignments across courses may find few instances where students have a chance to practice this skill. Answers to questions about instructional activities and expectations can be inventoried through checklists or matrixes. For example, faculty can complete a matrix for each of their courses that combines information about learning objectives with information about student assignments.

Raising these issues should prompt faculty conversations about learning. As Marchese (1997a) notes, insights about learning have come from such diverse sources as psychology, neuroscience, and archaeology. Insights have also come from the "wisdom of practice" of college and university teachers. Based on an exercise with faculty, Marchese captures the common threads that underlie the "powerful pedagogies" that have sprung up on many campuses (p. 92). Practices such as collaborative learning, service learning, case methods, capstone courses, and portfolios all emphasize the following:

1. Independence and choice for learners

2. Rich, timely feedback with opportunities for reflection

3. Active involvement, practice, and reinforcement

4. High-challenge, low-threat environments

5. Opportunities for creative and critical thinking

Characteristics such as these create opportunities for "deep" learning in which students become engaged in their work and seek meaning about what they are studying, in contrast to "surface" learning that is focused on short-term memorization of facts and concepts (Marchese, 1997a). Conversations about instructional strategies may be lively. As Palmer notes, some educators remain torn between the poles of teacher-centered instruction focused on rigor and student-centered instruction focused on active learning. He suggests that classrooms "should be neither teacher-centered nor student-centered but subject-centered," with teachers and students alike focused on the independent voice of the subject (1998, p. 116).

Timing of Curriculum Review and Inquiry

Curriculum questions can be raised simultaneously, as part of a formal review, or independently as a series of separate inquiries. Timing in relationship to assessment can also vary. Some faculty find it very useful to conduct a thorough review prior to embarking on traditional assessment activities. This review can help identify important issues for assessment. Other faculty find it more useful to begin by collecting information about student learning and development and to use this information to raise questions about their curriculum. If curriculum inquiry and assessment are continuous processes, then the two activities should be occurring simultaneously. An understanding of curricula will lead to better assessment questions and will improve the ability to understand and use assessment results. Certainly the information generated by each process should enrich the other. Curriculum awareness and assessment of student learning should be used together to improve the education of students.

Looking at Students' Experiences

Students have a role in what and how much they learn. A number of useful ways are available to examine the role students play in their own learning and development. Transcripts provide information about the courses students take while in college, and surveys and focus groups can be used to obtain self-reported information about other activities.

Transcript Analysis

All institutions maintain transcript files that identify the courses each student has taken. This information can answer many questions about student experiences. In addition, when coupled with information about student outcomes, transcript analysis can help faculty examine and understand the patterns of courses that best enhance the learning and development of students. However, this kind of project often requires expertise from staff in an institutional research office or computer center where records are typically maintained.

Some studies of transcripts are primarily descriptive. For example, faculty in a history department recently took a look at the courses taken by history majors during the past several years. Their interest was in determining whether students had taken a sufficient number of senior-level courses. The transcripts of all recent history graduates were examined to see how many courses they had taken at the 100 through 400 levels. Counts for each individual, as well as group averages, were calculated. The mix of courses was also examined. Because faculty discovered a haphazard pattern of course taking and a number of students who had taken only a few 400-level courses, they developed a set of prerequisites and upper-division requirements for all students.

Examining the impact of course-taking patterns on student learning could enhance the study just described. For example, if students who take several 400-level courses perform better on outcomes assessment measures than students who take few of these courses, a proposal for requiring additional advanced courses would have stronger justification. The approach of combining information from assessment measures with information about course-taking patterns has been greatly advanced by James L. Ratcliff and Elizabeth A. Jones working at the National Center on Postsecondary Teaching,

Learning, and Assessment at Pennsylvania State University. As they note, there is greater variation within colleges with respect to student learning than there is among colleges, often reflecting differences in course-taking patterns. With so much choice in course offerings, particularly within general education programs, students in the same graduating class may take few common courses (Ratcliff, 1994). Ratcliff and Jones (1993) have developed the Coursework Cluster Analysis Model to assess the impact of course-taking patterns in general education programs, particularly those that have a distribution plan with fairly wide choices among courses. In the model, students' residual scores (their actual performance on an outcomes assessment measure compared to their predicted performance) are sorted based on course-taking patterns observed on students' transcripts. Using this approach, the course-taking patterns of students who show large gains on assessment measures can be determined. For example, improvements in mathematics performance have been observed for students studying economics, music, and quantitative management, as well as mathematics. The work of Ratcliff and Jones shows that clusters rather than single courses are of importance in identifying differential gains in learning. Overall, Ratcliff (1997a) concludes, "students learn more from logical sequences of courses that build on one another than from independent and unrelated courses" (p. 149).

The model can be used to determine the most effective course-taking patterns associated with various institutional factors such as on-campus or off-campus study and student characteristics such as age or transfer status. The impact of various kinds of learning situations such as learning communities can also be examined. The model is premised on a number of specific assumptions: courses are the most important unit of learning in college, learning is developmental and cumulative, and undergraduate courses are relatively stable in content and instruction (Ratcliff and Jones, 1993, p. 265). In the view of Ratcliff and Jones, this model can help "identify the best fit of student and learning environment," rather than trying to identify a single environment that fits all students (p. 258). Transcripts or other records can also be used to document out-of-class experiences and to study the influence of these experiences on student learning and development. At the Sumter campus of the University of South Carolina, students who attend meetings or other approved events get credits that are recorded on an official student development transcript. Some area employers ask to see these transcripts when interviewing prospective employees (Banta and Kuh, 1998).

Students' Reports About Their Experiences

Transcripts can tell about the patterns of courses students have taken; students themselves can report on their other experiences. Several of the methods we discussed in earlier chapters can be used to gather information from students, including indirect assessment measures such as questionnaires, focus groups, and interviews. Direct assessment methods, such as portfolios, oral presentations, and written work, can also draw on students' experiences. Some faculty ask their students to keep journals recording their academic progress and experiences.

Many institutions have found it useful to administer the College Student Experiences Questionnaire (CSEQ). Originally developed by C. Robert Pace in 1979, the CSEQ has been revised several times. This widely used instrument is now available through the Indiana University Center for Postsecondary Research and Planning. The CSEQ provides a wealth of information about campus experiences. Students are asked about their activities during the current school year in eleven areas, including library usage, course learning, writing, experiences with faculty, and personal experiences. The current revision, developed by George Kuh, includes a section about the use of computer and information technology.

In addition to questions about activities, the CSEQ asks students to rate the emphasis their campus places on different aspects of student learning and development, such as intellectual and creative qualities, and to estimate their gains in these areas. Students are also asked for their overall opinions about their college or university. Because of the rich array of questions, survey responses lend themselves to various kinds of analysis. For example, institutional users can determine whether students who report the greatest gains in learning are those who engage in the broadest array of activities. Because survey items capture "quality of effort," researchers can examine the impact of this effort on student learning and satisfaction (Pace, 1992, p. 2). The CSEQ can be given at any point in students' careers, but is most often used at the freshman and senior levels. Institutional norms are available for comparison purposes.

Based on its CSEQ results, Wake Forest University introduced an annual theme day on campus to foster peer conversations about substantive matters and to more intentionally relate classroom learning with out-of-class activities. Faculty and staff have also used CSEQ results to foster conversations about desired outcomes of the undergraduate experience (Banta and Kuh, 1998).

Rather than using commercially available questionnaires, many institutions develop their own. With the increasing national emphasis on retention issues, some campuses have developed freshman-year experience surveys. Similar to the CSEQ, these surveys try to capture the activities of students. Local surveys can also address use of and satisfaction with campus services and programs. One recent local survey explored issues of class attendance in depth, asking students to rate the impact of several factors on their attendance. The study found that class attendance is related to personal factors such as time management and adjustment to college. As Ted Marchese (1996) points out, learning outcomes reflect not only a college's best effort but "a student's own motivation, effort, and time on task" (p. 4). He applauds institutions that place the assessment spotlight on students' use of time.

Just as questionnaires can address various student experiences and activities, so can focus groups and interviews. Focus groups are often used to probe issues with respect to particular campus services or programs. For example, residence hall directors may want to examine participation in hall activities. Focus groups for various target audiences can be conducted to collect comments and suggestions about programming. Portfolios offer another opportunity to obtain information about extracurricular activities. Students can be asked to write critiques about out-of-class events and to comment on how these events contributed to their learning and development. Asking students to keep logs or time diaries are additional approaches for learning about students' experiences (Schilling and Schilling, 1998).

Retention Analysis

Several institutions look closely at the retention and program completion rates of their students as part of their overall assessment programs. (Definitions for retention rates vary, but typically measure the return rate of a given group of students.) These rates provide global measures of student success in college. A recent national review based on statistics from ACT indicates that 24 percent of students at four-year colleges do not return for their second year, compared to 45 percent of those at two-year colleges (Mortenson, 1998). Students fail to return for both academic and nonacademic reasons.

Current thinking about student persistence has been influenced by the work of Vincent Tinto. In his 1993 book *Leaving College*, Tinto presents a longitudinal model of departure. This model argues that departures arise from interactions among students (with given attributes) and other members of the academic and social systems of the institution. Important student attributes include skills, resources, and dispositions, such as intentions and commitments. The experiences of students, as evidenced by their intellectual and social integration, cause them to continually modify their intentions and commitments. Negative experiences, whether through formal or informal interactions, can seriously weaken their institutional commitment. External commitments and influences also matter.

Thus this model notes the important role of academic and social integration on the departure decisions of students.

Based on Tinto's work, many investigators have looked at their own institutions to examine the role of academic systems, including the formal educational structure and informal faculty-staff interactions with students. They also examine the role of social systems, such as extracurricular activities and peer group interactions. Interviews of withdrawing students and telephone surveys of nonreturning students frequently are used to examine retention issues. Faculty at Chicago State University have found results from their Freshman Withdrawing Survey to be particularly significant. Based on information about financial difficulties of nonreturning students, the university was able to obtain a grant to establish a career development and placement center. For students in academic difficulty, it has linked financial aid to participation in a learning strategies course. All entering students are asked to complete multiple assessments of their knowledge, abilities, attitudes, and behaviors in order to identify at-risk students and provide them with appropriate academic and personal interventions (Lipscomb, 1995).

Some researchers combine background information obtained from their student databases with survey information about intentions, goals, commitments, and experiences in order to examine the factors contributing to persistence on their campuses. At The Pennsylvania State University, academic and student affairs staff have collaborated to design a longitudinal tracking study called the Class of 2000 Project (M. J. Dooris, personal communication, Sept. 10, 1997). In addition to factors related to retention of the Penn State class that entered in 1996, diversity issues and the impact of general education are being studied. Most often, factors in persistence studies are analyzed using multivariate statistics such as regression or discriminant analysis. The latter can be used to compare characteristics of returning students with characteristics of students who leave by choice or who do not return because they have been academically disqualified. Simple cross-classification tables and chi-square statistics can often help with initial data exploration.

Many institutions examine retention rates of particular groups of students before and after program changes are introduced. For example, if freshman seminars are introduced to help students adjust to campus life, retention rates of participating students may be tracked subsequently to see if the program had an effect. Institutions that have tracked retention for several years may be able to undertake time series analysis. Investigators at one university examined the relationship between the first-year retention rate for matriculating students and changes in the local economy as captured by the unemployment rate. Their results supported the hypothesis that a stronger economy with decreasing unemployment rates is associated with lower retention rates. Thus local investigators use several approaches to examine retention issues on their campuses.

Using Performance Indicators

Ewell's recent chapter in the *Handbook of the Undergraduate Curriculum* contains a thoughtful discussion about the use of performance indicators to convey "what is going on" (1997c, p. 608). In his view, indicators serve three purposes. They allow educators to compare relative performance of institutions or programs at a given time, to examine what is happening in a particular unit over a period of time, and to study the impact of a policy or program change by comparing results before and after the change takes place. Thus the main value of indicators is their use for comparative purposes. For those interested in performance measures, Ewell strongly supports the use of multiple indicators and warns against making comparisons across dissimilar settings.

Ewell defines an indicator as a "relevant, easily calculable statistic that reflects the overall condition of an enterprise" (1997c, pp. 608–609), but he cautions that indicators are proxies or indirect measures of an institution's or program's condition. Indicators do not necessarily convey information about causes. For example, the number of books checked out of the library in a given time does not necessarily convey causal information about the retention rate.

However, if faculty choose this measure as an indicator, it should convey information that is judged important.

Much of the current interest in performance indicators can be linked to the 1987 work led by Arthur W. Chickering and Zelda F. Gamson that was supported by the American Association for Higher Education, the Education Commission of the States, and the Johnson Foundation, Inc. Working with a number of noted educators, they developed the Seven Principles for Good Practice in Undergraduate Education. Institutions that implement good practice encourage activities such as student-faculty contact, cooperation among students, and active learning. They also give prompt feedback to students, communicate high expectations, emphasize time on task, and respect diverse talents and ways of learning. Clearly, "good practice" reflects experiences within and outside classrooms.

Along with several other educators, Chickering and Gamson have prepared three inventories that can be used to diagnose good practice on college campuses. These inventories are designed for use by institutions, faculty, and students, respectively. Each inventory addresses the seven areas of good practice. For example, students are asked if they set personal goals for learning in their courses, complete assignments promptly and accurately, and study with their classmates. Students are also asked a number of background questions, such as number of hours studied per week and importance of succeeding academically. The three inventories are available through the Seven Principles Resource Center at Winona State University in Minnesota.

In addition to distributing the inventories, Winona State University has been particularly active in identifying and implementing good practice. Based on collaborative meetings of students, faculty, and administrators, goals were identified for each of the seven principles, plans were drawn up to address these goals, and information from the inventories and other assessment activities was used to examine progress toward the goals. Information about interaction between faculty and students has been gathered from journal entries and classroom assessment techniques, as well as from inventories. Susan Hatfield and others have described results obtained from implementing and assessing good practice. For instance, based on their assessment findings, faculty in the Communication Studies Department have taken several actions to increase student-faculty contact, such as arriving to class early, learning students' names, and creating electronic mail lists to facilitate communication (Hatfield, Hatfield, and Krueger, 1996).

Noting the growing interest in performance measures, Ewell (1997c) suggests several possible indicators drawn from a variety of sources. For example, catalogue descriptions can indicate the number of courses available to fulfill a particular requirement, or the proportion of general education credits required in a particular area. Syllabi can be used to indicate the types of learning goals that are assessed in various kinds of courses and the number of assignments used to address these goals. Transcripts can be examined to reveal how many students are being permitted to substitute other courses for prerequisites. Self-reports of students can describe faculty-student contacts, discussions with peers, and use of student services.

Direct assessment measures are also useful as performance indicators. Portfolios, for example, are extremely valuable not only in measuring outcomes but in conveying information about what kinds of assignments are given to students and how well these assignments align with curriculum goals. In addition, Ewell suggests using pretests and posttests to examine intended connections between sequential courses (Ewell, 1997c).

Evaluating Campus Services and Programs

Only some of the experiences students encounter are generated through in-class curricula. Almost all students draw on services such as advising and financial aid, and most participate in extracurricular programs. In their recent book *Assessment in Student*

Affairs, M. Lee Upcraft and John H. Schuh (1996) provide several reasons why those who provide services and programs may want to assess their units. In most cases the issue will be whether the unit is providing high-quality service rather than whether it should continue. Demonstrating quality may involve comparisons with professional standards or with other institutions. Similar to academic departments, service units and programs must have goals and objectives against which they can measure performance. Issues of cost and affordability may arise. Perhaps a service is needed and valuable but could be offered in an alternative, more cost-effective way. Assessment can help service units with strategic planning, focusing on big issues and preparing for the future, and can also assist with immediate decisions such as how to improve services and reach appropriate audiences.

Focus of Assessment

Upcraft and Schuh (1996) articulate several assessment issues that can be raised by service units and programs. First, service units may want to focus on characteristics of their clients. Although numbers of users may be large, important target audiences may not be represented. For instance, professionals may want freshmen to participate in leadership programs but find instead that they are only reaching juniors and seniors. For this reason, units may want to keep track of client characteristics such as age, student classification, gender, and race. This is much easier for services where clients register and more difficult for programs, such as speeches or presentations, where open attendance is encouraged. In cases where social security numbers of participants can be determined, student records maintained at the institutional level can usually provide additional information about descriptive characteristics. Once the information has been extracted, units may wish to create their own databases to maintain relevant records. In addition to information about clients, service providers should also keep records on the types and frequency of activities they have offered.

A second issue for service units is whether they are serving their clients' needs. As Upcraft and Schuh point out, asking clients is only one way to determine this. Because clients are likely to reveal wants rather than needs, it is important that the knowledge of staff, institutional expectations, and available research on service programs be considered in program design. Few student needs and wants for parking are met, yet most campuses have given careful consideration to providing this service. At Ball State University, staff from several areas, including career services, counseling, and residence halls, came together to design a needs assessment survey that was sent to a representative sample of students. The survey was organized around a "wellness" model. Students were asked about their concerns in areas grouped under the headings of emotional, social, academic, spiritual, occupational, and physical wellness. The concerns of various groups of students were revealed by the survey, and participating service areas were able to use findings to help plan appropriate support programs (R. Hyman and P. Donn, personal communication, Sept. 12, 1997).

A third issue for assessment of service units is that of client satisfaction, which of course is not unrelated to the first two issues. Clients will use services and be satisfied with them if they feel their needs are met. To examine client satisfaction, many service units provide brief questionnaires for their clients to complete upon finishing some activity. Other units conduct focus groups of representative clients. Telephone surveys can also be used to follow up with clients. Satisfaction studies usually concentrate on reactions to specific services as well as overall strengths and weaknesses of the unit, and generally ask for suggestions for improvement. Clients can be asked about various aspects of service delivery such as availability and competence. Directly observing interactions between clients and service providers is another approach for collecting information about the reactions of clients.

Carl A. Ruby (1998) has adapted the business-oriented SERVQUAL instrument for use on college campuses. Based on a study of 748 students at ten institutions, he concludes this instrument can be helpful in evaluating the quality of campus support services. The instrument asks students to rate the importance of twenty-two factors relevant to quality service and to indicate how strongly they agree that these factors are descriptive of services provided on their own campuses. In addition to tangible factors such as office appearance, dimensions of service quality addressed by the instrument include empathy, reliability, responsiveness, and assurance. The last captures the ability of employees to earn students' confidence by acting in a knowledgeable and professional manner.

Some institutions embed questions about satisfaction with services and programs within surveys that are designed to be comprehensive. For example, surveys developed for graduating seniors can ask students whether they used particular services and, if so, whether they were satisfied with them.

In addition to client satisfaction, service providers should also examine whether their units have had the intended effects on clients. Do users of services show relative gains in important areas such as leadership skills, self-confidence, or academic success? Providing measurement inventories for program participants on a pre-post basis, requiring portfolios and other assessment measures, and using self-reported information from clients can help investigate whether service programs have had the desired impact. For assessment of service units and programs to be meaningful, these units must have statements of intended outcomes. Upcraft and Schuh's book (1996) is directed at student affairs professionals, but their observations about evaluating campus programs are applicable to all units that provide services to students, including those in academic affairs and business affairs. Service units in all areas can benefit from assessment.

Implementing and Assessing Seamless Learning

George Kuh has called for faculty and student affairs staff to work together to examine the impact of out-of-class experiences on student learning. As he notes, the "impact of college is most potent when in-class and out-of-class experiences are complementary" (1997, p. 70). When this connection is recognized by professionals within various areas of a college or university, the chance that students will be able to link their in-class and out-of-class experiences and apply what they are learning to their own lives is maximized.

The American College Personnel Association has developed a document called the Student Learning Imperative, which has been endorsed by several other organizations. This statement calls for institutions of higher education to create "conditions that motivate and inspire students to devote time and energy to educationally-purposeful activities" (American College Personnel Association, 1994, p. 1). As Kuh (1997) notes, the document calls for student affairs professionals and staff to help students connect their out-of-class experiences with their in-class experiences and to focus their efforts on achieving overall institutional goals for learning and development. In addition, it argues for collaboration across all areas of the campus.

In June 1998, the American Association for Higher Education, the American College Personnel Association, and the National Association of Student Personnel Administrators issued a joint report called *Powerful Partnerships: A Shared Responsibility for Learning*. This report provides ten principles about learning, each illustrated by a set of exemplary collaborative practices. The report provides a strong reason for areas of the campus to work together on behalf of a shared mission. As the authors note, "Learning is a social activity, and modeling is one of the most powerful learning tools" (p. 1). Jane Fried (1995) notes several promising areas for collaboration, including experiential education, service learning programs, orientation programs and courses, and leadership programs.

As one example of collaboration, personnel from academic affairs and student affairs at Virginia Commonwealth University worked together on a large-scale study of freshman experiences. During the course of the first semester, students in English classes were asked to write short, anonymous essays in response to questions about adjustment, learning experiences, social experiences, and expectations for college life. For example, students were asked to write about feedback they were receiving in their classes and about the role of partying in their lives. A team of twenty-five faculty and student affairs staff read more than ten thousand essays. The study provided several insights about the freshman year. It revealed that exposure to VCU's diverse campus contributed to students' growth in open-mindedness about people and ideas (Fuhrmann, 1995).

Several campuses have begun to actualize the ideas expressed in the Student Learning Imperative. For instance, the use of learning communities provides a compelling opportunity for areas of the campus to work together to strengthen in-class and out-of-class experiences for students. Students who participate in learning communities generally take courses that link two or more disciplines and explore a common theme. This allows students to view courses as complementary rather than isolated. Early models were implemented at Evergreen State College, SUNY Stony Brook, and the University of Maryland at College Park. As Matthews and her coauthors note in their review, purposes for learning communities vary across campuses (Matthews, Smith, MacGregor, and Gabelnick, 1997). Some campuses are particularly concerned with retention issues; others may view learning communities as a way to enhance overall general education goals or to develop particular skills such as writing and oral communication.

Learning communities have been introduced for various groups, from honors students to those who are underprepared. Learning communities for freshmen are particularly popular. On several campuses, entering students not only take courses together, they also live in small communities in residence halls. This proximity enhances opportunities to link in-class and out-of-class experiences. In particular, study groups among students are usually encouraged. Many freshman community programs provide peer mentors who are upper-division students.

Evidence supports the success of learning communities in helping students make a successful transition to college life (Matthews,

Smith, MacGregor, and Gabelnick, 1997). These communities enhance communication between students and faculty, help students build supportive relationships with their peers, and result in greater perceived gains with respect to intellectual development (Tinto, Love, and Russo, 1994; Tinto, 1997). Learning communities provide a real opportunity to be "more intentional about building connections between our disciplines, with each other, and with our students" (Matthews, Smith, MacGregor, and Gabelnick, 1997, p. 473).

Published research is quite positive, but those who introduce learning communities will want to obtain assessment information so that they can understand and improve what is happening on their own campuses. The ideas Upcraft and Schuh (1996) have presented for evaluating service programs apply quite well to assessing learning communities. Those managing the process need to know how many students are participating and to have descriptive information about the characteristics of these students. Faculty and staff involved in the program should keep logs or other records of the activities they provide. Journals and feedback surveys completed by program leaders can be very helpful. In addition, surveys and other assessment methods can gauge the reactions of students. Information should be examined to see if the program is achieving its goals; the impact of learning communities on persistence rates is often of particular interest. The impact of programs on aspects of learning such as critical thinking and communication skills may be important as well.

To study freshman learning communities on its campus, Ball State University followed a panel of students throughout the first year. Descriptions of the activities of students and their reactions to their experiences were collected on a continuous basis, using several instruments patterned on the classroom assessment techniques popularized by Tom Angelo and K. Patricia Cross (1993). Panelists provided specific insights about learning communities indicating they wanted more interaction with peer mentors and more information about program purposes. Panelists also provided comments

about obstacles students face during their first year of college, including the need to learn better time management and study skills.

Several aspects of student experiences can be examined to provide valuable information for assessment purposes. Asking the right
questions will help tap this rich information.

11

Reporting and Using Assessment Results

USE (v.): apply to a given purpose

Assessment information is of little use if it is not shared with appropriate audiences and used in meaningful ways. In this chapter, we review some strategies for analyzing, reporting, and using assessment results. We start with a brief reconsideration of our definition of assessment, then discuss several factors that contribute to the ultimate usefulness of assessment information. Because the way information is analyzed and reported is a key to its usefulness, we end the chapter with a closer look at these two important factors.

Reconsidering Our Definition of Assessment

In Chapter One, we defined assessment as the process of collecting, reviewing, and using information about academic programs in order to improve student learning and development. Some authors stop short of this view. For example, James L. Ratcliff (1997a) distinguishes between *measurement*, which involves gathering and quantifying information, *assessment*, which involves analyzing and interpreting information, and *evaluation*, which involves applying judgments to assessment efforts (p. 22). Upcraft and Schuh draw a similar distinction. In their view, "evaluation is any effort to use assessment evidence to improve institutional, departmental, divisional, or agency effectiveness" (1996, p. 19). In other words, evaluation applies judgment to data that are gathered and interpreted through assessment. According to their definition, evaluators use all kinds of evidence, including information about outcomes such as cost-effectiveness and client satisfaction, as well as student learning.

In contrast, Barbara Wright views assessment as a process that turns data into useful information and, in addition, actually "uses the evidence and interpretations: it follows through with change" (1997, p. 573). In Wright's view, to define assessment more narrowly would "perpetuate a false dichotomy between improvement and accountability" (p. 573). In our view, as well, assessment can and should be used for both purposes.

The closer the generation of assessment information is to the point of use, the less meaningful it is to distinguish between assessment and evaluation. Faculty using classroom assessment techniques are both collecting and using information in a continuous process. As Angelo and Cross (1993) describe it, classroom assessment involves planning, implementing, and responding to what is learned. Likewise, departmental faculty serving on a curriculum and assessment committee will both examine and use assessment information without concern for labels. On some campuses, program review, planning and budgeting, and/or quality improvement initiatives are well-defined processes. In these cases, using assessment can mean that the information it generates is considered and valued as part of these strategies for decision making. For example, assessment results can be used to develop proposals for change that are acted on in the planning and budgeting cycle. The important question is not how assessment is defined but whether assessment information is used, and how assessment relates to well-established campus practices.

In fact, on some campuses faculty make little use of the word assessment. They speak instead of self-study or improving teaching and learning. Among the most valuable aspects of assessment are the clarity it brings to goals and objectives for learning, the systematic look it encourages educators to take at issues of student learning and development, and the emphasis it places on improvement. In some cases, it is appropriate to give the act of using assessment information a special label such as evaluation or planning. The choice should depend on the particular campus and the language that is comfortable to faculty on that campus.

Responding to Various Audiences

In a completely voluntary assessment world, faculty and staff would come together at their own initiative to examine issues that affect student learning and development. In reality, internal interests and external needs all have an impact on assessment. In this section, we briefly describe the role of internal and external audiences in shaping the assessment process.

Internal Audiences

If assessment is a faculty-owned process aimed at improving what occurs in classrooms, then the most important audience for assessment information is faculty themselves. At campuses where assessment is driven primarily by faculty, their own questions and interests shape the process. Faculty in various disciplines proceed in their own ways to collect, review, and use assessment information. Student affairs and other professionals also examine assessment-related questions and work with faculty to examine issues of mutual interest. It is still important, however, to have a generally agreed upon plan for assessment activities and to analyze, report, and use information in systematic ways.

Even on campuses where assessment arises primarily from interests of faculty in various disciplines, additional internal audiences may shape the process. Most campuses have created committees or other structures that influence assessment. These committees may establish timetables and outlines for reports required from campus units asking for information about unit assessment activities. Once approved and in place these internal structures and requirements often play a dominant role in assessment of both general education and the major. In many cases these internal structures are created in response to external pressures such as those described next.

External Audiences

Various external audiences have influenced the current shape of assessment, both through external reporting needs and through their influence on how faculty and staff proceed internally. Often they have provided a real stimulus to campus assessment efforts, what Peter Ewell calls a "triggering" opportunity (1997d, p. 6).

Regional Accreditors

Regional accrediting bodies have had a significant impact on the direction assessment has taken. Specifics differ, but all six accrediting bodies now require member institutions to collect and use assessment information for improvement. Although they provide recommendations, no regional accreditation association requires the use of specific assessment processes or instruments (Cole, Nettles, and Sharp, 1997). The position of the Middle States Association of Colleges and Schools (1996) is typical: outcomes assessment is a standard that must be met for accreditation by its Commission on Higher Education, but this commission "believes it is an institution's prerogative to determine how best to implement assessment" (p. 1). However, it does expect institutions to use information from assessment to answer questions about institutional effectiveness.

The Commission on Institutions of Higher Education of the North Central Association of Colleges and Schools (1997) issued a statement about student academic achievement in 1989. This statement, as well as subsequent revisions, clearly sets forth the expectation that all accredited institutions will have a program in place to document student academic achievement. The commission did not issue a new criterion for assessment. Instead, it reaffirmed that information about student learning was always expected as part of existing requirements. The commission's third criterion for accreditation requires institutions to demonstrate that "The institution is accomplishing its educational and other purposes" (p. 40). The role of assessment is examined under this criterion as well as under criterion four that requires institutions to demonstrate they can continue to accomplish their purposes.

The North Central Association expects institutions to use assessment information for improvement purposes. By March 1996, the commission had issued a set of observations based on initial reviews of assessment plans or site visits for more than four hundred of its members. Among many other insights, evaluators who reviewed campus plans and activities pointed out the critical link between assessment results and planning and budgeting. This commission now expects all members to have fully functioning assessment programs in place (Lopez, 1996, p. 5). Although regional accrediting bodies do not require any particular organizational structures, it is unlikely that as many campuses would be engaged in assessment today in the absence of the impetus they provide.

Professional Accreditors

During the past decade, many professional accrediting bodies have made substantial changes in the way they examine institutions. For example, AACSB—the International Association for Management Education, formerly the American Assembly of Collegiate Schools of Business—has moved from an input-driven model of accreditation to a goal-based model. As a condition of accreditation, business schools are now expected to establish appropriate goals and to provide evidence they are meeting their goals. These schools are asked to describe their processes for curriculum planning, evaluation, and revision. Assessment activities are expected as part of these processes. AACSB explicitly asks its members to provide an analysis of educational outcomes, including information from stakeholders such as alumni and employers. AACSB does not prescribe how student assessment should be carried out, but clearly expects a program of assessment to be in place (American Assembly of Collegiate Schools of Business, 1994).

The American Speech-Language-Hearing Association has made similar changes in its accreditation process. In the view of members of this association, the purpose of accreditation is to monitor and enhance the efficacy of educational programs by means of continuous self-study and improvement (Goldsmith, 1997). As a third example, the National Council for Accreditation of Teacher Education (NCATE) revised its standards in 1995 to emphasize performances of prospective teachers. The new accreditation standards ask schools of education to monitor and evaluate the progress of their students and to use performance assessments in this process. The skills emphasized by NCATE come from the principles for licensing systems that were developed by the Interstate New Teacher Assessment and Support Consortium. These changes are part of a national movement to develop a system in which standards for accreditation, licensing, and certification of teachers are all consistently focused on expected knowledge, skills, and dispositions of teachers (Wise, 1998).

Many other disciplinary accrediting bodies have undergone similar shifts in emphasis from input-based accreditation to accreditation focused on student learning. These bodies have influenced assessment primarily at the division, department, and academic program level, rather than at the institutional level. Several institutions that require assessment of the major allow departments to report on an internal time line that is consistent with external needs and to use the materials and reports developed for their professional accrediting bodies for internal purposes. The expertise and commitment of faculty resulting from their engagement in discipline-specific assessment has helped greatly the implementation of assessment at the institutional level.

State Governments

A third important impetus has come from state governments, often through board-mandated requirements rather than written legislation. Whereas accrediting bodies have been quite clear in their emphasis on using information for improvement, in several states legislators and state leaders have focused on issues of accountability. As Marchese (1994) notes, most of the ideas for assessment have come from within the academy, but these initiatives may not be enough to answer questions from state governments and the public. Some states require periodic reporting of results and a few maintain testing programs for all students (Ewell, 1996). Ewell's regular column in *Assessment Update* helps keep readers up to date on the view *From the States*. In his opinion, current state approaches to assessment are directed toward "assuring quality" for external audiences, rather than encouraging improvements in local practice (1997a, p. 12). He notes that the relationship between assessment and accountability has "always been rich and strange" (1997a, p. 8). Ewell sees an increased emphasis on performance indicators that emphasize efficiency more than quality. South Carolina recently enacted a law requiring that 100 percent of all funding for higher education be allocated on the basis of performance measures. Several of these indicators capture elements of educational "good practice" such as collaboration and cooperation. Ewell reports that at least seven states incorporate student outcomes information in their performance funding schemes, often influencing campus choice about assessment approaches. He also notes that over time such systems tend to place increasing weight on hard measures in order to avoid charges of biased judgment (Ewell, 1997b). More recently, he reports renewed interest in statewide standardized testing with intentions to judge institutions comparatively (Ewell, 1998). These audiences clearly influence assessment questions. Accordingly, they also influence assessment practice.

Using Assessment Results

Because the specifics of assessment vary from campus to campus, assessment practitioners need to think about the kinds of actions that will foster the use of assessment information on their own campuses.

Laying Appropriate Groundwork

The potential of assessment information to be useful starts with faculty and staff discussions about its overall purposes and about specific goals for assessment. Is there concern about out-of-class experiences? What about retention and graduation rates? Can assessment information help inform faculty development efforts? Answers to these questions provide direction for the types of information collected, shared, and used.

Laying the groundwork for assessment usage requires thinking through the ways institutions or units are organized to respond to assessment information. A key decision for the future of assessment is the makeup of an assessment committee, particularly in relationship to other key committees. Because most programs already have curriculum committees in place, assessment may be added to this committee's responsibilities. Then, faculty who are looking at curriculum issues will also be aware of the relationship among assessment questions, findings, and the curriculum. If these two committees exist separately, assessment information still needs to be considered in curriculum deliberations. One approach to coordination is to have overlapping membership between the two committees; another is to ask the separate committees to hold one or more joint meetings each year. Some institutions or units have found it helpful to adopt a rule that no changes in the curriculum will be approved without assessment information to support the change. In a recent *Campus Trends* study, 76 percent of responding institutions indicated they had made curriculum or program changes based on assessment findings (El-Khawas, 1995). Because assessment brings such important information to the table, the number of changes that are made in the absence of assessment results should be small.

Assessment responsibilities can also be added to those of other existing committees, such as strategic planning or faculty development. As an alternative to a committee structure, smaller units can identify assessment coordinators who share information with the entire faculty at regularly scheduled meetings. Many approaches are possible as long as the location of responsibility is recognized. As Hutchings and Marchese (1990) have pointed out, "To endure, assessment needs to find a home within ongoing institutional mechanisms" (p. 34).

Linking Assessment to Internal Processes

We have noted the close link between the processes of curriculum development and assessment. If assessment is to be successful, it must be linked to other processes as well.

Continuous Improvement

In a 1994 *Assessment Update* article, Ted Marchese argues persuasively for linking assessment to quality improvement initiatives. In particular, he urges the use of Total Quality Management (TQM) or Continuous Quality Improvement (CQI) to provide a context for assessment. In his words, "a campus devoted to CQI in all its endeavors would feel compelled to do assessment" (p. 2). Why this belief? As Marchese notes, the quality movement brings with it a "sense of collective responsibility for learning, a habit of listening to the people we serve, a preference for data, an ethic of continuous improvement, a determination to develop fully the talent of every learner, and an acknowledgment that we are professionally accountable to one another and to those we serve for results" (p. 2). The quality movement uses flowcharts and graphs to monitor processes and show how steps relate to one another. Marchese notes that such approaches could easily be adapted for use in curriculum planning.

Each aspect of the quality movement is enhanced by the practice of assessment, providing a much-needed context for assessment initiatives. In Marchese's view, the quality movement has the potential to transform organizations in ways that are consistent with assessment. As Marchese's article acknowledges, assessment alone has not always been successful at making this kind of transformation. Marchese's 1994 article was based on his keynote presentation at the AAHE Assessment and Quality Conference in June 1993. It marked the first of several conferences in which AAHE explored the view that assessment and continuous improvement are complementary activities.

More recently, Peter Ewell (1997c, p. 610) has noted that "colleges and universities are beginning to adopt new management approaches based on Total Quality Management," and that these concepts are expanding beyond administrative support areas into academic functions. On the basis of her review of several institutions practicing CQI, Susan West Engelkemeyer (1998) also notes a natural evolution from a focus on short-term processes in administrative areas to long-term initiatives focused on student learning. According to Marchese (1997b), quality initiatives seem to have greatest appeal to faculty in professional schools such as engineering and business who are most likely to adopt its ideas by creating student study or project teams or expanding the use of student and teacher feedback. Quality ideas have also been applied to course and curriculum design, leading to elimination of duplication and overlap in course sequences.

As Ewell points out, the focus of TQM on continuous data gathering and on ways that various functions fit together provides a useful example for assessment. Ewell recognizes the impact of processes such as TQM on helping assessment move beyond its early emphasis on "inspection at the end" (1997c, p. 610). TQM prompts campuses to search constantly for improvement, to study problems in depth, and to redistribute decision making beyond top levels of the hierarchy (Yudof and Busch-Vishniac, 1996).

At the University of Maryland College Park, assessment and CQI are integrated in the Office of Continuous Quality Improvement (D. Moore, personal communication, Sept. 15, 1997). Academic units can call on the CQI office for facilitation services and assessment support. A cross-functional team in the School of Public Affairs asked for help in collecting data from three sources in preparation for a faculty retreat. An alumni survey was conducted, expert reviews of the curriculum were obtained, and a CQI office staff member queried potential employers and advisory board members via telephone to identify skills and knowledge that graduates of public policy schools would need to be successful. The three sources of information were brought together in briefing material for faculty prior to the retreat. CQI staff interviewed faculty to help frame the retreat agenda, then facilitated discussions at the retreat.

Just as there are those who resist assessment because of its language and agenda, there are those who resist the quality movement. The 1993 issue of *Campus Trends* noted that only 11 percent of responding institutions were engaged in extensive activity with respect to TQM, compared to 43 percent with student outcomes assessment (El-Khawas, 1993). In his recent review of quality initiatives, Marchese (1997b) estimates there may be about a hundred campuses where the pursuit of quality initiatives is a daily fact of life, and perhaps ten where the culture of quality is a dominant norm.

It appears unlikely that TQM will be widely adopted, particularly outside administrative units, and even less likely that it will overtake assessment in widespread use. However, the discussion about the potential of TQM and the realization that educators need to regularly collect and examine information about student learning and development as well as institutional processes have been very beneficial to assessment practitioners. The ideas of TQM have permeated many campuses even if the language has not. As Yudof and Busch-Vishniac (1996) point out, "The most obvious negative of TQM is simply its name and language" (p. 26).

Program Review

Some colleges and universities have found it useful to link assessment with the broader process of program review, which has a longer history on many campuses. These institutions ask their departments to conduct formal self-studies at regular intervals, perhaps every five to seven years. Peer review is involved, and often the information is used for external as well as internal reporting. As the name implies, program review covers many dimensions of the way a unit is functioning. A great deal of descriptive information is typically reported, including average class size, number of majors, and faculty resources. Information about student learning and development is only one of many aspects of the unit that is examined.

At institutions where program review is in place, faculty sometimes view the introduction of assessment as a redundant process. In these cases, building on the existing process of program review may be best. Strengthening review guidelines asking for information about student learning is one possibility (Ewell, 1997c). Because the review of a particular unit is conducted only once every few years, the unit should collect at least some assessment information in the interim. Faculty understand that basic statistics such as enrollment and student credit hours are meaningless if reported only once every five or six years. Assessment practitioners need to build on this understanding when making the case for providing regular and timely assessment information.

Since the State of Illinois implemented an eight-year cycle of program reviews, Douglas Eder reports that during that process, assessment information is peer reviewed and useful in an official sense at Southern Illinois University Edwardsville (SIUE). As the SIUE Assessment Office assists departments in preparing for reviews, faculty learn that much of the information collected for the self-study is available annually and they begin to request it regularly (personal communication, Sept. 22, 1997).

Planning and Budgeting

Another important connection for assessment is the planning and budgeting process. Planning generally deals with decisions about future programs; budgeting provides resources to put these programs in place. Although some changes based on assessment results will have little impact on budgeted dollars, the potential of assessment to have a substantial impact will be limited if the information it generates is not respected and valued in planning and budgeting decisions. Many institutions ask campus units to prepare annual reports on their accomplishments and needs and to accompany these reports with requests for necessary funding. In some cases, requests from campus units are presented to planning committees made up of institution-wide representatives who are asked to rank or otherwise evaluate the merits of the proposals. In other cases, requests are made directly to high-level decision makers. If assessment information is to be valuable, it must be included in this process. Institutions that require assessment information in order to justify budget requests for new programs or substantial revisions in existing programs help guarantee that assessment will be seen as a valuable process. Some institutions put aside blocks of money to be awarded on a competitive basis. Assessment information should be considered, if not required, in proposals for these incentive funds.

At Virginia Tech, where assessment is more than a decade old, gaps in student learning have been used to argue successfully for new faculty to teach new or better courses in the area where the gap was identified (J. A. Muffo, personal communication, Sept. 16, 1997). Assessment data showing that students learn math more effectively when technology is appropriately used convinced the central administration and several deans to reallocate funds for a 250-computer math laboratory that may be doubled in size within two years. Recently the provost invested $400,000 in grants to departments that proposed to improve undergraduate retention and chart progress using assessment data. At the end of the first year some of the projects were not continued, but some that had strong supporting assessment data were funded again at a higher level.

Teaching and Learning

Assessment must contribute to the heart of higher education—the teaching and learning that takes place both inside and outside the classroom. If it does not, there is little chance that faculty or students will continue to engage in assessment. Proponents of classroom assessment, classroom research, and the use of classroom assignments for assessment all point to their close links with teaching and learning, providing a strong rationale for their use. These methods can also contribute to programmatic assessment, further enhancing opportunities to improve teaching and learning.

Some of the most dramatic improvements in teaching and learning as a result of assessment have occurred at two-year institutions. At Oakton Community College, changing pedagogy to a more active learning mode, improving advising, and initiating remediation for high-risk students have helped increase the passing rate on the national nurse licensing exam from 55 to 94 percent (T. Bers and M. Mittler, personal communication, Sept. 15, 1997). Revising objectives and tests in areas of demonstrated weakness on the registry exam for medical lab technician majors at Spartanburg Technical College was one of a number of actions that helped raise some subscores on the registry exam above the national average for the first time (J. E. Cantrell, personal communication, Sept. 15, 1997).

All assessment methods should be evaluated to determine whether they can contribute to improved teaching and learning. Can a survey project provide meaningful insights to classroom teachers about their programs? Does a performance assessment allow for feedback to students and provide them with opportunities to respond? Can new faculty development programs be introduced based on what is learned through a portfolio project? Perhaps faculty would benefit from learning more about providing feedback to students or designing scoring rubrics. Based on their assessment results, Austin Peay State University has offered faculty development seminars on improving communication and critical thinking skills, on learning styles, and on other issues of teaching and learning (Rudolph, 1996).

Improving Assessment

In addition to using assessment information to enrich other processes, the results of assessment must be used to improve assessment itself. Thus faculty should critically examine the assessment process to see if it is providing the information they need for themselves and their students and to make sure that numerous opportunities are provided for sharing and discussing information. If assessment brings improvements to curriculum design or teaching and learning, a fresh look may need to be taken at the type of information that is being collected. Perhaps faculty will need to focus assessment efforts on new academic programs or approaches to learning. Perhaps learning objectives will need to be revised or updated. Similar to all good processes for change, assessment needs to be seen as ongoing, rather than tied to some particular completion date (Rowley, Lujan, and Dolence, 1997).

Analyzing, Reporting, and Sharing Results

Raw data and reams of tables are unlikely to have much impact on teaching and learning. Making information useful requires assessment practitioners to decide about relevant analyses, draw helpful comparisons, create various kinds of reports, and distribute them to appropriate individuals. Because information can often be interpreted in more than one way, the process of drawing conclusions should be open to all those who are likely to be affected by the results of an assessment project. Faculty and others should engage in extended conversations before analysis, conclusions, and recommendations are finalized. As Peter Ewell (1985, p. 117) notes, "different perspectives can be immensely valuable in the interpretation of data on outcomes."

Communicating Use of Information

One of the most convincing ways to let others know about the value of assessment is to make sure they are aware of how this information has been used in the past. Information about courses that have been added or modified, classroom assignments that have been changed, teaching strategies that have been introduced, and other improvements resulting from assessment findings need to be shared. Campuses have introduced these kinds of changes, but faculty, staff, or students may be unaware of the role assessment information played in decision making. Poster sessions and newsletters are particularly useful for increasing awareness about the impact of assessment.

Faculty at Chicago State University have made many curricular and instructional changes on the basis of assessment findings, including course additions, deletions, and revisions and the development of supplemental instruction (D. Lipscomb, personal communication, Oct. 17, 1997). Assessment findings are shared with faculty continuously and there is a campuswide expectation that student learning will increase if faculty use assessment to guide improvements in teaching and curriculum. Explanations of assessment—how it works and how it is intended to help students—appear in department view books, student resource guides, and other publications distributed during orientation and at student meetings scheduled by departmental faculty.

Factors That Discourage Use

A number of factors can inhibit the use of assessment information, including the failure to inform interested individuals in advance about the purposes and scope of assessment projects. Another serious problem is raising questions and focusing energy on issues that are not important. Too many data collection efforts fail to ask the right questions of the right individuals. Even if the right questions are asked, competing agendas or lack of resources may account for a lack of action on recommendations. Faculty and staff involved in assessment need to be realistic in proposing suggestions for action. Encouraging decision makers to prepare a plan for implementing recommendations, including assignment of responsibility and a time frame for actions, can be a crucial step in ensuring that changes actually occur (Farmer and Napieralski, 1997).

Helpful Administrative Actions

Faculty are not alone in ensuring that assessment information is used. On many campuses, administrators help set the overall tone for assessment but then defer to faculty to implement the program. At the time recommendations are made, the value of leadership is greatest. Administrative leaders need to be willing to support recommendations that are based on assessment findings and to provide resources to carry out these recommendations. Agreeing on an implementation plan and providing administrative support to carry it out are important steps that leaders can take.

Analyzing Assessment Information

Faculty and staff need to think about how information will be examined before it is actually collected (Ewell, 1994b). What kinds of questions need to be answered? What kinds of comparisons will be made? Anticipating the way data will be analyzed helps assessment planners identify the types of information needed, appropriate methods and sources to obtain this information, and the number of cases to be examined. Here we describe some useful ways to examine assessment information.

Descriptive and Comparative Information

In many cases, faculty are primarily interested in the basic descriptive information that is generated from assessment projects. This includes responses to various questions on surveys, such as the percentage of students who were "very satisfied" with their majors, mean scores on assessment examinations, and summaries of scores assigned to various products and performances. Descriptive information about individuals who participated in the study, including the number of cases and some indication of how well they represent the overall group of interest on key characteristics, should be included. However, faculty often want additional information. Comparisons among various groups of students, comparisons to previous findings, and, in some cases, more sophisticated analyses that attempt to examine causal factors in performance and satisfaction are common.

Because there is strong evidence that student learning and development vary within institutions as well as across them, one of the most useful approaches for understanding information is to compare results for various groups of students (Ratcliff, 1994; Pascarella and Terenzini, 1991). As Ewell (1994b) describes, students can be grouped in several ways. Many reports compare students according to demographic characteristics such as gender and race. For example, the responses of males and females to questions about involvement and adjustment in college may be compared. Are males and females similar in their willingness to seek help? Do they report similar study habits? Do they achieve similar results on performance assessments?

Assessment results are often compared for students who are grouped according to their educational backgrounds, including descriptors such as high school class rank and SAT or ACT scores. High school class rank, which captures student behaviors during a four-year period, can be a good predictor of many aspects of college life. For example, class attendance and study behaviors in college often differ among students grouped according to their high school class ranks. Both high school class rank and test scores are useful in predicting college grade point averages. High school class size, high school grade point average, and program of study in high school are other background characteristics included in some studies.

A third category for comparison purposes includes descriptors related to college activities and experiences. Assessment results are often examined based on students' current classification levels. Test results may be compared for entering freshmen and upper-class students. Comparisons across majors are also common. Results based on participation in various programs such as distance education or freshman learning communities may be of interest. Comparing performances of students on related assessment instruments can be helpful. Scores on a writing examination may be correlated with those on a critical thinking inventory. Scores on assessment instruments may be compared with information about success after graduation.

In addition to comparing results across subgroups of students, other kinds of comparisons can be made. Comparing results on similar instruments across a period of years can be extremely helpful. Comparisons can be made for groups of students or for the same students at different times. Institutions that administer surveys to students at regular intervals frequently compare results for these students at two or more points in time. For example, life goals that students endorse when they are freshmen can be compared to those they later endorse as seniors. Where external norms are available, local students can be compared to students elsewhere and results on tests or other performance assessments can be compared to agreed-upon targets or standards.

If social security numbers are available, the information used to conduct these comparisons can be obtained from various on-campus sources. Usually an institutional research, computer center, or student affairs information office will be able to provide background data. Information about performance on related assessment instruments may also be available from these units. In cases where instruments are given anonymously, background questions for comparisons must be included on the instrument itself.

Many assessment studies collect information from groups other than current or previous students. Recruiters, employers, and professionals in the field often participate in assessment projects, allowing for comparisons among these groups. Responses of employers about the types of knowledge and skills they consider important on the job can also be compared with responses from students to these same questions. Background questions on employer surveys allow for comparisons of their answers within groups. For example, responses of firms can be compared based on the number of individuals they employ.

The Impact of Various Response Scales on Analysis

To a great extent, the specific assessment measures faculty use determine subsequent analyses. Certain response scales limit the types of statistics that can be calculated. Responses that are expressed in *categories* such as gender and race can be reported in tables showing the number or percentage of cases in each group, but do not allow researchers to calculate means or medians. This is because the data have no natural order. For example, analysts could report on the percentage of females first and then the percentage of males, or the reverse; the order is not meaningful. However, the mode can be used to illustrate the category that is represented most frequently.

Content analysis applied to open-ended questions on surveys or comments from focus groups represents one way to generate categorical data. Comments are coded and sorted into various categories. Researchers can report on the number or percentage of cases in each of the categories, but cannot calculate most other statistics.

Both medians and modes can be calculated for response scales that capture *ranks* or *orders*, such as "strongly disagree" to "strongly agree." Occasionally analysts also report means for this information, but need to remember that applying numbers such as one to five to these responses implies an assumption that the distance between the categories is equal. *Scaled* or *interval data* such as age and height are expressed in meaningful numbers. Thus these data lend themselves to several kinds of analyses, including descriptive statistics such as means, medians and modes, and multivariate analysis such as regression and analysis of variance.

Scoring scales used for performance assessment and portfolios represent rank or order data. Although they can be used to calculate means, the difference between one and two is not necessarily the same as the difference between five and six. Although judgment is applied in deciding the weights to be assigned to various questions, scores on multiple-choice and other objective tests are treated as interval data and can be used in multivariate analyses.

Possibilities for analysis of comparative data also depend on the type of information collected. For example, when comparing results for males and females on a survey item that asks for reasons why students have chosen to study on the campus, cross-classification tables can be used to display results in categories. Then researchers can use chi-square analysis to see if the distribution of responses across categories differs significantly by gender. If, however, researchers are comparing test scores for students taking distance-education classes with those of students on campus, they will be able to calculate means and use t-tests to see if scores differ significantly. If comparing test scores across several sites, analysis of variance can be used rather than t-tests. Linda A. Suskie's 1992 book, *Questionnaire Survey Research: What Works*, has an excellent discussion about appropriate choices of statistical techniques.

Use of Multivariate Analysis

A number of investigators have used multivariate statistics to examine assessment-related issues. For example, student satisfaction with the campus may be of interest to those planning academic or cocurricular programs. In this case, researchers can examine a model that relates student satisfaction to academic and social experiences, as well as to a set of background characteristics. Numbers can be assigned to students' overall satisfaction levels, as determined by questions on a senior survey. Several independent variables that capture demographic and educational characteristics can be included in the model. Age, grade point average, and time to degree are all possibilities. The numbers of hours typically spent studying, working, and on other out-of-class activities may be used to capture academic and social behaviors. Characteristics such as gender can be included in the model by creating "dummy" variables. Students can be assigned a value of one if they are females and zero if they are males (or vice versa). Including this variable allows investigators to determine the average increment to satisfaction with the campus for students who are females. Analysis of variance or regression can then be used to examine the relationship between student satisfaction and the set of independent variables that has been identified. Similar approaches can be used to examine such things as grade point averages, time to degree, and hours spent studying. Several campuses examine models to explain retention rates.

Another common use of multivariate analysis is with respect to test scores. Rather than directly comparing pretest scores to posttest scores, in some analyses predicted posttest scores are developed based on pretest scores and background educational characteristics such as high school class rank and entry-level test scores. Actual posttest scores are then compared with predicted posttest scores.

Reporting Results

Anyone who has responsibility for report writing must anticipate the kinds of audiences that will receive reports, as well as specific needs and interests of these audiences. In fact, report writers often need to prepare different reports for different audiences.

Selecting Report Formats

We begin with some suggestions for sharing information that has been generated through campuswide assessment projects. A significant challenge for those who collect campuswide information is to make it meaningful to various audiences. One way to maintain interest is to share information in various formats.

Comprehensive Reports Based on Campuswide Projects

A number of faculty, as well as senior administrators, will want to see a thorough report of the entire project. This kind of comprehensive report includes descriptions of purposes, methods, results, and conclusions. Quantitative results can include basic descriptive statistics and comparisons. Qualitative results can include selected items such as comments derived from surveys or focus groups. Several campuses sort comments from student surveys into topic areas, such as comments about academic issues, service areas, and out-of-class learning. Although time-consuming to prepare, comprehensive reports provide a valuable record that can be used for reference purposes. We provide a more detailed description of thorough project reports later in the chapter.

Theme Reports

Faculty may be more interested in particular issues than in seeing all results at once. Thus extracting information from a larger project that focuses on a particular theme is helpful. For instance, a senior survey may include several questions about students' plans for the future and about other career issues such as self-ratings of preparation for work and satisfaction with advice about careers. Results for these questions can be combined in a single newsletter or note that focuses on a career theme. A theme report can also focus on topics such as class attendance, study behaviors, or how students use their time. Evidence about a particular skill such as critical thinking or writing could also be the focus of a theme report. Organizing reports around problems or issues is a similar strategy.

Institutional Report Cards and Other Summaries

A number of campuses combine results from several different projects into institutional report cards. These generally include performance indicators that reflect assessment results and curriculum measures. Midlands Technical College has developed an annual Institutional Effectiveness Report Card that includes indicators about current student satisfaction and retention as well as about posteducation satisfaction and success. In the report card, actual performances on the indicators are compared to standards or expectations. One standard calls for a 90 percent satisfaction rate among continuing students with respect to instruction, and another calls for a 90 percent rate of employment or continuing education for graduates. The report card presents evidence from various assessment instruments indicating how well the standard has been met. Plans for continued assessment activities are also described (Gray, 1998).

Generally, institutional report cards capture evidence about what students know and can do in a few important summary measures.

Any kind of short report that captures findings from several assessment studies in a single document can be helpful in letting faculty know the scope of campuswide assessment and its general findings. Overview reports such as these are most effective if they relate results to important goals. For example, results from freshmen can provide an indication of their entering levels of knowledge and skills, and results from alumni can be used to illustrate what is known about students' success after college.

Sometimes results can be summarized in a flyer or brochure that can be distributed outside the campus as well. For example, results from several studies could be organized around themes such as acquiring knowledge, interacting with faculty, and continuing to learn. Ball State University has created a brochure called *Expressions* that captures findings from student surveys organized around these and other themes.

Reports for Specific Audiences

In addition to general reports that have fairly widespread circulation, a number of reports may be prepared for specific audiences, such as accrediting bodies, state governments, and internal committees. The last may have specific reporting requirements for general education assessment or expect annual reports about assessment of the major. The institutions' board of trustees or alumni association may also benefit from focused reports.

Students make up another important audience for assessment information. Flyers and short brochures that contain important findings often capture their interest. Freshmen may be curious about how their class compares to previous classes. A brief report with graphs and bar charts comparing results for two or more years can be used to illustrate differences. For some projects, students will receive individual reports on their own performance. These reports should include some interpretation of what the results imply. For instance, a career interest inventory may indicate that a student would benefit from career counseling. If so, the student should be made aware of this.

Extracts for Colleges and Departments

A number of campuses provide extracts from campuswide studies that include specific results for colleges and departments. Generally, each department is provided with its own results as well as campuswide averages. Extracts can provide overviews of an entire study, or can concentrate on particular themes such as those just described. Reports can include qualitative as well as quantitative information. For example, many senior and alumni surveys ask students to provide overall comments. Any reflections students provide about experiences in their majors are most useful if provided to the relevant departments.

Reports Prepared in Departments

Comprehensive project reports, summaries of projects, and theme reports can be generated within units as well as at the institutional level. The timing and content of departmental reporting is usually guided by requirements of professional accrediting bodies or by internal reporting needs. Timetables for reports to professional accreditors differ greatly. Some accrediting bodies expect full reports only once every ten years, others review programs more frequently, and some ask for interim reports between campus visits. Internally, departments may be called upon to prepare program reviews every five to seven years. Annual reports may be required by internal assessment committees dealing with general education or the major. Often a report outline is made available asking the unit to provide a description of learning goals, assessment activities, and important findings. In order to provide some summary information, the Office of University Assessment at Oklahoma State University regularly asks each academic program for a one-page report about its assessment methods and general results (Shaw, McKinley, and Robinson, 1996).

In cases where there are no regular reporting requirements for assessment, there may be a temptation to obtain frequency distributions, accumulate computer printouts, and save these tables for future reference. Although this reduces work in the short run, it can greatly complicate matters in the long run. We recommend that at least some kind of summary report be prepared annually, or on some other periodic basis, so that a record will exist of what has taken place.

Oral and Web-Based Reports

Although sometimes overlooked, oral reports can be a very useful way of sharing information. In fact, administrative leaders may expect an oral summary of important project findings. Departmental faculty can also benefit from internal discussion of assessment results. Providing opportunities for conversations both before and after written reports are prepared can be very helpful in encouraging the use of assessment information. Chaffee and Jacobson warn planners not to assume that "issuing a report satisfies the need for communication" (1997, p. 241). They recommend bringing oral, written, and visual information into campus gatherings. Oral reports can be presented informally at brown bag lunches or with brief presentations at open forums. Poster sessions are appealing because they combine elements of both written and oral reports. At poster sessions, faculty who have conducted assessment projects may summarize the highlights of their work in outline form, then make themselves available to answer questions and engage in informal discussion.

An increasing number of institutions are using the Web for report distribution. The Web page for the Information Management and Institutional Research Office at IUPUI, maintained by Victor Borden, contains links to assessment surveys and a form for faculty to submit requests for information from the university database. Those who are reading assessment reports can toggle back and forth among survey questions, tables, and charts (Connolly and Lambert, 1997).

Displaying Results

Several possibilities exist for displaying information. In addition to narrative descriptions and tables, most reports will include some graphic displays. Pie charts may be constructed to show how parts of a whole are distributed. For example, a pie chart can be used to show the percentages of students who are working in jobs categorized as in their major, related to their major, or not in their major. Pie charts are useful if results fall into no more than five or six (generous) slices. Categories represented by very small percentages do not show well on a pie chart. Bar charts may also be used to show percentages or counts of cases in various categories such as years, majors, or classification levels. Line graphs connecting means for various groups are also popular for displaying results. Several line graphs can be shown on the same display. Results for freshmen on several subscores of a test could be represented by one line, with a second line showing results for juniors. All charts and tables must be clearly labeled if they are to be useful to readers.

Elements of a Thorough Report

In this section, we share some basic components of strong project reports. The topics we suggest can be used to develop an outline for annual reports requested from campus units as well as for describing campuswide projects.

Introduction and Project Objectives

Helpful reports begin with an explanation of project objectives—a narrative that lets readers know why the project was undertaken. A general description of who was studied and for what purpose should be included here. Important audiences for the information should be identified. An acknowledgment of those who were involved in designing the approach, carrying out the project, or writing the report should be included. A common purpose of an assessment report is to examine whether students know and can do what educators have collectively determined is important with respect to their learning and development. In this case, it is certainly helpful, if not necessary, to describe goals and objectives for learning. If the statement is extensive, it may be included in an appendix rather than the main body of the report.

Methodology

Next, describe methods. How was it determined whether students learned what faculty wanted them to learn? Because most programs require their students to develop in several areas, a variety of approaches will probably be used. For example, faculty assessing whether their students have mastered important areas of a general education program may include surveys and tests, as well as performance measures. The methodology section of a project report should clearly explain which objectives were examined by which methods and why these methods were chosen. It should also ensure that all objectives for goals and learning were actually addressed by assessment measures. Once this is done, the methods themselves should be described. What exactly was collected in student portfolios? How were portfolios evaluated? In addition, the methodology section should describe carefully the target groups studied. If sampling was used, the method should be described. It is also important to indicate when and where information was collected.

Results

This section should start with a comparison of those who were included in the study to those who were eligible. For example, many students who are sent survey instruments fail to complete and return them. In addition to reporting a response rate, it is helpful for readers to know whether the characteristics of those who returned the survey were different from the group of all eligible students. Comparisons of demographic characteristics such as gender and race and educational descriptors such as class level and grade point average can be very helpful. If there are differences between the respondents and the population, readers can keep these in mind as they examine results. Alternatively, the report can present project results that are weighted by the actual percentage of each group in the population. Upcraft and Schuh (1996) strongly recommend the latter approach.

This section should include specific findings. What were scores on a test instrument? How well did students do on a writing assignment? How did respondents answer survey questions? If standards are in place, this section of the report should indicate how well students performed compared to the standards. For example, if an 80 percent score indicates mastery of particular material, the report should tell the percentage of students that achieved this score.

Survey projects can generate a great deal of information. Some reports may contain responses to all of the questions that were asked, but there are occasions when it is more appropriate to be selective in what is reported. In this case, it is appropriate for the report writer to let the information tell its own story. This means reporting enough information to clarify major points, but not so much as to overwhelm the reader. It is perfectly acceptable for the writer to make selections about what to report. Additional details can be provided in an appendix or technical report (Upcraft and Schuh, 1996).

Whether to report negative results is a question some investigators may face. To provide a complete picture, negative results need to be reported along with the positive. As Upcraft and Schuh note, "in no way should results be toned down or omitted because certain audiences will be offended or threatened" (1996, p. 284). We all have an obligation to report honestly. However, findings should be reported in ways that are not judgmental. Also, when results are controversial or surprising it may be important to conduct personal visits with those who could be affected. They may need a reminder that negative findings often present the greatest opportunities for improvement.

Conclusions and Recommendations

Numerical or descriptive results are important parts of any report. In addition, some self-evaluation needs to be included. What can be concluded based on the information collected? How well are goals being achieved? Are assessment results what faculty and staff hoped they would be? Answers to these questions should reflect faculty discussion and consensus, not just the opinion of the report writer. A section about conclusions can be followed (or combined) with a section of recommendations. Recommendations should indicate the actions that those responsible for planning the assessment project will take themselves, as well as the actions they will request others to take. Perhaps faculty development efforts or additional budget dollars will be requested. Any recommendations should be quite clear about the location of responsibility for action.

Use of Results

Occasionally action already has been taken by the time a report is written, permitting the addition of a section describing use of results. A description of what action was taken, and by whom, can be very valuable to readers. It is helpful to describe how the collection and use of assessment information affected various audiences. If additional writing assessments were introduced, what initial effect did this have on students and faculty? What long-term effect did this have?

Observations About the Process

A thorough assessment report will contain some observations and recommendations about the assessment methodology that was used. Was the survey instrument easy to understand? Was it too long? Did the rating scheme for performance assessment work? Future plans for assessment should also be described. Although not always included in assessment reports, readers often appreciate an indication of lessons learned, hints, and reflections for those who might use similar approaches or methods. If assessment had unexpected benefits or created unanticipated problems, these can be described as well.

Executive Summary

The type of extensive report we have just described benefits greatly from an executive summary that provides an overview. An executive summary should contain one or two pages that capture main points, and should be able to stand alone as a brief review of the project.

Confidentiality

When thinking about preparing reports, writers need to consider who will likely see results and what type of information should be shared. In general, it pays to operate on the assumption that reports will circulate widely, even if that was not the intention.

Many assessment studies include a promise of confidentiality to students. When students are identified by names or numbers on surveys or other instruments, they are often told that, except for individual feedback to them, they will not be identified in any way in reports. It is important to respect this promise.

A related issue is what to do with results for individual instructors. For example, an assessment instrument that is administered to students in multiple sections of a course often produces results that can be disaggregated by instructors. A decision should be made in advance of data collection as to how these data will be reported. It might be appropriate to provide results to individual instructors at their own request, but not to circulate this information. Reasons for varying results among sections may not be immediately obvious. Characteristics of students such as class attendance or prerequisite skills may differ greatly across sections. Given normal apprehensions about assessment, it would be unwise to imply that instructors are being compared. For similar reasons, faculty names should be deleted from reports containing students' comments.

Institutional research and assessment offices also need to be careful about how they report results for individual departments. It is best to avoid the appearance that specific comparisons are being made.

Report Distribution

Each report should have a distribution plan. Those who are most likely to be affected by the results should have the opportunity to examine them first. Then related reports can be distributed according to a timetable. Comprehensive project reports can be provided first to interested administrators and faculty. This can be followed with a theme report, or a summary report of the results, which is distributed to all faculty. At about the same time, a one-page flyer containing report highlights can be sent to students. The student newspaper may want to feature an assessment study and provide background information on the project. A useful distribution plan considers the needs of various audiences and the appropriate sequence of report sharing. As T. Dary Erwin indicates, "The reporting process is one of continuous and varying communication" (1991, p. 140), most useful when accomplished in a carefully planned and timely manner.

Can We Determine the Impact of Assessment?

This chapter has included suggestions for analyzing, reporting, and using assessment results. Our observation is that much of what we recommend is occurring on campuses all over the country. As a result of their assessment efforts, many institutions can report specific changes based on assessment findings. Courses have been modified, added, or dropped. New programs have been introduced. Resources have been provided. Advising and other student services have been improved (Banta, Lund, Black, and Oblander, 1996; Hyman, Beeler, and Benedict, 1994; Banta and Associates, 1993; Peterson, 1998). It pays to remember, however, that not every assessment project will result in a specific change. Many times the impact of assessment findings is more subtle and is felt only over time. Rarely is assessment information the only factor that contributes to the introduction of change. Often, specific assessment findings reinforce other information. Similarly, minor changes in academic programs should not be expected to produce large changes in measured outcomes (Pace, 1985).

Much of the value of assessment comes from the systematic way it makes educators question, discuss, share, and observe. As a result, assessment contributes greatly to the understanding of what educators do and to the choices they make about future directions for their work. Although in many cases, as Hutchings and Marchese note, "the possibility of proving a cause-and-effect relationship between assessment and improved learning is likely to remain elusive" (1990, p. 35), many institutions report great benefits from assessment.

12

A Matter of Choices

CHOICE (n.): the chance to select

In several previous chapters, we made the point that assessment can be conducted in various ways. As such, the process of planning and implementing assessment programs requires many choices. The most important choice, of course, is to undertake a meaningful assessment program. Once committed to this endeavor, several selections must be made. What are the purposes of the program? What approaches will be used? How will the information be shared? We addressed these topics in prior chapters; here we revisit some of the most important choices that give shape and character to assessment. Among others, we consider the choice between accountability and improvement as rationales for assessment, and between qualitative and quantitative approaches as ways to collect information. In most cases, we conclude that these choices are not a matter of either/or, but offer instead the chance to find a balance that works.

Accountability Versus Improvement

Across the country, at conferences and national meetings (Ewell, 1997a), and locally in faculty conversations, there is still much discussion of assessment purposes. Most educators realize the potential of assessment to help improve academic programs, but they also recognize the external audiences that drive the process. Barbara Wright (1997) cautions against treating these two purposes as "mutually exclusive." As she notes, assessment practitioners are often warned that "the same methods cannot and should not be used for both purposes" (p. 572). Yet in her view, as well as ours, the two should not be treated as totally separate purposes. States that require assessment often defer to institutions to set their own agendas, as long as the focus is on improving quality. Virginia has long followed this approach. Likewise, faculty at many institutions understand the need to be accountable to their students and peers, as well as to the external public, for what they do. Often information and reports prepared for external audiences provide useful information for internal purposes.

The biggest challenge for assessment with respect to serving dual purposes is to generate information based on locally developed methods that can be reported to external audiences in meaningful ways. Educators often make the assumption that the public understands only numbers and therefore favors large-scale commercial testing. Yet many individuals place great value on narrative and descriptive approaches. Educators need to find ways to use these approaches to communicate with the public. Portfolios that are evaluated with scoring scales containing easily understood labels offer some potential. Peter Elbow (1994a, 1994b) has recommended that readers of portfolios assign only two scores, excellent and poor/unsatisfactory, to portfolios at the margin and no scores to other portfolios. Karl L. Schilling and Karen Maitland Schilling urge faculty to be creative in conveying what they do, to tell a descriptive story "supported by credible evidence" about college experiences with the aim of generating a "constructive dialogue" about their work (1993b, p. A40).

Although using locally developed methods leaves the public without a way to compare institutions, some strategies exist to provide peer information. One strategy is to voluntarily create peer groups for the purpose of exchanging information. Typically these groups include institutions that reside in differing states, but nevertheless provide real potential for campuses or programs to learn from others that are most like them. For example, Indiana University–Purdue University Indianapolis exchanges information with a peer group of urban schools.

Another promising area is that of benchmarking—the process of identifying and learning from institutions that are recognized for their outstanding practices. Benchmarking generally includes careful study of "best practice" institutions to see how they proceed and to gather information and examples for other campuses to use in solving problems. The American Productivity & Quality Center engages in benchmarking studies that involve both industries and educational institutions. In 1997, it identified several best practice institutions with respect to measuring performance outcomes and the following year, in collaboration with University of Maryland University College, identified best practice institutions with respect to assessing learning outcomes (Brown and Newhouse, 1998).

Peter Ewell (1997a) makes a strong case for improving the peer review process with the aim of developing a "meaningful academically owned, nongovernmental approach to quality assurance." Ewell believes that institutional accrediting agencies should concentrate on the "academic integrity of the degree," focusing on issues such as outcomes assessment, curriculum, and educational practice, and reducing emphasis on finance and governance procedures already addressed by other government agencies (p. 18). He urges attention to processes involved in general education, perhaps including reviews of institutional portfolios and peer visits similar to those conducted in England, Scotland, and Hong Kong. In addition, Ewell recommends that accrediting agencies treat their reviews of institutional quality assurance and improvement processes as the centerpiece of their approach rather than as an add-on to other requirements. David D. Dill and his coauthors (1996) also argue that accrediting bodies should focus on internal quality assurance procedures.

William R. Dill (1998) believes that rather than asking campuses to "document and justify how things are," accreditors and others concerned with quality should "unleash as many resources as we can for tangible efforts to see how good we can make them become" (p. 17). Presently, the Western Association of Schools and Colleges is experimenting with approaches that will put assessment and learning at the center of its accreditation process (Cole, Nettles, and Sharp, 1997).

These suggestions provide ways to learn from others about what they are doing and to provide assurances to external audiences that educators are concerned about their own performances. Those of us in higher education need to "mind our own business" or others will do it for us.

Course-Based Versus Programmatic Assessment

As faculty and staff begin to design assessment programs and to select their approaches to assessment, they often ask whether they should use course-based assessment or programmatic assessment. The growing popularity of course-based approaches has increased the frequency of this question. Focusing assessment on learning in individual courses has many advantages. It helps faculty clearly see which learning objectives are being addressed, as well as how well these objectives are being met. Because of its link to the classroom, course-based assessment contributes to understanding and improving the curriculum. Although new assessment instruments such as tests, writing exercises, and surveys may be created for use in the classroom, course-based assessment provides an opportunity for faculty to use materials they already have developed for grading purposes.

The success of using course-based assessment for programmatic improvement rests on the willingness of classroom teachers to share what they are doing. Faculty teaching general education courses at Raymond Walters College are asked to follow one of two possible scenarios as they share materials developed through primary trait analysis. The first scenario calls for department meetings where individual faculty present their results, including their plans to improve the critical thinking and quantitative reasoning skills of their students. The second scenario asks faculty to meet in groups of two or three, with group reports later presented to the whole department (Denton and Ritchey, 1998). Strategies like these, with specific procedures that foster faculty discussion and sharing, help ensure that results from course-based assessment can be used to improve academic programs. In our view, course-based assessment should be seen as one of many valuable approaches to achieving programmatic assessment, not as an alternative to it.

Assessing Individual Students Versus Assessing Programs

One of the greatest benefits of assessment is the emphasis it places on examining academic programs in holistic ways. Because the focus is often on aggregated information, faculty sometimes can learn what they need to know by looking at results for groups of students rather than at results for individual students. Faculty can use group forms of testing that do not provide individual results or can ask a sample of students to participate in locally designed assessment activities that are examined for overall rather than individual results.

An early notion about programmatic assessment was that it should have no effect on individual students, that it should aim at evaluating programs rather than providing feedback to students (Schilling and Schilling, 1998). More recently, assessment practitioners have begun to take a different view, that assessment should indeed have an effect on individual students. This approach helps increase student motivation, often an issue with respect to large-scale assessment projects that seem unrelated to classroom activities.

As Ted Marchese (1998) has pointed out, the best forms of assessment are those that are educative for students, that provide students an opportunity to learn from activities in which they engage. The Schillings believe that the most valuable assessment approaches are those that "serve both the student and the institution" (1998, p. 263). We believe assessment should directly improve student learning both through the types of activities that are conducted and the ways that results are used. Thus the possibility that assessment methods will shape and influence in addition to measure (Terenzini, 1989) may be seen as a strength rather than a weakness.

If individual students are to benefit, they need feedback about how they have performed on assessment activities. As Doherty and her coauthors note, "we need to promote purposeful and self-reflective behavior" (1997, p. 185) to make assessment criteria public and to provide feedback that is both "diagnostic and prescriptive" pointing students toward future learning and performance (p. 187). Writing competence exams accompanied by constructive feedback are one example, comprehensive senior projects with feedback from external reviewers are another. Course-based approaches that draw on existing classroom materials also hold potential in this regard. Results from these activities can be used to assess individual performances, provide feedback to students, and examine the overall academic program. Often a representative committee of faculty members reexamines classroom materials such as tapes of in-class presentations or a sample of essays. In these cases, the results from assessing individual students provide the basis for programmatic assessment.

Using course materials often means that assessment activities will be required rather than voluntary and will have consequences for students in terms of their grades and progress through their programs. If so, these consequences should reflect primarily the importance of the activity in the curriculum, not the value of the activity to programmatic assessment. Faculty need to consider the higher levels of reliability and validity required when using assessment activities to make decisions about individual students. They also need to find ways to look at the ability of students to integrate what they have learned, perhaps through assessment occurring in capstone courses. Also important, educators must remember that programmatic assessment is more than grading individual students; it requires looking at academic programs in holistic ways.

Qualitative Versus Quantitative Approaches

A number of authors have pointed out the value and increasing acceptance of using qualitative information to assess academic programs (Upcraft and Schuh, 1996; Wright, 1997; Farmer and Napieralski, 1997). Although there are many possible definitions, *quantitative methods* are distinguished by their emphasis on numbers, measurement, experimental design, and statistical analysis. Researchers typically work with a small number of predetermined response categories to capture various experiences and perspectives of individuals. Often emphasis is on analyzing a large number of cases using carefully constructed instruments that have been evaluated for their reliability and validity (Patton, 1990). Techniques include questionnaires, structured interviews, and tests.

In contrast, *qualitative methods* such as in-depth, open-ended interviews, observations of activities, behaviors, and interactions, and analysis of written documents yield direct quotations, descriptions, and excerpts rather than numbers. As Michael Patton (1990) indicates, information for qualitative studies often comes from fieldwork where the researcher spends time making firsthand observations about the situation or program under study. Thus validity and reliability depend on the skill and integrity of the researcher: "the researcher is the instrument" (p. 14).

Qualitative approaches such as analysis of group discussions and journal writing rely on discovery, subjectivity, and interpretation (Farmer and Napieralski, 1997). The Schillings (1998) note how an interview project conducted with graduating seniors at Miami University helped faculty gain an understanding of students' learning styles and often caused them to change their strategies for teaching.

In the Schilling's view, face-to-face interviews between faculty and students provide participants an excellent opportunity to reflect on college life. Examination of portfolio materials to identify student assignments and use of free writing exercises that ask students to reflect on their experiences in relation to particular developmental goals have also been used with success at Miami University (Schilling and Schilling, 1993a).

Farmer and Napieralski (1997) see great potential in qualitative methods that allow for discovery of the insider's perspective. What do people associated with a program think, and why? Using an ethnographic approach, interviewers may work without a specific agenda, allowing questions to proceed in promising directions. Qualitative approaches allow for goal-free evaluation, the chance to discover the unintended and accidental effects of a program as well as the intended effects. It allows faculty to discover if students are learning in unexpected ways—ways not specified in intended outcome objectives.

Barbara Wright (1997) notes that assessment methods such as examining written commentary provided by students in portfolios is free of the "invidious statistical comparisons that many faculty fear, for themselves or their campuses" (p. 578). Descriptive results can stimulate faculty thinking, as well as provide material for communicating with the public. Farmer and Napieralski (1997) note that qualitative approaches can be particularly appealing to liberal arts faculty who sometimes lack respect for traditional scientific, experimental models because they value complexity and discovery more than simplification and verification. Some observers believe that placing excessive emphasis on standardization, content validity, and reliability washes out what is important about learning (Marchese, 1998). For programs involved in a self-study process, Farmer and Napieralski recommend relying on institutional research offices to supply needed quantitative data allowing faculty to spend more time on qualitative assessment and on what data mean.

The contrast between quantitative and qualitative methods is an important one. Just as some faculty are more comfortable with descriptive approaches, others are more comfortable with quantitative approaches. In disciplines such as nursing and engineering where there is substantial agreement about expected knowledge for students, nationally normed measures are widely used. Likewise, many faculty choose to develop local examinations (Schilling and Schilling, 1998; Banta, 1996b). It is particularly important that the needs of faculty in various disciplines be respected. We strongly encourage faculty to choose methods that are most comfortable to them. In many cases, this will involve a mix of quantitative and qualitative approaches.

Value-Added Versus Comprehensive Longitudinal Designs

Although very popular at the beginning of the current assessment movement and still in use for some purposes, there has been a decided shift away from value-added assessment designs. Criticized for being mechanical, sometimes irrelevant, and often misleading, test-retest designs have been replaced in emphasis by studies that are truly longitudinal (Ewell, 1991). This shift has paralleled the movement toward using assessment information for improvement of both individual and programmatic performances.

Institutions remain concerned about their effects on student growth and development, but the notion that these effects can be captured by one particular measurement approach has long been abandoned (Ewell, 1991). Comprehensive longitudinal studies now make use of information about students' characteristics, goals, motivation, and experiences in addition to their scores on particular instruments. These techniques draw on both quantitative and qualitative information such as survey research and interviews as well as performance measures. Information is collected at regular intervals with the intent of examining the impact of college on students. These studies often draw heavily on institutional information available through student records. Portfolios offer a particularly striking example of longitudinal design. As Ewell (1991) points out, however, such designs can be costly and time consuming, and require rather large samples if generalizations are to be made. Many projects require expertise in terms of statistical analysis.

Technology Versus Traditional Approaches

The 1990s have seen a proliferation of opportunities for using technology to enhance assessment. CyberCATs, surveys on the Web, computer-administered examinations that provide individual scores and feedback, and electronic portfolios are now available to enhance assessment projects. Practitioners at Indiana University–Purdue University Indianapolis are developing software for computer scoring of essays and have found promising results for the reliability of scores assigned by computers compared to those assigned by readers. On several campuses, students are placed in appropriate courses based on results from computer-adapted testing in which the difficulty of test items reflects performance on prior questions. Some institutions use software that can link administrative records to portfolios developed by students. Other campuses now have classrooms that contain electronic audience response systems allowing for immediate tallying and graphing of students' answers to quizzes or to questions posed with classroom assessment techniques. Many institutions use the Web to share information about their assessment programs. *Assessment Update* has added a regular column, "Web Corner," compiled by Ephraim Schechter, Cel Johnson, and Alec M. Testa, that shares information about Web-based resources. The emergence of technology-driven, self-paced courses may bring a new role for assessment in directly credentialing students based on their ability to demonstrate competence (Ewell, 1997e).

A great deal of work is under way to assess the differences between new assessment approaches and traditional methods, but few conclusions have been reached yet. We recommend that campuses monitor the use of these innovations to see if response rates or results differ greatly from traditional methods and, if so, to investigate why. Otherwise, we heartily endorse their use.

Local Development Versus Technical Precision

One of the distinguishing characteristics of successful assessment programs is the extent to which they engage faculty and others in the process. Faculty plan the program, design instruments, collect information, interpret results, and utilize findings. Meaningful assessment needs consensus, agreement, and collaboration among all those who are involved. Quite clearly, assessment is a group activity that requires faculty and staff to be more public and open about what they do than in the past. Assessment requires faculty to move away from the view that each course is "the intellectual property of the faculty member offering it" (Schneider, 1997, p. 253). Instead, faculty accept a shared responsibility for helping students learn.

Institutions that have been most successful in securing widespread involvement in assessment are often those where participants develop local instruments and techniques. As Ewell asks, does the trend toward using locally developed materials mean that "anything goes" (1991, p. 110)—that technical quality will be lacking, as some observers imply? We do not think this needs to be the case. In fact, local instruments often offer the best chance for content validity. Faculty who develop their own approaches can match their instruments to the local curriculum. In several chapters, we stressed the value of drawing on local campus expertise when constructing instruments and also noted the importance of faculty development efforts. Both strategies increase the quality of locally developed instruments. It is true that local instruments lack national norms, but the latter offer no guarantee of instrument validity.

Ewell has pointed out the importance of validation procedures in ensuring the value of locally developed instruments. As educators create ways to assess complex, integrated abilities, they must be "precise up front about the nature of the ability being investigated and how it might be recognized at different stages of development" (1991, p. 113). They must place the design of instruments in context, continually seeking faculty comments about the appropriateness of assessment instruments given typical requirements in college classrooms. Practitioners' judgments about the applicability and usefulness of what students are asked to do are also important. In addition, we all must be careful to guard against inappropriate uses of assessment results. Keeping these cautions in mind, we encourage faculty and staff on local campuses to continue the imaginative work they have already done in creating assessment instruments.

Campuswide Versus Program-Level Assessment

It is extremely important for assessment activities to reflect what is going on in individual programs and to draw on classroom activities as much as possible. However, there are a number of benefits to campuswide assessment activities as well. When planned by faculty, staff, and students who represent a broad cross section of the campus and communicated in meaningful ways, these activities help campus units see what they have in common as an institution. These activities serve as a reminder of institutional values and help in examining how well overall goals are being met. Activities such as senior or alumni surveys, writing competence examinations, and common projects for seniors can provide valuable information at the institutional and, through disaggregation, the program level as well. Institutional studies can be based on comprehensive longitudinal designs such as those described earlier and can provide results for subsets of students as well as for all students. Campuswide activities should support those that are occurring in individual programs, providing an additional source of information as faculty seek to improve what they do. In fact, institutions represent programs in the aggregate. Educators need to know that campuses are functioning well overall as well as in individual units.

Cultural Change Versus Additional Responsibility

Some individuals view assessment as something extra to do, as one more responsibility, or as an activity that warrants only minimal attention. In contrast, many others see it as a valuable way of learning about their institutions and programs, a process that has great potential to help them improve. Assessment leaders at Truman State University indicate that their institution was transformed by assessment. This campus was able to develop "a culture of assessment that has served its students and faculty—as well as the citizens of its state—very well" (Magruder, McManis, and Young, 1997, p. 28). Is this something all campuses can and should aspire to achieve? And if so, what would foster this change?

As Pat Hutchings points out, many campuses are seeking to build a culture "in which teaching and learning are the subject of sustained, public attention and inquiry, and where members of the academic community take seriously their shared responsibility for ensuring and improving the quality of the educational experience" (1996, p. 4). Assessment can and should be part of this larger concern with issues of teaching and learning. In fact, assessment is best viewed as a reflection of the value placed on student learning and development. In Marcia Mentkowski's words, "the assessment cart builds on the lead of the learning horse" (1998, p. 2).

Campus cultures are made up of the assumptions, ideas, customs, and languages that are shared and transferred to others. They reflect demographics and history as well as external influences (Mentkowski, 1998). How can educators help ensure the place of assessment in institutional cultures? Cultural change is fostered by planned conversations among individuals. In Marcia Mentkowski's view, faculty involvement is "less a matter of motivation, than of connection" (p. 5). Institutional structures that consciously focus on student learning are needed. Pat Hutchings (1996) suggests the use of "teaching circles" whose members meet regularly to talk about their teaching and students' learning in conversations that draw on information and evidence. She suggests discussions based on the use of classroom assessment techniques and strongly encourages conversations across disciplines. Discussions about assessment among faculty from across the campus can be very beneficial even for faculty who are drawing primarily on their own classroom activities. Although disciplines may differ, faculty have much to share when it comes to the practice of assessment. Ewell notes the all-too-common problem of "missed opportunities for discussing assessment results" (1997e, p. 377). In his view, retreats and workshops should center on recognized campus issues addressed by assessment information.

Ideas must be shared with those who are new to institutions. Truman State University acknowledges that its culture of assessment "requires constant nurturing and care" (Magruder, McManis, and Young, 1997, p. 27). Assessment leaders recognize that faculty as well as students regularly leave the institution and that newcomers must be integrated to the values of assessment.

Cultural change requires a look at basic assumptions about how individuals proceed (Chaffee and Jacobson, 1997). For example, it is important that rewards place value not only on teaching but also on the substantial energy faculty devote to assessment. A key assumption relates to the campus view of improvement. Without a conscious desire to improve, assessment may appear to have little purpose. Pat Hutchings aptly notes that "all the tools in the world are beside the point if there's no sense that improvement is an urgent need" (1996, p. 8). We must not think of this need as something pejorative, as some observers do! Instead, we must foster a shared cultural value on improvement, perhaps focusing and monitoring progress on a few key results (Chaffee and Jacobson, 1997).

As Marchese notes, whether for an individual or a program, "Assessment is a process in which, rich usable, credible *feedback* . . . comes to be *reflected* upon by an academic community, and then is *acted* on by that community . . . within its commitment to get smarter and better at what it does" (1997a, p. 93). That commitment must be strong for assessment to succeed.

In the process of examining assumptions, educators need to build on a shared language to help participants understand underlying theories and models and the thinking that governs actions (Brown, 1997). Faculty at Alverno consider their "language of learning as part of the connective tissue of the social context for learning" (Mentkowski, 1998). Barr and Tagg (1995) have argued effectively for educators to truly put learning first—to speak about whether institutions produce learning rather than provide instruction. Likewise, Pascarella and Terenzini have called for "learning-centered management" with decision making that reflects potential consequences for student learning (1991, p. 656). Campuses need to examine whether or not they do this.

Cultural change starts from a shared vision of what an institution wants to become (Chaffee and Jacobson, 1997). Educators need to set high expectations not only for students but also for themselves with respect to teaching, learning, and assessment (Hutchings, 1996). As Barr and Tagg (1995) propose, educators can set the inspiring goal that each graduating class learns more than the previous one. Judy Sorum Brown (1997, p. 6) questions, "Why is it so difficult for an institution of learning to be a learning organization?" If, as she notes, creative tension is found in the gap between vision and reality, assessment can help provide the information to bridge that gap, to help provide energy for change. Combined with a renewed emphasis on teaching and learning, the practice of assessment can help communicate a shared vision. Assessment's special role in this vision is its focus on student learning and development and its emphasis on using evidence for improvement. Wolff and Harris (1994) advocate developing a "culture of evidence" supported by an attitude of open inquiry. By helping us all articulate and make public our expectations, assessment should help raise expectations for students and ourselves. The practice of assessment can encourage *mindfulness*, an openness to new information and an awareness of multiple perspectives (Marchese, 1997a; Langer, 1997). Perhaps of most importance, the practice of assessment reminds us all that we are learners, something that is greatly valued in learning organizations (Brown, 1997).

Is There a Choice About Doing Assessment?

This book is based on the assumption that we all care about what we are doing and want to tap the potential of assessment to help improve—that assessment is valuable and useful even if not required. If practiced wisely, assessment itself can help achieve many of the elements of educational "good practice" described by Ewell and Jones (1996). It can help create high expectations for students, provide opportunities for synthesizing experiences, create opportunities for active learning, and give prompt feedback. Many faculty appreciate the benefits assessment has to offer and work with others to capture its rewards. In our view, assessment should be seen as a natural responsibility to our students and each other. We hope this book has helped you learn about assessment, as we have learned from writing it.

References

American Assembly of Collegiate Schools of Business. *Achieving Quality and Continuous Improvement Through Self-Evaluation and Peer Review: Standards for Accreditation, 1994–95.* St. Louis, Mo.: American Assembly of Collegiate Schools of Business, 1994.

American Association for Higher Education, American College Personnel Association, National Association of Student Personnel Administrators (joint report). *Powerful Partnerships: A Shared Responsibility for Learning,* June 2, 1998.

American College Personnel Association. *The Student Learning Imperative.* Washington, D.C.: American College Personnel Association, 1994.

Angelo, T. A. "Classroom Assessment: Involving Faculty and Students Where It Matters Most." *Assessment Update,* 1994, 6(4), 1–2, 5, 10.

Angelo, T. A. "Improving Classroom Assessment to Improve Learning: Guidelines from Research and Practice." *Assessment Update,* 1995, 7(6), 1–2, 12–13.

Angelo, T. A. *A One-Day Colloquium on Classroom Assessment and Classroom Research.* American Assocation for Higher Education Assessment Forum, Washington D.C., June 8, 1996.

Angelo, T. A. "Challenging (and Changing) Common (Mis)Perceptions About Outcomes Assessment." A keynote plenary session at the 1998 AACSB Outcomes Assessment Seminar in Nashville, Tenn., Mar. 1998.

Angelo, T. A., and Cross, K. P. *Classroom Assessment Techniques: A Handbook for College Teachers.* (2nd ed.) San Francisco: Jossey-Bass, 1993.

Appelbaum, M. I. "Assessment Through the Major." In C. Adelman and others, *Performance and Judgment: Essays on Principles and Practice in the Assessment of College Student Learning.* Washington, D.C.: U.S. Department of Education Office of Educational Research and Improvement, 1988.

Association of American Colleges. *Integrity in the College Curriculum: A Report to the Academic Community.* Washington, D.C.: Association of American Colleges, 1985.

Association of American Colleges. *Strong Foundations: Twelve Principles for Effective General Education Programs.* Washington, D.C.: Association of American Colleges, 1994.

Astin, A. W. *Achieving Educational Excellence: A Critical Assessment of Priorities and Practices in Higher Education.* San Francisco: Jossey-Bass, 1985.

Astin, A. W. *Assessment for Excellence: The Philosophy and Practice of Assessment and Evaluation in Higher Education.* New York: American Council on Education/Macmillan, 1991.

Banks, D. "Community College Strategies: Virginia Community College System." *Assessment Update,* 1996, 8(2), 8.

Banta, T. W. "Use of Outcomes Information at the University of Tennessee, Knoxville." In P. T. Ewell (ed.), *Assessing Educational Outcomes.* New Directions for Institutional Research, no. 47. San Francisco: Jossey-Bass, 1985.

Banta, T. W. "Editor's Notes: The Power of a Matrix." *Assessment Update,* 1996a, 8(4), 3, 13.

Banta, T. W. "Using Assessment to Improve Instruction." In R. J. Menges and M. Weimer, *Teaching on Solid Ground: Using Scholarship to Improve Practice.* San Francisco: Jossey-Bass, 1996b.

Banta, T. W., and Kuh, G. D. "A Missing Link in Assessment: Collaboration Between Academic and Student Affairs Professionals." *Change: The Magazine of Higher Learning,* 1998, 30(2), 40–46.

Banta, T. W., Lund, J. P., Black, K. E., and Oblander, F. W. (eds.) *Assessment in Practice: Putting Principles to Work on College Campuses.* San Francisco: Jossey-Bass, 1996.

Banta, T. W., Rudolph, L. B., Van Dyke, J., and Fisher, H. S. "Performance Funding Comes of Age in Tennessee." *Journal of Higher Education,* 1996, 67(1), 23–45.

Banta, T. W., and Associates. *Making a Difference: Outcomes of a Decade of Assessment in Higher Education.* San Francisco: Jossey-Bass, 1993.

Barker, J. R., and Folger, J. "Assessing Student Achievement in the Major: Assessment for Program Improvement. Focus on an Academic Major." In T. W. Banta, J. P. Lund, K. E. Black, and F. W. Oblander (eds.), *Assessment in Practice: Putting Principles to Work on College Campuses.* San Francisco: Jossey-Bass, 1996.

Barr, R. B., and Tagg, J. "From Teaching to Learning—A New Paradigm for Undergraduate Education." *Change: The Magazine of Higher Learning,* 1995, *27*(6), 12–25.

Barrows, H. S. "How Can We Assess What Is Valued in the World Outside the Classroom?" Presentation at the Indiana University–Purdue University Indianapolis Assessment Conference in Indianapolis, Ind., Nov. 1997.

Belanoff, P. "Portfolios and Literacy: Why?" In L. Black, D. A. Daiker, J. Sommers, and G. Stygall (eds.), *New Directions in Portfolio Assessment: Reflective Practice, Critical Theory, and Large-Scale Scoring.* Portsmouth, N.H.: Boynton/Cook, 1994.

Bennion, D. H., Collins, R. W., and Work, S. "Techniques for Communicating and Building Trust for Assessment in a Large University." Presentation at the American Association for Higher Education's Ninth Annual Conference on Assessment and Quality, June 14, 1994.

Bennion, D. H., and Work, S. "Using an Assessment Expo (Fair) to Communicate Eastern Michigan University Assessment Successes to Faculty and Staff at EMU and Local Two- and Four-Year Colleges and Universities." Poster session, 1998 American Association for Higher Education (AAHE) Assessment Conference, June 15, 1998.

Bers, T., Davis, D., and Taylor, W. "Syllabus Analysis: What Are We Teaching and Telling Our Students?" *Assessment Update,* 1996, *8*(6), 1–2, 14–15.

Beyer, B. K. *Practical Strategies for the Teaching of Thinking.* Needham Heights, Mass.: Allyn & Bacon, 1987.

Black, L. C. "Portfolio Assessment." In T. W. Banta and Associates, *Making A Difference: Outcomes of a Decade of Assessment in Higher Education.* San Francisco: Jossey-Bass, 1993.

Bloom, B. S. (ed.). *Taxonomy of Educational Objectives: The Classification of Educational Goals. Handbook I: Cognitive Domain.* White Plains, N.Y.: Longman, 1956.

Bloomsburg University of Pennsylvania. *Undergraduate Catalogue 1995–1997.* Bloomsburg: University of Pennsylvania, 1995.

Bogue, E. G., and Saunders, R. L. *The Evidence for Quality.* San Francisco: Jossey-Bass, 1992.

Boyer, E. L. *Selected Speeches 1979–1995.* Princeton, N.J.: Carnegie Foundation for the Advancement of Teaching, 1997.

Brookfield, S. D. *Developing Critical Thinkers.* San Francisco: Jossey-Bass, 1987.

Brookfield, S. D. *Becoming a Critically Reflective Teacher*. San Francisco: Jossey-Bass, 1995.

Brown, J. S. "On Becoming a Learning Organization." *About Campus*, Jan.–Feb. 1997, pp. 5–10.

Brown, M. M., and Newhouse, B. "Best Practices in Measuring Institutional Performance Outcomes." Presentation at the American Association for Higher Education 1998 Assessment Conference, Cincinnati, Ohio, June 13–17, 1998.

Butler University Elementary/Early Childhood Team. *Butler University Elementary/Early Childhood Portfolio Defense*. Indianapolis, Ind.: Butler University, 1997.

Byham, W. C. "Using the Assessment Center Method to Measure Life Competencies." In C. Adelman and others, *Performance and Judgment: Essays on Principles and Practice in the Assessment of College Student Learning*. Washington, D.C.: U. S. Department of Education Office of Educational Research and Improvement, 1988.

Carter-Wells, J. "Raising Expectations for Critical Reading." In E. A. Jones (ed.), *Preparing Competent College Graduates: Setting New and Higher Expectations for Student Learning*. New Directions for Higher Education, no. 96. San Francisco: Jossey-Bass, 1996.

Chaffee, E. E., and Jacobson, S. W. "Creating and Changing Institutional Cultures." In M. W. Peterson, D. D. Dill, L. A. Mets, and Associates, *Planning and Management for a Changing Environment: A Handbook on Redesigning Postsecondary Institutions*. San Francisco: Jossey-Bass, 1997.

Chandler, J. V., and Horne, B. "When in Doubt, Ask! The Exit Interview." *Assessment Update*, 1995, 7(3), 10.

Cherry, R. D., and Meyer, P. R. "Reliability Issues in Holistic Assessment." In M. M. Williamson and B. A. Huot (eds.), *Validating Holistic Scoring for Writing Assessment: Theoretical and Empirical Foundations*. Cresskill, N.J.: Hampton Press, 1993.

Chickering, A. W. *Education and Identity*. San Francisco: Jossey-Bass, 1969.

Chickering, A. W., and Gamson, Z. F. "Seven Principles for Good Practice in Undergraduate Education." *AAHE Bulletin*, 1987, 39(7), 3–7.

Chickering, A. W., and Reisser, L. *Education and Identity*. (2nd ed.) San Francisco: Jossey-Bass, 1993.

Click, B.A.L., III. "Educating Students to Write Effectively." In E. A. Jones (ed.), *Preparing Competent College Graduates: Setting New and Higher Expectations for Student Learning*. New Directions for Higher Education, no. 96. San Francisco: Jossey-Bass, 1996.

Cole, J.J.K., Nettles, M. T., and Sharp, S. *Assessment of Teaching and Learning for Improvement and Accountability: State Governing, Coordinating Board and Regional Accreditation Association Policies and Practices.* Ann Arbor: University of Michigan, National Center for Postsecondary Improvement, 1997.

Conference on College Composition and Communication Committee on Assessment. "Writing Assessment: A Position Statement." *College Composition and Communication,* 1995, 46(3), http://www.missouri.edu/~cccc/assessment.html.

Connolly, M., and Lambert, J. "Assessment's Greatest 'Hits' Using the World Wide Web to Enhance Assessment Efforts." *Assessment Update,* 1997, 9(2), 1–2, 12–13.

Courts, P. L., and McInerney, K. H. *Assessment in Higher Education: Politics, Pedagogy, and Portfolios.* New York: Praeger, 1993.

Cross, K. P. "What's in That Black Box? Or, How Do We Know What Students Are Learning?" Howard R. Bowen Lecture presented at the Claremont Graduate School, Claremont, Calif., Nov. 1989.

Cross, K. P., and Angelo, T. A. *Classroom Assessment Techniques: A Handbook for Faculty.* San Francisco: Jossey-Bass, 1988.

Cross, K. P., and Steadman, M. H. *Classroom Research: Implementing the Scholarship of Teaching.* San Francisco: Jossey-Bass, 1996.

Crouch, M. K., and Fontaine, S. L. "Student Portfolios as an Assessment Tool." In D. F. Halpern and Associates, *Changing College Classrooms: New Teaching and Learning Strategies for an Increasingly Complex World.* San Francisco: Jossey-Bass, 1994.

Crowl, T. K. *Fundamentals of Educational Research.* Madison, Wis.: Brown & Benchmark, 1993.

Crowl, T. K. *Fundamentals of Educational Research.* (2nd ed.) Boston: McGraw-Hill, 1996.

Cullen, J. A., and Cook, P. R. "Memos Linking Domains of Learning to Program Outcomes Through Critical Thinking." *Assessment Update,* 1998, 10(5), 16.

Curry, L., and Wergin, J. F. "Professional Education." In J. G. Gaff, J. L. Ratcliff, and Associates, *Handbook of the Undergraduate Curriculum: A Comprehensive Guide to Purposes, Structures, Practices, and Change.* A publication of the Association of American Colleges and Universities. San Francisco: Jossey-Bass, 1997.

Delandshere, G., and Petrosky, A. R. "Capturing Teachers' Knowledge: Performance Assessment." *Educational Researcher,* 1994, 23(5), 11–18.

Denney, L. *Assessment of Student Learning and Development Progress Report 1996*. Dayton, Ohio: Sinclair Community College, 1996.

Denton, J. M., and Ritchey, L. H. "Using Embedded Assessment to Improve Student Learning and Institutional Effectiveness." Presentation at the American Association for Higher Education 1998 Assessment Conference, Cincinnati, Ohio, June 13–17, 1998.

Diamond, R. M. *Designing and Assessing Courses and Curricula: A Practical Guide*. San Francisco: Jossey-Bass, 1998.

Dill, D. D. "Focusing Institutional Mission to Provide Coherence and Integration." In M. W. Peterson, D. D. Dill, L. A. Mets, and Associates, *Planning and Management for a Changing Environment: A Handbook on Redesigning Postsecondary Institutions*. San Francisco: Jossey-Bass, 1997.

Dill, D. D., Massy, W. F., Williams, P. R., and Cook, C. M. "Accreditation and Academic Quality Assurance: Can We Get There from Here?" *Change: The Magazine of Higher Learning*, 1996, 28(5), 17–24.

Dill, W. R. "Guard Dogs or Guide Dogs? Adequacy Versus Quality in the Accreditation of Teacher Education." *Change: The Magazine of Higher Learning*, 1998, 30(6), 12–17.

Dillon, W. T. "Involving Community in Program Assessment." *Assessment Update*, 1997, 9(2), 4, 11, 15.

Doherty, A., Chenevert, J., Miller, R. R., Roth, J. L., and Truchan, L. C. "Developing Intellectual Skills." In J. G. Gaff, J. L. Ratcliff, and Associates, *Handbook of the Undergraduate Curriculum: A Comprehensive Guide to Purposes, Structures, Practices, and Change*. A publication of the Association of American Colleges and Universities. San Francisco: Jossey-Bass, 1997.

Domholdt, E. "Poster Session Showcases Assessment Efforts." *Assessment Update*, 1996, 8(5), 5–6, 15.

Dougherty, B. C., and Fantaske, P. "Defining Expectations for Problem-Solving Skills." In E. A. Jones (ed.), *Preparing Competent College Graduates: Setting New and Higher Expectations for Student Learning*. New Directions for Higher Education, no. 96. San Francisco: Jossey-Bass, 1996.

Driscoll, A., and others. *Assessing the Impact of Service Learning: A Workbook of Strategies and Methods*. Portland, Ore.: Center for Academic Excellence, Portland State University, 1998.

Eder, D. J. "Assessing Student Achievement in the Major: The Departmentally Owned Senior Assignment as an Assessment Mechanism." In T. W. Banta, J. P. Lund, K. E. Black, and F. W. Oblander (eds.), *Assessment in Practice: Putting Principles to Work on College Campuses*. San Francisco: Jossey-Bass, 1996.

Ehrlich, T. "Foreword." In B. Jacoby and Associates, *Service-Learning in Higher Education: Concepts and Practices*. San Francisco: Jossey-Bass, 1996.

Elbow, P. "How Portfolios Show Us Problems with Holistic Scoring, but Suggest an Alternative." *Assessment Update*, 1994a, 6(4), 4–5.

Elbow, P. "Will the Virtues of Portfolios Blind Us to Their Potential Dangers?" In L. Black, D. A. Daiker, J. Sommers, and G. Stygall (eds.), *New Directions in Portfolio Assessment: Reflective Practice, Critical Theory, and Large-Scale Scoring*. Portsmouth, N.H.: Boynton/Cook, 1994b.

Elbow, P. "Writing Assessment: Do It Better; Do It Less." In E. M. White, W. D. Lutz, and S. Kamusikiri (eds.), *Assessment of Writing: Politics, Policies, Practices*. New York: Modern Language Association of America, 1996, pp. 120–134.

Elder, L., and Paul, R. "Universal Intellectual Standards." Rohnert Park, Calif.: Center for Critical Thinking, 1996, <http://www.sonoma.edu/CTHINK/University/univlibrary/unistan.nclk>

El-Khawas, E. *1989 Campus Trends Survey*. Washington, D.C.: American Council on Education, 1989.

El-Khawas, E. *Campus Trends, 1990*. Higher Education Panel Report No. 80. Washington, D.C.: American Council on Education, 1990.

El-Khawas, E. *Campus Trends, 1993*. Higher Education Panel Report No. 83. Washington, D.C.: American Council on Education, 1993.

El-Khawas, E. *Campus Trends, 1995*. Higher Education Panel Report No. 85. Washington, D.C.: American Council on Education, 1995.

El-Khawas, E., and Knopp, L. *Campus Trends, 1996*. Higher Education Panel Report No. 86. Washington, D.C.: American Council on Education, 1996.

Ellison, V. G., and Heard, M. H. "Assessing Student Achievement in the Major: America's Challenge—Assessing the Present, Preparing for the Future." In T. W. Banta, J. P. Lund, K. E. Black, and F. W. Oblander (eds.), *Assessment in Practice: Putting Principles to Work on College Campuses*. San Francisco: Jossey-Bass, 1996.

Engelkemeyer, S. W. "What Happened to CQI?" *AAHE Bulletin*, 1998, 50(7), 11–16.

Erwin, T. D. *Assessing Student Learning and Development: A Guide to the Principles, Goals, and Methods of Determining College Outcomes*. San Francisco: Jossey-Bass, 1991.

Erwin, T. D. "Assessment and Policy: Selected Institutions Utilizing Assessment Results." Prepared for the Student Outcomes Pilot—Cognitive Group National Postsecondary Education Cooperative, Aug. 1998 (rev. Sept. 1998).

Erwin, T. D., and Fuller, R. "Using Assessment to Improve General Education." Presentation at the American Assocation for Higher Education 1998 Assessment Conference, Cincinnati, Ohio, June 13–17, 1998.

Ewell, P. T. "Some Implications for Practice." In P. T. Ewell (ed.), *Assessing Educational Outcomes*. New Directions for Institutional Research, no. 47. San Francisco: Jossey-Bass, 1985.

Ewell, P. T. "To Capture the Ineffable: New Forms of Assessment in Higher Education." In G. Grant (ed.), *Review of Research in Education*, no. 17. Washington D.C.: American Educational Research Association, 1991.

Ewell, P. T. "A Matter of Integrity: Accountability and the Future of Self-Regulation." *Change: The Magazine of Higher Learning*, 1994a, 26(6), 24–29.

Ewell, P. T. *A Policy Guide for Assessment: Making Good Use of Tasks in Critical Thinking*. Princeton, N.J.: Educational Testing Service, 1994b.

Ewell, P. T. *Student Tracking: New Techniques, New Demands; Working Over Time: The Evolution of Longitudinal Student Tracking Data Bases*. New Directions for Institutional Research, no. 87. San Francisco: Jossey-Bass, 1995.

Ewell, P. T. "The Current Pattern of State-Level Assessment: Results of a National Inventory." *Assessment Update*, 1996, 8(3), 1–2, 12–13, 15.

Ewell, P. T. "Accountability and Assessment in a Second Decade: New Looks or Same Old Story?" In *Assessing Impact: Evidence and Action—Presentations from the 1997 American Association for Higher Education Conference on Assessment and Quality*. Washington, D.C.: American Association for Higher Education, 1997a.

Ewell, P. T. "From the States: Putting It All on the Line—South Carolina's Performance Funding Initiative." *Assessment Update*, 1997b, 9(1), 9, 11.

Ewell, P. T. "Identifying Indicators of Curricular Quality." In J. G. Gaff, J. L. Ratcliff, and Associates, *Handbook of the Undergraduate Curriculum: A Comprehensive Guide to Purposes, Structures, Practices, and Change*. A publication of the Association of American Colleges and Universities. San Francisco: Jossey-Bass, 1997c.

Ewell, P. T. "Organizing for Learning: A New Imperative." In T. J. Marchese (ed.), *AAHE Bulletin*, Dec. 1997d, 50(4), 3–6.

Ewell, P. T. "Strengthening Assessment for Academic Quality Improvement." In M. W. Peterson, D. D. Dill, L. A. Mets, and Associates, *Planning and Management for a Changing Environment: A Handbook on Redesigning Postsecondary Institutions*. San Francisco: Jossey-Bass, 1997e.

Ewell, P. T. "From the States: Statewide Testing: The Sequel." *Assessment Update*, 1998, 10(5), 12–13.

Ewell, P. T., and Jones, D. P. Indicators of "Good Practice" in Undergraduate Education: A Handbook for Development and Implementation. Boulder, Colo.: National Center for Higher Education Management Systems, 1996.

Ewing, S. C. "Alternative Assessment: Popularity, Pitfalls, and Potential." Assessment Update, 1998, 10(1), 1–2, 11–12.

Facione, P. A. "Critical Thinking: A Statement of Expert Consensus for Purposes of Educational Assessment and Instruction." Executive Summary, "The Delphi Report." Millbrae, Calif.: California Academic Press, 1990.

Facione, P. A., and Facione, N. C. "The California Critical Thinking Dispositions Inventory." INQUIRY: Critical Thinking Across the Disciplines. Millbrae, Calif.: California Academic Press, 1992.

Facione, P. A., and Facione, N. C. "The California Critical Thinking Skills Test." CCTST Form A and Form B Test Manual. Millbrae, Calif.: California Academic Press, 1994a.

Facione, P. A., and Facione, N. C. Holistic Critical Thinking Scoring Rubric. Millbrae, Calif.: California Academic Press, 1994b.

Facione, P. A., Facione, N. C., and Giancarlo, C.A.F. "The Motivation to Think in Working and Learning." In E. A. Jones (ed.), Preparing Competent College Graduates: Setting New and Higher Expectations for Student Learning. New Directions for Higher Education, no. 96. San Francisco: Jossey-Bass, 1996.

Facione, P. A., Sanchez, C. A., Facione, N. C., and Gainen, J. The Disposition Toward Critical Thinking. Journal of General Education, 1995, 44(1), 1–25.

Farmer, D. W., and Napieralski, E. A. "Assessing Learning in Programs." In J. G. Gaff, J. L. Ratcliff, and Associates, Handbook of the Undergraduate Curriculum: A Comprehensive Guide to Purposes, Structures, Practices, and Change. A publication of the Association of American Colleges and Universities. San Francisco: Jossey-Bass, 1997.

Ferren, A. "Faculty Resistance to Assessment: A Matter of Priorities and Perceptions." AAHE Conference Discussion Papers, 8th Annual Assessment Conference and 1st Continuous Quality Improvement Conference. Chicago, June 9–12, 1993, pp. 1–12.

Fink, A. The Survey Handbook, The Survey Kit. Thousand Oaks, Calif.: Sage, 1995.

Fink, A., and Kosecoff, J. How to Conduct Surveys: A Step-by-Step Guide. (2nd ed.) Thousand Oaks, Calif.: Sage, 1998.

Forrest, A., and a study group on portfolio assessment. Time Will Tell: Portfolio-Assisted Assessment of General Education. Washington, D.C.: AAHE Assessment Forum, American Association for Higher Education, 1990.

Francis, M. C., Mulder, T. C., and Stark, J. S. *Intentional Learning: A Process for Learning to Learn in the Accounting Curriculum*. Accounting Education Series, Vol. 12. Sarasota, Fla.: Accounting Education Change Commission and American Accounting Association, 1995.

Freeman, R., and Lewis, R. *Planning and Implementing Assessment*. London: Kogan Page, 1998.

Freidus, H. "Mentoring Portfolio Development." In N. Lyons (ed.), *With Portfolio in Hand: Validating the New Teacher Professionalism*. New York: Teachers College Press, 1998.

Fried, J., and Associates. *Shifting Paradigms in Student Affairs: Culture, Context, Teaching, and Learning*. Lanham, Md.: University Press of America, 1995.

Friedman, S. J. "Evaluating Assessment Reports from Departments and Programs." *Assessment Update*, 1995, 7(5), 8–9.

Fuhrmann, B. S. "The Integration of Professional and Liberal Studies." Presentation at the Association for General and Liberal Studies Conference, 1994.

Fuhrmann, B. S. "Campus Strategies: The 'Prompts' Project Prompts Academic and Student Affairs Collaboration." *Assessment Update*, 1995, 7(6), 10.

Gaff, J. G. "Tensions Between Tradition and Innovation." In J. G. Gaff, J. L. Ratcliff, and Associates, *Handbook of the Undergraduate Curriculum: A Comprehensive Guide to Purposes, Structures, Practices, and Change*. A publication of the Association of American Colleges and Universities. San Francisco: Jossey-Bass, 1997.

Gainen, J., and Facione, P. A. "Assessing Student Achievement in General Education: Pilot Assessment of Learning Outcomes in a General Education Core Curriculum." In T. W. Banta, J. P. Lund, K. E. Black, and F. W. Oblander (eds.), *Assessment in Practice: Putting Principles to Work on College Campuses*. San Francisco: Jossey-Bass, 1996.

Gainen, J., and Locatelli, P. *Assessment for the New Curriculum: A Guide for Professional Accounting Programs*. Sarasota, Fla.: American Accounting Association, 1995.

Gandolfo, A., and Carver, C. A. "Electronic Classroom Assessment Techniques: Assessment Beyond the Classroom in a Networked Environment." *Assessment Update*, 1995, 7(6), 3.

Gardiner, L. F. *Planning for Assessment: Mission Statements, Goals, and Objectives*. Trenton, N.J.: Office of Learning Assessment, Department of Higher Education, 1989.

Gardiner, L. F. *Redesigning Higher Education: Producing Dramatic Gains in Student Learning*. Report No. 7. Washington, D.C.: Graduate School of Education and Human Development, George Washington University, 1994.

Gardiner, L. F., Anderson, C., and Cambridge, B. L. (eds.), *Learning Through Assessment: A Resource Guide for Higher Education*. Washington, D.C.: American Association for Higher Education Assessment Forum, 1997.

Gardner, P. D. "Are College Seniors Prepared to Work?" In J. N. Gardner, G. Van der Veer, and Associates, *The Senior Year Experience: Facilitating Integration, Reflection, Closure, and Transition*. San Francisco: Jossey-Bass, 1998.

Gibson-Groshon, S. S., and Miller, S. "Campus Strategies: User-Friendly Portfolio Assessment." *Assessment Update*, 1995, *7*(2), 15.

Gold, R. G., and Hewitt, R. "Faculty Development to Promote Assessment: Using Grants to Initiate Assessment Activities." In T. W. Banta, J. P. Lund, K. E. Black, and F. W. Oblander (eds.), *Assessment in Practice: Putting Principles to Work on College Campuses*. San Francisco: Jossey-Bass, 1996.

Goldsmith, S. "Transforming Specialized Accreditation." Presentation to American Association for Higher Education Conference on Assessment and Quality, Rockville, Md., June 1997.

Gray, P. J. "Campus Profiles: Indiana University Bloomington." *Assessment Update*, 1995a, *7*(6), 14–15.

Gray, P. J. "Campus Profiles: Western Carolina University." *Assessment Update*, 1995b, *7*(2), 8–9.

Gray, P. J. "Campus Profiles: Institutional Effectiveness at Midlands Technical College." *Assessment Update*, 1998, *10*(5), 8–9, 15.

Gray, P. J., and Banta, T. W. (eds.). *The Campus-Level Impact of Assessment: Progress, Problems, and Possibilities*. New Directions for Higher Education, no. 100. San Francisco: Jossey-Bass, 1997.

Green, R. "Quality Standards for Academic Program Evaluation Plans." *Assessment Update*, 1993, *5*(6), 4–5.

Hagerty, B.M.K., and Stark, J. S. "Comparing Educational Accreditation Standards in Selected Professional Fields." *Research in Higher Education*, 1989, *60*(1), 1–20.

Haswell, R. H., and Wyche-Smith, S. "Assessing Student Achievement in General Education: Two-Tier Rating Procedure for Placement Essays." In T. W. Banta, J. P. Lund, K. E. Black, and F. W. Oblander (eds.), *Assessment in Practice: Putting Principles to Work on College Campuses*. San Francisco: Jossey-Bass, 1996.

Hatfield, S., Hatfield, T., and Krueger, D. "Using Seven Principle Based Assessment to Promote Optimal Learning." Presentation at the American Association for Higher Education Conference on Assessment and Quality, Washington, D.C., June 1996.

Hatfield, S., Krueger, D., and Hatfield, T. "Starting Points: Developing a Department Assessment Plan." Presentation at the American Association for Higher Education Assessment Conference, Cincinnati, Ohio, June 13–17, 1998.

Herman, J. L., Aschbacher, P. R., and Winters, L. *A Practical Guide to Alternative Assessment.* Alexandria, Va.: Association for Supervision and Curriculum Development, 1992.

Herman, J. L., and Winters, L. "Portfolio Research: A Slim Collection." *Educational Leadership,* 1994, *52*(2), 48–55.

Hilgers, T., and Bayer, A. S. "Student Voices and the Assessment of a New Core Writing Requirement at the University of Hawaii." *Assessment Update,* 1993, *5*(4), 4–5.

Hill, I. B. "Assessing Student Achievement in the Major: Setting the Context for Assessment." In T. W. Banta, J. P. Lund, K. E. Black, and F. W. Oblander (eds.), *Assessment in Practice: Putting Principles to Work on College Campuses.* San Francisco: Jossey-Bass, 1996.

Hill, I., Hoban, J., Stone, C., and Zivney, T. *Assessment Techniques: College of Business Undergraduate Core Program, Ball State University.* Muncie, Ind.: College of Business, Ball State University, 1993.

Hinson, F. D., and Stillion, J. M. "Assessing Student Achievement in General Education: Faculty Led Assessment." In T. W. Banta, J. P. Lund, K. E. Black, and F. W. Oblander (eds.), *Assessment in Practice: Putting Principles to Work on College Campuses.* San Francisco: Jossey-Bass, 1996.

Hogan, T. P., and Stamford, A. M. "Encouraging Departments to Engage in Assessment Activities." *Assessment Update,* 1997, *9*(5), 4–5, 14.

Holt, D., and Janzow, F. "Assessing General Education Using Aggregated Student Course Ratings." *Assessment Update,* 1995, *7*(4), 1–2, 5.

Holton III, E. F. "Preparing Students for Life Beyond the Classroom." In J. N. Gardner, G. Van der Veer, and Associates, *The Senior Year Experience: Facilitating Integration, Reflection, Closure, and Transition.* San Francisco: Jossey-Bass, 1998.

Hummer, A. "An Innovative Measurement of Communication Outcomes: Self-Perception." *Assessment Update,* 1998, *10*(1), 6–7, 15.

Hurtgen, J. R. "Assessment of General Learning: State University of New York College at Fredonia." In P. J. Gray and T. W. Banta (eds.), *The Campus-Level Impact of Assessment: Progress, Problems, and Possibilities.* New Directions for Higher Education, no. 100. San Francisco: Jossey-Bass, 1997.

Hutcheson, P. A. "Structures and Practices." In J. G. Gaff, J. L. Ratcliff, and Associates, *Handbook of the Undergraduate Curriculum: A Comprehensive*

Guide to Purposes, Structures, Practices, and Change. A publication of the Association of American Colleges and Universities. San Francisco: Jossey-Bass, 1997.

Hutchings, P. "Learning Over Time: Portfolio Assessment." *AAHE Bulletin*, Apr. 1990, pp. 6–8.

Hutchings, P. "Building A New Culture of Teaching and Learning," *About Campus*, Nov.-Dec. 1996, pp. 4–8.

Hutchings, P., and Marchese, T. "Watching Assessment: Questions, Stories, Prospects." *Change: The Magazine of Higher Learning*, 1990, *22*(5), 12–38.

Hutchings, P., Marchese, T., and Wright, B. *Using Assessment to Strengthen General Education*. Washington, D.C.: American Association for Higher Education Assessment Forum, 1991.

Hyman, R., Beeler, K. J., and Benedict, L. G. "Outcomes Assessment and Student Affairs: New Roles and Expectations." *NASPA Journal*, 1994, *32*(1), 20–30.

Imasuen, E. "Institution-Wide Classroom Assessment." *Assessment Update*, 1998, *10*(3), 9.

Impara, J. C., and Plake, B. S. (eds.). *The Thirteenth Mental Measurements Yearbook*. Lincoln: University of Nebraska Press, 1998.

Jacksonville State University. *Jacksonville State University Catalogue 1996–97*. Vol. 87, No. 1. Jacksonville, Ala.: Jacksonville State University, 1996.

Jacobs, L. C., and Chase, C. I. *Developing and Using Tests Effectively: A Guide for Faculty*. San Francisco: Jossey-Bass, 1992.

Jacoby, B. "Service-Learning in Today's Higher Education." In B. Jacoby and Associates, *Service-Learning in Higher Education: Concepts and Practices*. San Francisco: Jossey-Bass, 1996.

Johnson, R., McCormick, R., Prus, J., and Rogers, J. "Assessment Options for the College Major." In T. W. Banta and Associates, *Making a Difference: Outcomes of a Decade of Assessment in Higher Education*. San Francisco: Jossey-Bass, 1993.

Joint Committee on Standards for Educational Evaluation. *The Program Evaluation Standards: How to Assess Evaluations of Educational Programs*. (2nd ed.) Thousand Oaks, Calif.: Sage, 1994.

Jones, E. A. "Communications Outcomes Expected by Faculty, Employers, and Policymakers." *Assessment Update*, 1996a, 8(6), 7–8, 15.

Jones, E. A. "Editor's Notes." In E. A. Jones (ed.), *Preparing Competent College Graduates: Setting New and Higher Expectations for Student Learning*. New Directions for Higher Education, no. 96. San Francisco: Jossey-Bass, 1996b.

Jones, E. A., Hoffman, L. M., Ratcliff, G., Tibbets, S., and Click III, B. A. *Essential Skills in Writing, Speech and Listening, and Critical Thinking for College Graduates: Perspectives of Faculty, Employers, and Policymakers*. NCTLA Project Summary, 1994.

Kalina, M. L., and Catlin, A. "The Effects of the Cross-Angelo Model of Classroom Assessment on Student Outcomes: A Study." *Assessment Update*, 1994, 6(3), 5, 8.

Katz, A. M. "Assessing Student Achievement in General Education: Solving Logistical Problems That Impede Assessment." In T. W. Banta, J. P. Lund, K. E. Black, and F. W. Oblander (eds.), *Assessment in Practice: Putting Principles to Work on College Campuses*. San Francisco: Jossey-Bass, 1996.

Kinnick, M. K., and Walleri, R. D. "Assessment of Behavioral Change and Performance." In J. O. Nichols (ed.), *A Practitioner's Handbook for Institutional Effectiveness and Student Outcomes Assessment Implementation*. Edison, N.J.: Agathon Press, 1995.

King, P. M., and Kitchener, K. S. *Developing Reflective Judgment: Understanding and Promoting Intellectual Growth and Critical Thinking in Adolescents and Adults*. San Francisco: Jossey-Bass, 1994.

Knight, M. E., and Gallaro, D. (eds.). *Portfolio Assessment: Applications of Portfolio Analysis*. Lanham, Md.: University Press of America, 1994.

Kramp, M. K., and Humphreys, W. L. "Narrative, Self-Assessment, and the Habit of Reflection." *Assessment Update*, 1995, 7(1), 10–13.

Krotseng, M., and Pike, G. "Cognitive Assessment Instruments: Availability and Utilization." In J. O. Nichols (ed.), *A Practitioner's Handbook for Institutional Effectiveness and Student Outcomes Assessment Implementation*. New York: Agathon, 1995.

Krueger, R. A. *Focus Groups: A Practical Guide for Applied Research*. Thousand Oaks, Calif.: Sage, 1994.

Kuh, G. "Working Together to Enhance Student Learning Inside and Outside the Classroom: New Looks or Same Old Story?" In *Assessing Impact: Evidence and Action—Presentations from the 1997 AAHE Conference on Assessment and Quality*. Washington, D.C.: American Association for Higher Education, 1997.

Kuratko, D. F. "Assessing Student Achievement in the Major: New Venture Creation—The Ultimate Business Course Assessment." In T. W. Banta, J. P. Lund, K. E. Black, and F. W. Oblander (eds.), *Assessment in Practice: Putting Principles to Work on College Campuses*. San Francisco: Jossey-Bass, 1996.

Langer, E. *The Power of Mindful Learning*. New York: Addison-Wesley, 1997.

Leslie, D. W., and Fretwell, E. K. *Wise Moves in Hard Times: Creating and Managing Resilient Colleges and Universities*. San Francisco: Jossey-Bass, 1996.

Light, R. J. *The Harvard Assessment Seminars: Second Report 1992*. Cambridge, Mass.: Harvard University Graduate School of Education and Kennedy School of Government, 1992.

Lincoln, Y. S., and Denzin, N. K. "The Fifth Moment." In N. K. Denzin and Y. S. Lincoln (eds.), *Handbook of Qualitative Research*. Thousand Oaks, Calif.: Sage, 1994.

Linn, R. L., and Baker, E. L. "Can Performance-Based Student Assessments Be Psychometrically Sound?" In J. B. Baron and D. P. Wolf (eds.), *Performance-Based Student Assessment: Challenges and Possibilities, Ninety-Fifth Yearbook of the National Society for the Study of Education, Part 1*. Chicago: University of Chicago Press, 1996.

Lipscomb, D. "Campus Strategies: Linking Assessment to Retention of First-Year Students." *Assessment Update*, 1995, 7(5), 6–7.

Loacker, G., and Mentkowski, M. "Creating a Culture Where Assessment Improves Learning." In T. W. Banta and Associates, *Making a Difference: Outcomes of a Decade of Assessment in Higher Education*. San Francisco: Jossey-Bass, 1993.

Lopez, C. *Opportunities for Improvement: Advice from Consultant-Evaluators on Programs to Assess Student Learning*. North Central Accreditation Commission on Institutions of Higher Education, March, 1996.

Lyons, N. "Constructing Narratives for Understanding: Using Portfolio Interviews to Scaffold Teacher Reflection." In N. Lyons (ed.), *With Portfolio in Hand: Validating the New Teacher Professionalism*. New York: Teachers College Press, 1998a.

Lyons, N. "Portfolios and Their Consequences: Developing as a Reflective Practitioner." In N. Lyons (ed.), *With Portfolio in Hand: Validating the New Teacher Professionalism*. New York: Teachers College Press, 1998b.

Magruder, J., McManis, M. A., and Young, C. C. "The Right Idea at the Right Time: Development of a Transformational Assessment Culture." In P. J. Gray and T. W. Banta (eds.), *The Campus-Level Impact of Assessment: Progress, Problems, and Possibilities*. New Directions for Higher Education, no. 100. San Francisco: Jossey-Bass, 1997.

Marchese, T. J. "Third Down, Ten Years to Go." *AAHE Bulletin*, 1987, 40, 3–8.

Marchese, T. J. "Assessment, Quality, and Undergraduate Improvement." *Assessment Update*, 1994, 6(3), 1–2, 12–14.

Marchese, T. J. "Editorial: Resetting Expectations." *Change: The Magazine of Higher Learning*, 1996, 28(6), 4.

Marchese, T. J. "The New Conversations About Learning." In *Assessing Impact: Evidence and Action—Presentations from the 1997 AAHE Conference on Assessment and Quality.* Washington, D.C.: American Association for Higher Education, 1997a.

Marchese, T. J. "Sustaining Quality Enhancement in Academic and Managerial Life." In M. W. Peterson, D. D. Dill, L. A. Mets, and Associates, *Planning and Management for a Changing Environment: A Handbook on Redesigning Postsecondary Institutions.* San Francisco: Jossey-Bass, 1997b.

Marchese, T. J. "Thinking About Learning in Relation to Assessment: A Conversation." Presentation at the American Association for Higher Education Assessment Conference, Cincinnati, Ohio, June 13–17, 1998.

Marcic, D., and Seltzer, J. *Organizational Behavior: Experiences and Cases.* (5th ed.) Cincinnati, Ohio: South-Western, 1998.

Marienau, C., and Fiddler, M. "Enhancing Your Career Through Self-Assessment." *Journal of AHIMA,* 1997, 68(10), 30–33.

Matthews, R. S., Smith, B. L., MacGregor, J., and Gabelnick, F. "Creating Learning Communities." In J. G. Gaff, J. L. Ratcliff, and Associates, *Handbook of the Undergraduate Curriculum: A Comprehensive Guide to Purposes, Structures, Practices, and Change.* A publication of the Association of American Colleges and Universities. San Francisco: Jossey-Bass, 1997.

McCarthy, M. D. "One-Time and Short-Term Service-Learning Experiences." In B. Jacoby and Associates, *Service-Learning in Higher Education: Concepts and Practices.* San Francisco: Jossey-Bass, 1996.

McClain, C. J., and Krueger, D. W. "Using Outcomes Assessment: A Case Study in Institutional Change." In P. T. Ewell (ed.), *Assessing Educational Outcomes.* New Directions for Institutional Research, no. 47. San Francisco: Jossey-Bass, 1985.

McGourty, J., Sebastian, C., and Swart, W. "Performance Measurement and Continuous Improvement of Undergraduate Engineering Education Systems." Paper presented at the Frontiers in Education conference, Pittsburgh, Nov. 1997.

Mentkowski, M. "Paths to Integrity: Educating for Personal Growth and Professional Peformance." In S. Srivastva and Associates, *Executive Integrity: The Search for High Human Values in Organizational Life.* San Francisco: Jossey-Bass, 1988.

Mentkowski, M. "Creating a Culture of Assessment: A Look Through the Lens of Assessment Update: Assessment Trends: What Have We Learned From a Decade of "Assessment Update?" An interactive session at the American Association for Higher Education Assessment Conference, Cincinnati, Ohio, June 13–17, 1998.

Mentkowski, M., and Doherty, A. "Abilities That Last a Lifetime: Outcomes of the Alverno Experience." *AAHE Bulletin*, 1984, *37*, 8–14.

Messick, S. "The Once and Future Issues of Validity: Assessing the Meaning and Consequences of Measurement." In H. Wainer and H. Braun (eds.), *Test Validity*. Hillsdale, N.J.: Erlbaum, 1988.

Meyers, C., and Jones, T. B. *Promoting Active Learning: Strategies for the College Classroom*. San Francisco: Jossey-Bass, 1993.

Middle States Association of Colleges and Schools, Commission on Higher Education. *Framework for Outcomes Assessment*. Philadelphia: Middle States Association of Colleges and Schools, Commission on Higher Education, 1996.

Miller, P. M. "Peer Feedback at the Executive MBA Level on Interpersonal Skills Team Building Skills and Oral Presentation Skills." Presentation at the AAHE Assessment Conference, Miami, June 1997.

Millward, R. E. "Assessment Centers." In T. W. Banta and Associates, *Making a Difference: Outcomes of a Decade of Assessment in Higher Education*. San Francisco: Jossey-Bass, 1993.

Minnesota Community College Faculty. *Open to Change: Strategies in Thinking, Writing and Classroom Assessment*. St. Paul, Minn.: Minnesota Community Colleges, 1994.

Minnesota Community College Teaching for Thinking Project. *Four Kinds of Thinking Which Can Be Developed and Integrated Across the Curriculum*. St. Paul, Minn.: Minnesota Community Colleges, 1996.

Mintz, S. D., and Hesser, G. W. "Principles of Good Practice in Service-Learning." In B. Jacoby and Associates, *Service-Learning in Higher Education: Concepts and Practices*. San Francisco: Jossey-Bass, 1996.

Moden, G., and Williford, A. "Assessing Student Development and Progress: Applying Alumni Assessment Research to Academic Decision Making." In T. W. Banta, J. P. Lund, K. E. Black, and F. W. Oblander (eds.), *Assessment in Practice: Putting Principles to Work on College Campuses*. San Francisco: Jossey-Bass, 1996.

Moore, D. "Shaping Department Goals and Objectives for Assessment." In C. Palomba and others, *Assessment Workbook*. Muncie, Ind.: Ball State University, 1992.

Morris, S. M. "Assessing Employer Needs Through the Use of Focus Groups." *Assessment Update*, 1995, *7*(5), 1–2, 7.

Mortenson, T. G. *Postsecondary Educational Opportunity*. Oskaloosa, Iowa: T. G. Mortenson, Aug. 1998.

Morton, K. "Issues Related to Integrating Service-Learning into the Curriculum." In B. Jacoby and Associates, *Service-Learning in Higher Education: Concepts and Practices*. San Francisco: Jossey-Bass, 1996.

Moss, P. A. "Rethinking Validity for the Assessment of Teaching." In N. Lyons (ed.), *With Portfolio in Hand: Validating the New Teacher Professionalism.* New York: Teachers College Press, 1998.

Muffo, J. A. "Lessons Learned from a Decade of Assessment." *Assessment Update,* 1996, 8(5), 1–2, 11.

Murphy, P. D., and Gerst, J. "Beyond Grades and 'Satisfactory' in Assessing Graduate Student Learning." *Assessment Update,* 1997, 9(3), 12–13.

National Education Goals Panel. *The National Education Goals Report: Building A Nation of Learners 1992.* Washington, D.C: National Education Goals Panel, 1992.

National Governors Association. *Time for Results: The Governors' 1991 Report on Education.* Washington, D.C.: National Governors' Association, 1986.

National Institute of Education, Study Group on the Conditions of Excellence in American Higher Education. *Involvement in Learning: Realizing the Potential of American Higher Education.* Washington, D.C.: U.S. Government Printing Office, 1984.

National Science Foundation, Foundation Coalition. *Assessment and Evaluation: A Key to Successful Program Improvement.* Arlington, Va.: National Science Foundation, n.d.

Nichols, J. O. *Assessment Case Studies: Common Issues in Implementation with Various Campus Approaches to Resolution.* New York: Agathon, 1995a.

Nichols, J. O. *A Practitioner's Handbook for Institutional Effectiveness and Student Outcomes Assessment Implementation.* New York: Agathon, 1995b.

Nilson, L. B. *Teaching at Its Best: A Research-Based Resource for College Instructors.* Bolton, Mass.: Anker, 1998.

Norris, S. P., and Ennis, R. H. *The Practitioners Guide to Teaching Thinking Series: Evaluating Critical Thinking.* Pacific Grove, Calif.: Critical Thinking Press and Software, 1989.

North Central Association of Colleges and Schools. *Handbook of Accreditation 1994–96.* Chicago: North Central Association of Colleges and Schools, Commission on Institutions of Higher Education, 1994.

North Central Association of Colleges and Schools. *Handbook of Accreditation.* (2nd ed.) Chicago: North Central Association of Colleges and Schools, Commission on Institutions of Higher Education, 1997.

Nummedal, S. G. "How Classroom Assessment Can Improve Teaching and Learning." In D. F. Halpern and Associates, *Changing College Classrooms: New Teaching and Learning Strategies for an Increasingly Complex World.* San Francisco: Jossey-Bass, 1994.

Olds, B. M., and Miller, R. L. "Using Real-Life Projects to Teach Total Quality Management." *Assessment Update,* 1997, 9(3), 1–2, 14–15.

Oshiro, E. "Assessing Student Achievement in General Education: Evaluation of the Senior Project." In T. W. Banta, J. P. Lund, K. E. Black, and F. W. Oblander (eds.), *Assessment in Practice: Putting Principles to Work on College Campuses.* San Francisco: Jossey-Bass, 1996.

Outcomes Assessment Council at Ferris State. *Outcomes Assessment Planning Part One: Outcomes Assessment Plans; Part Two: Planning for Change.* Big Rapids, Mich.: Ferris State University, 1994.

Pace, C. R. "Perspectives and Problems in Student Outcomes Research." In P. T. Ewell (ed.), *Assessing Educational Outcomes.* New Directions for Institutional Research, no. 47. San Francisco: Jossey-Bass, 1985.

Pace, C. R. *College Student Experiences Questionnaire: Norms for the Third Edition, 1990.* Los Angeles: UCLA Center for the Study of Evaluation, 1992.

Palmer, P. J. *The Courage to Teach: Exploring the Inner Landscape of a Teacher's Life.* San Francisco: Jossey-Bass, 1998.

Palomba, C. A. "Assessment at Ball State University." In P. J. Gray and T. W. Banta (eds.), *The Campus-Level Impact of Assessment: Progress, Problems, and Possibilities.* New Directions for Higher Education, no. 100. San Francisco: Jossey-Bass, 1997.

Palomba, C. A., and others. *Assessment Workbook.* Muncie, Ind.: Ball State University, 1992.

Palomba, N. A. "Assessment in Ball State University's College of Business—A Challenging Journey." Presentation to AACSB Southern Business Deans Annual Meeting, New Orleans, Nov. 17, 1997.

Pascarella, E. T., and Terenzini, P. T. *How College Affects Students: Findings and Insights from Twenty Years of Research.* San Francisco: Jossey-Bass, 1991.

Patton, G. W., Dasher-Alston, R., Ratteray, O.M.T., and Kait, M. B. "Outcomes Assessment in the Middle States Region: A Report on the 1995 Outcomes Assessment Survey." Philadelphia: Commission on Higher Education of the Middle States Association of Colleges and Schools, 1996.

Patton, M. Q. *Qualitative Evaluation and Research Methods.* (2nd ed.) Newbury Park, Calif.: Sage, 1990.

Peterson, M. W. "Assessing Institutional Support for Student Assessment." *Assessment Update,* 1998, *10*(4), 1–2, 7–8.

Peterson, M. W., Dill, D. D., and Mets, L. A. *Planning and Management for a Changing Environment: A Handbook on Redesigning Postsecondary Institutions.* San Francisco: Jossey-Bass, 1997.

Peterson, M. W., and Einarson, M. K. "Analytic Framework of Institutional Support for Student Assessment." Paper presented at the annual meeting of the AERA, San Diego, Calif., 1998; NCPI Project 5.2. Ann Arbor: University of Michigan, 1998.

Peterson, M. W., Einarson, M. K., Trice, A. G., and Nichols, A. R. *Improving Organizational and Administrative Support for Student Assessment: A Review of Research Literature.* NCPI Project 5.2. Ann Arbor: University of Michigan, 1997.

Pike, G. R. "Assessment Measures: The Reflective Judgment Interview." *Assessment Update,* 1996, 8(5), 14–15.

Pitts, B., Lowe, B. T., Ranieri, P., and Palomba, C. "Using Assessment to Improve General Education." Presentation at the AAHE Assessment Conference, Miami, Fla., June 1997.

Poje, D. J. "Assessing Student Achievement in General Education: Student Motivation and Standardized Testing for Institutional Assessment." In T. W. Banta, J. P. Lund, K. E. Black, and F. W. Oblander (eds.), *Assessment in Practice: Putting Principles to Work on College Campuses.* San Francisco: Jossey-Bass, 1996.

Porter, D. B. "Assessment: The Good, the Bad and the Ugly." In R. W. Tucker (ed.), *Adult Assessment Forum: Journal of Quality Management in Adult-Centered Education,* 1998, 8(3), 11–14.

Prus, J., and Tebo-Messina, M. "Campus Profiles: Assessment of Student Learning and Development at Winthrop University: An Update." *Assessment Update,* 1996, 8(6), 9, 10.

Ratcliff, J. L. "Assessment's Role in Strengthening the Core Curriculum." In D. F. Halpern and Associates, *Changing College Classrooms: New Teaching and Learning Strategies for an Increasingly Complex World.* San Francisco: Jossey-Bass, 1994.

Ratcliff, J. L. "Quality and Coherence in General Education." In J. G. Gaff and J. L. Ratcliff (eds.), *Handbook of the Undergraduate Curriculum: A Comprehensive Guide to Purposes, Structures, Practices, and Change.* A publication of the Association of American Colleges and Universities. San Francisco: Jossey-Bass, 1997a.

Ratcliff, J. L. "What Is a Curriculum and What Should It Be?" In J. G. Gaff, J. L. Ratcliff, and Associates, *Handbook of the Undergraduate Curriculum: A Comprehensive Guide to Purposes, Structures, Practices, and Change.* A publication of the Association of American Colleges and Universities. San Francisco: Jossey-Bass, 1997b.

Ratcliff, J., and Jones, E. A. "Coursework Cluster Analysis." In T. W. Banta and Associates, *Making a Difference: Outcomes of a Decade of Assessment in Higher Education.* San Francisco: Jossey-Bass, 1993.

Reardon, M. F., and Ramaley, J. A. "Building Academic Community While Containing Costs." In J. G. Gaff and J. L. Ratcliff (eds.), *Handbook of the*

Undergraduate Curriculum: A Comprehensive Guide to Purposes, Structures, Practices, and Change. A publication of the Association of American Colleges and Universities. San Francisco: Jossey-Bass, 1997.

Reason, P. (ed.). *Participation in Human Inquiry.* Thousand Oaks, Calif.: Sage, 1994.

Rest, J. *Guide for the Defining Issues Test: How to Use the Optical Scan Forms and the Center's Scoring Service.* Version 1.3. Minneapolis: University of Minnesota Center for the Study of Ethical Development, Jan. 1993.

RiCharde, R. S. *Learning-Thinking Styles Inventory.* Lexington: Virginia Military Institute, 1992.

Rogers, G. M., and Sando, J. K. *Stepping Ahead: An Assessment Plan Development Guide.* Terre Haute, Ind.: Rose-Hulman Institute of Technology, 1996.

Rowley, D. J., Lujan, H. D., and Dolence, M. G. *Strategic Change in Colleges and Universities: Planning to Survive and Prosper.* San Francisco: Jossey-Bass, 1997.

Rubin, R. B., and Morreale, S. P. "Setting Expectations for Speech Communication and Listening." In E. A. Jones (ed.), *Preparing Competent College Graduates: Setting New and Higher Expectations for Student Learning.* New Directions for Higher Education., no. 96. San Francisco: Jossey-Bass, 1996.

Ruby, C. A. "Assessing Satisfaction with Selected Student Services Using SERVQUAL, a Market-Driven Model of Service Quality." *NASPA Journal,* Summer 1998, *35*(4), 331–341.

Rudolph, L. B. "Assessing Student Achievement in General Education: Looking Beneath Standardized Test Scores." In T. W. Banta, J. P. Lund, K. E. Black, and F. W. Oblander (eds.), *Assessment in Practice: Putting Principles to Work on College Campuses.* San Francisco: Jossey-Bass, 1996.

Rust, C. "Assessing What Really Matters in the Major and the Degree: A British Perspective on Moves to Better Practice in Assessment." *Assessment Update,* 1997, *9*(6), 6–7.

St. Ours, P. A., and Corsello, M. "Faculty-Driven Assessment: A Collaborative Model That Works." *Assessment Update,* 1998, *10*(4), 6–8.

Sax, L. J., Astin, A. W., Korn, W. S., and Mahoney, K. M. *The American Freshman: National Norms for Fall 1997.* Los Angeles: Higher Education Research Institute, UCLA, 1997.

Schalinske, R. A., Patterson, R. A., and Smith, G. L. "Assessing Student Achievement in General Education: An Assessment of a Core Curriculum." In T. W. Banta, J. P. Lund, K. E. Black, and F. W. Oblander (eds.), *Assessment in Practice: Putting Principles to Work on College Campuses.* San Francisco: Jossey-Bass, 1996.

Schilling, K. L., and Schilling, K. M. "Descriptive Approaches to Assessment: Moving Beyond Meeting Requirements to Making a Difference." In North Central Association of Colleges and Schools, Commission on Institutions of Higher Education (ed.), *A Collection of Papers on Self-Study and Institutional Improvement*. Chicago: North Central Association of Colleges and Schools, 1993a, pp. 171–174.

Schilling, K. L., and Schilling, K. M. "Professors Must Respond to Calls for Accountability." *Chronicle of Higher Education*, Mar. 24, 1993b, p. A40.

Schilling, K. L., and Schilling, K. M. "Looking Back, Moving Ahead: Assessment in the Senior Year." In J. N. Gardner, G. Van der Veer, and Associates, *The Senior Year Experience: Facilitating Integration, Reflection, Closure, and Transition*. San Francisco: Jossey-Bass, 1998.

Schneider, C. G. "The Arts and Sciences Major." In J. G. Gaff, J. L. Ratcliff, and Associates, *Handbook of the Undergraduate Curriculum: A Comprehensive Guide to Purposes, Structures, Practices, and Change*. A publication of the Association of American Colleges and Universities. San Francisco: Jossey-Bass, 1997.

Schön, D. A. *The Reflective Practitioner: How Professionals Think in Action*. New York: Basic Books, 1983.

Senge, P. M. *The Fifth Discipline: The Art and Practice of the Learning Organization*. New York: Doubleday, 1990.

Shaeiwitz, J. A. "Capstone Experiences: Are We Doing Assessment Without Realizing It?" *Assessment Update*, 1996, 8(4), 4, 6.

Sharkey, S. R. "Assessment and Improving General Education: Perspectives, General Education Revisited." *Journal of the Association for General and Liberal Studies*. Waterloo, N.Y.: In House Graphic Design, 1992.

Shaw Jr., B. F., McKinley, K. H., and Robinson, S. P. "Developing A Campuswide Approach to the Assessment of Institutional Effectiveness: Encouraging Faculty Involvement Through Mini-Grants." In T. W. Banta, J. P. Lund, K. E. Black, and F. W. Oblander (eds.), *Assessment in Practice: Putting Principles to Work on College Campuses*. San Francisco: Jossey-Bass, 1996.

Shulman, L. "Teacher Portfolios: A Theoretical Activity." In N. Lyons (ed.), *With Portfolio in Hand: Validating the New Teacher Professionalism*. New York: Teachers College Press, 1998.

Singell, L., and Palmer, M. "Outcomes Assessment for Continuous Improvement." Presentation at the AACSB Outcomes Assessment Seminar, Nashville, Tenn., Spring 1998.

Snyder, J., Lippincott, A., and Bower, D. "Portfolios in Teacher Education: Technical or Transformational?" In N. Lyons (ed.), *With Portfolio in Hand: Validating the New Teacher Professionalism*. New York: Teachers College Press, 1998, pp. 123–142.

Spicuzza, F. J. "An Evaluation of Portfolio Assessment: A Student Perspective." *Assessment Update*, 1996, 8(6), 4–6, 13.

Stark, J. S., and Lattuca, L. R. *Shaping the College Curriculum: Academic Plans in Action*. Boston: Allyn & Bacon, 1997.

Stark, J. S., and others. *Planning Introductory College Courses: Influences on Faculty*. Ann Arbor: National Center for Research to Improve Postsecondary Teaching and Learning, University of Michigan, 1990.

Steadman, M. H. "CATs for Community Colleges: Changing Both Sides of the Teaching-Learning Equation." Sarasota Springs, N.Y.: National Center on Adult Learning, 1995.

Steele, J. M. "Postsecondary Assessment Needs: Implications for State Policy." *Assessment Update*, 1996, 8(2), 1–2, 12–13, 15.

Suskie, L. A. *Questionnaire Survey Research: What Works*. Tallahassee, Fla.: Association for Institutional Research, 1992.

Tebo-Messina, A., and Sarow, M. "Faculty Development to Promote Assessment: Learning Research—An Interdisciplinary Faculty Approach to General Education Assessment." In T. W. Banta, J. P. Lund, K. E. Black, and F. W. Oblander (eds.), *Assessment in Practice: Putting Principles to Work on College Campuses*. San Francisco: Jossey-Bass, 1996.

Terenzini, P. T. "Assessment with Open Eyes: Pitfalls in Studying Student Outcomes." *Journal of Higher Education*, 1989, 60(6), 644–664.

Terenzini, P. T. "Cross-National Themes in the Assessment of Quality in Higher Education." *Assessment Update*, May-June 1993, 5(3), 1–2, 4, 13.

Tinto, V. *Leaving College: Rethinking the Causes and Cures of Student Attrition*. Chicago: University of Chicago Press, 1993.

Tinto, V. "Classrooms as Communities: Exploring the Educational Character of Student Persistence." *Journal of Higher Education*, 1997, 68(6), 599–623.

Tinto, V., Love, A. G., and Russo, P. *Building Learning Communities for New College Students: A Summary of Research Findings of the Collaborative Learning Project*. Syracuse, N.Y.: National Center on Postsecondary Teaching Learning and Assessment, Syracuse University, 1994.

University of Texas at San Antonio. *1998–99 Undergraduate Catalog*. San Antonio: University of Texas at San Antonio, 1998.

Upcraft, M. L., and Schuh, J. H. *Assessment in Student Affairs: A Guide for Practitioners*. San Francisco: Jossey-Bass, 1996.

U.S. Department of Education. "Secretary's Procedures and Criteria for Recognition of Accrediting Agencies." *Federal Register*, 1988, *53*(127), 25088–25099.

U.S. Department of Education, National Center for Education Statistics. *Student Outcomes Information for Policy-Making*. NCES 97–991, prepared by Patrick Terenzini. Washington, D.C.: Council of the National Postsecondary Education Cooperative Working Group on Student Outcomes from a Policy Perspective, 1997.

U.S. Department of Education, National Center for Education Statistics. *Definitions and Assessment Methods for Critical Thinking, Problem Solving, and Writing*. Prepared by T. Dary Erwin. Washington, D.C.: Council of the National Postsecondary Education Cooperative Working Group on Student Outcomes, Panel on Cognitive Outcomes, 1998.

Van Dyke, J., and Williams, G. W. "Assessing Student Achievement in the Major: Involving Graduates and Employers in Assessment of a Technology Program." In T. W. Banta, J. P. Lund, K. E. Black, and F. W. Oblander (eds.), *Assessment in Practice: Putting Principles to Work on College Campuses*. San Francisco: Jossey-Bass, 1996.

Vaughn, S., Schumm, J. S., and Sinagub, J. *Focus Group Interviews in Education and Psychology*. Thousand Oaks, Calif.: Sage, 1996.

Vavrus, L. "Put Portfolios to the Test." *Instructor*, 1990, *100*(1), 48–53.

Walker, C. J. "Assessing Group Process: Using Classroom Assessment to Build Autonomous Learning Teams." *Assessment Update*, 1995, *7*(6), 4–5.

Walker, R. D., and Muffo, J. A. "Assessing Student Achievement in the Major: Alumni Involvement in Civil Engineering." In T. W. Banta, J. P. Lund, K. E. Black, and F. W. Oblander (eds.), *Assessment in Practice: Putting Principles to Work on College Campuses*. San Francisco: Jossey-Bass, 1996.

Walvoord, B. E. "But Is It Valid?" Issues in Performance Assessment, Towson, Md. Presentation at the AAHE Assessment Forum, Washington, D.C., June 1996.

Walvoord, B. E., and Anderson, V. J. "An Assessment Riddle." *Assessment Update*, 1995, *7*(6), 8–9, 11.

Walvoord, B. E., and Anderson, V. J. *Effective Grading: A Tool for Learning and Assessment*. San Francisco: Jossey-Bass, 1998.

Walvoord, B. E., Bardes, B., and Denton, J. "Closing the Feedback Loop in Classroom-Based Assessment." *Assessment Update*, 1998, *10*(5), 1–2, 10–11.

Watson, G., and Glaser, E. M. *Watson-Glaser Critical Thinking Appraisal Manual.* Orlando: The Psychological Corporation/Harcourt Brace, 1980.

White, E. M. "Portfolios as an Assessment Concept." In L. Black, D. A. Daiker, J. L. Sommers, G. Stygall (eds.), *New Directions in Portfolio Assessment: Reflective Practice, Critical Theory, and Large-Scale Scoring.* Portsmouth, N.H.: Boynton/Cook, 1994.

Wiggins, G. "A True Test: Toward a More Authentic and Equitable Assessment." *Phi Delta Kappan,* 1989, 70, 703–713.

Wiggins, G. "The Truth May Make You Free But the Test May Keep You Imprisoned: Toward Assessing Worth of the Liberal Arts." In *Assessment 1990: Understanding the Implications.* Washington, D.C.: AAHE Assessment Forum, 1990, pp. 54–65.

Wiggins, G. *Assessing Student Performance: Exploring the Purpose and Limits of Testing.* San Francisco: Jossey-Bass, 1993.

Wiggins, G. "Feedback: How Learning Occurs." In *Assessing Impact: Evidence and Action—Presentations from the 1997 AAHE Conference on Assessment and Quality.* Washington, D.C.: American Association for Higher Education, 1997.

Wiggins, G. *Educative Assessment: Designing Assessments to Inform and Improve Student Performance.* San Francisco: Jossey-Bass, 1998.

Williford, A. M. "Ohio University's Multidimensional Institutional Impact and Assessment Plan." In P. J. Gray and T. W. Banta (eds.), *The Campus-Level Impact of Assessment: Progress, Problems, and Possibilities.* New Directions in Higher Education, no. 100. San Francisco: Jossey-Bass, 1997.

Williford, A., and Moden, G. O. "Using Assessment to Enhance Quality." In T. W. Banta and Associates, *Making a Difference: Outcomes of a Decade of Assessment in Higher Education.* San Francisco: Jossey-Bass, 1993.

Wingspread Group on Higher Education. *An American Imperative: Higher Expectations for Higher Education.* Racine, Wis.: Johnson Foundation, 1993.

Wise, A. "NCATE's Emphasis on Performance: Presidential Perspectives." Washington, D.C.: National Council for Accreditation of Teacher Education, 1998.

Wolf, B. *Handbook on Assessment Strategies: Measures of Student Learning and Program Quality.* Bloomington: Office of the Vice Chancellor for Academic Affairs and Dean of Faculties, Indiana University, 1993.

Wolff, R. A., and Harris, O. D. "Using Assessment to Develop a Culture of Evidence." In D. F. Halpern and Associates, *Changing College Classrooms: New Teaching and Learning Strategies for an Increasingly Complex World.* San Francisco: Jossey-Bass, 1994.

Wood, P. K. "Assessment Measures: Critical Thinking Assessment at the University of Missouri, Columbia." *Assessment Update*, 1997 9(6), 11–13, 16.

Wood, P. K., and Lynch, C. L. "Campus Strategies: Using Guided Essays to Assess and Encourage Reflective Thinking." *Assessment Update*, 1998, *10*(2), 14–15.

Wresch, W. "Finding Balance in General Education Assessment." *Assessment Update*, 1998, *10*(5), 4, 15.

Wright, B. D. "Evaluating Learning in Individual Courses." In J. G. Gaff, J. L. Ratcliff, and Associates, *Handbook of the Undergraduate Curriculum: A Comprehensive Guide to Purposes, Structures, Practices, and Change.* A publication of the Association of American Colleges and Universities. San Francisco: Jossey-Bass, 1997.

Young, C. C. "Assessing Student Achievement in the Major: Triangulated Assessment of the Major." In T. W. Banta, J. P. Lund, K. E. Black, and F. W. Oblander (eds.), *Assessment in Practice: Putting Principles to Work on College Campuses.* San Francisco: Jossey-Bass, 1996.

Yudof, M. G., and Busch-Vishniac, I. J. "Total Quality: Myth or Management in Universities?" In N. Weise (ed.), *Change: The Magazine of Higher Learning*, 1996, *28*(6), 18–27.

Zhang, Z., and RiCharde, R. S. *Assessing College Students' Development: A Repeated-Measures Analysis Using a Mixed Model.* Paper presented at the Annual Meeting of the American Education Research Association, San Diego, Calif., April 1998.

Name Index

Subject Index